通向中国

# Chinese Odyssey

## Innovative Chinese Courseware

**SIMPLIFIED & TRADITIONAL**

**Vol. 1 • TEXTBOOK**

Xueying Wang, Li-chuang Chi, and Liping Feng

王学英　　祁立庄　　冯力平

CHENG & TSUI COMPANY Boston

12  11  10  09  08          2  3  4  5  6

Published by
Cheng & Tsui Company, Inc.
25 West Street
Boston, MA 02111-1213 USA
Fax (617) 426-3669
www.cheng-tsui.com
"Bringing Asia to the World"

Library of Congress Cataloging-in-Publication Data

Wang, Xueying.
Chinese odyssey : innovative Chinese courseware / Xueying Wang,
  Li-chuang Chi, and Liping Feng.
      p. cm.
  Includes an index.
  Chinese and English.
  ISBN 10:  0-88727-538-9
  ISBN 13:  978-0-88727-538-8
  1. Chinese language—Textbooks for foreign speakers—English.
I. Chi, Li-chuang. II. Feng, Liping. III. Title.
PL1129.E5W385 2004
495.1'82421—dc22

                                    2004063504

Simplified & Traditional Character Edition

Printed in Canada

*Chinese Odyssey* includes multimedia products, textbooks, workbooks, and audio products. Visit www.cheng-tsui.com for more information on the other components of *Chinese Odyssey*.

# Table of Contents

## Simplified Character Lessons

## Traditional Character Lessons

# Publisher's Note

Despite the increasing use of technology in foreign language education, there have been few multimedia courses in Chinese that focus on all four skills and span all levels of language instruction. At long last, we are pleased to present *Chinese Odyssey*, unique because it is the first stand-alone multimedia series designed for multi-year classroom instruction. *Chinese Odyssey's* pace and oral/aural emphasis are geared to the American high school and college instructional environments, and its combination of multimedia, audio, and book products allows educators the flexibility to use it independently as a multimedia course, or to combine multimedia and paper formats.

In this edition of *Chinese Odyssey*, we combine both simplified and traditional characters in the same book. In Volumes 1 & 2, which cover the first year of study, we present the traditional and simplified character editions in separate sections. This layout is meant to provide ready access to both traditional and simplified characters without overwhelming beginning students. In Volumes 3–6, which cover the second and third years of study, we present the two character sets together on facing pages. We switch to facing pages in the higher levels in order to encourage fluency for intermediate and advanced-level students who wish to study and compare both character sets.

The Cheng & Tsui Chinese Language Series is designed to publish and widely distribute quality language learning materials created by leading instructors from around the world. We welcome readers' comments and suggestions concerning the publications in this series. Please send feedback to our Editorial Department (e-mail: editor@cheng-tsui.com), or contact the following members of our Editorial Board.

# Preface

Welcome to *Chinese Odyssey*, an innovative multimedia language course-ware for learning Mandarin Chinese. *Chinese Odyssey* is designed to provide a comprehensive curriculum, laying the groundwork for building your Chinese language skills from beginning to advanced levels over a period of three years. Designed for high school, college, and adult learners, *Chinese Odyssey* teaches the full scope of language learning skills—listening, speaking, reading, and writing—in addition to grammar. And because it is completely multimedia-based, *Chinese Odyssey* provides unique access to video, audio, images, and interactive exercises, adding a new dimension of flexibility and richness to the language learning experience.

## Year-by-Year Learning Objectives

### *First Year (Volumes 1 and 2)*

The first year is designed to teach the basic survival skills you will need to communicate in Chinese. The exercises concentrate heavily on spoken language and pronunciation, with a special focus on pinyin and tones in Volume 1. In Volume 2, pronunciation exercises are gradually replaced by more communicative and grammar-based exercises.

### *Second Year (Volumes 3 and 4)*

In your second year of studying Chinese, you will complete the basic groundwork in Chinese, and you'll learn more about Chinese grammar. At this point, you should become more comfortable with Chinese customs and will be able to communicate about daily tasks with Chinese people. By the end of this year, you will have gained the necessary language skills for living in China.

### *Third Year (Volumes 5 and 6)*

At this level, you will be continuously honing your language skills and cultural understanding. You will develop the skills necessary to carry on a high-level discussion in Chinese, expressing your opinions as you talk about issues related to current events, Chinese society, politics, economics, the education system, and aspects of Chinese culture such as food, holidays, and Chinese medicine. You will also begin to learn the written form of Chinese (书面语/書面語), which is different from the modern spoken form of the language.

# *Chinese Odyssey's* Pedagogical Approach

## Why Multimedia

In the past, most education took place in a classroom environment and was based primarily on interaction between the teacher and student. Today, people of all ages and backgrounds are seeking to enhance their language experience with multimedia tools. As a completely stand-alone multimedia courseware, *Chinese Odyssey* lets you effectively manage your own learning. Using the multimedia CD-ROMs, you can instantly see whether you've completed an exercise correctly, get explanations of answers, and record your exercise scores. You can participate in a variety of interactive situations that allow you to practice what you have learned. Thus, you can set your own pace and focus on your perceived areas of weakness.

The multimedia format easily accommodates students of varying backgrounds, skill levels, and aptitudes. For example, beginning students can spend more time learning to write Chinese characters by following animated stroke order, or focus on pronunciation drills. In the second and third years, students can take advantage of online resources—such as links to Internet pages related to lesson topics—which will enrich their learning experience. In short, for students, using the multimedia program is like having a private tutor.

Within the realm of traditional classroom-based instruction, the *Chinese Odyssey* courseware enables instructors to more effectively use their limited instructional hours for interaction with their students rather than for mechanical drills. For example, using the multimedia CD-ROM, students can do drills and exercises as well as review the lesson on their own time. This frees up class time for more meaningful interaction between teachers and students. Because the courseware contains a score-keeping function, language instructors don't have to spend lots of time grading students' homework. Instructors can simply ask students to print out their exercise score reports, which will automatically indicate the students' performance as well as the time taken to complete the exercise. Moreover, students absent from class can take their portable CDs with them in order to keep up with lessons, without having to use too much of the instructor's time to make up the class.

## A Note about the Exercises

*Chinese Odyssey* contains sophisticated multimedia exercises in grammar and the four basic language skills—listening, speaking, reading and writing. In order to prepare you to take the *Hanyu Shuiping Kaoshi* (HSK), the Chinese Proficiency Test given by the Chinese government, some of the exercises are in HSK format (see "How *Chinese Odyssey* Provides Preparation for the HSK" below). Other multimedia exercises include matching games and pre-recorded dialogues that you can engage in with the computer; we hope that such activities are able to bring some fun and interaction to Chinese learning.

## Why We Introduce Idiomatic Colloquial Speech

Rather than teaching artificial textbook "language," which is heavily limited by vocabulary and grammar, we introduce authentic idiomatic colloquial speech to make learning more real and the everyday spoken language more accessible. Heritage students and those who are highly motivated to learn can simply memorize the colloquial speech without a need to analyze the grammar. Those who have limited time do not have to memorize the idiomatic colloquial speech.

## Topics in *Chinese Odyssey*

The course material contains practical topics such as greeting people, entertaining guests, opening a bank account, or going to the post office, as well as contemporary topics such as dating and opening a cell phone account. Before writing *Chinese Odyssey*, we held a series of discussions with our students in order to select topics that would be, from a learners' perspective, both interesting and practical. For example, dating is a topic that students love because it helps to bring Chinese learning from academia into their everyday world.

## Settings in *Chinese Odyssey*

The settings in *Chinese Odyssey* are designed to mirror the real experiences of students learning Chinese. In the first year, most students begin their language-learning journey in their home country. During the second and third years, however, students tend to travel abroad to enhance their language-learning experience in the target country of their chosen language. Thus, in parallel, our courseware begins in the home country of the novice Chinese learner, and then shifts to China, with increasingly sophisticated scenes as the students themselves advance in their language skills.

## Curriculum Planning

Each year of *Chinese Odyssey* covers two volumes of material, with 20 lessons for each of the first two years (approximately 5–6 instructional hours per lesson), and 10 lessons for the third year (approximately 9–10 instructional hours per lesson). To facilitate learning and teaching, we have tightly controlled the number of vocabulary words and the length of the text in each lesson.

Grammar is graded in terms of level of difficulty, and difficult grammar points such as 的, 了, and verb complements usually appear more than once: first to introduce basic concepts and later with increasingly detailed explanations and practice.

## Cultural Information

Cultural information is imbedded in the lessons themselves. For example, culture is introduced by way of idioms, language notes, and situations that reveal different aspects of Chinese life and customs.

## How *Chinese Odyssey* Provides Preparation for the HSK

In addition to providing a rigorous Chinese language course, *Chinese Odyssey* is designed to prepare you for taking the *Hanyu Shuiping Kaoshi* (HSK), a proficiency-based, standardized aptitude test issued by the Chinese government. If you want to study abroad or work in China, you will eventually have to take this test. *Chinese Odyssey*'s testing software is modeled after the HSK, to give you a sense of what the actual exam is like and help you prepare for the exam.

## A Tour through *Chinese Odyssey*

### *Textbook*

#### Text

Each lesson is introduced with a dialogue, which we refer to as the lesson's "text." Based on the experiences of a group of friends studying Chinese, the dialogues reflect the daily life of a typical university student. The situations in each of the lessons are real-life situations that you might encounter upon visiting or preparing to visit China, such as asking for directions, ordering food at a restaurant, or applying for a visa to study abroad. We have also incorporated a range of cultural material, including common idioms and slang, to enhance your working knowledge of Chinese culture and tradition.

#### Vocabulary

Because Chinese is a non-alphabetic language, it is often fascinating but time-consuming for beginning students to learn the written form. To make it easier, we have divided the vocabulary in Volume 1 of the first year into the following two types:

- Basic: Basic vocabulary consists of common words that are used in every-day conversation. You will practice listening, speaking, and reading these words, but will not be responsible for writing them by hand.

- Core: From the pool of basic vocabulary words, there is a smaller set of core vocabulary, which you should learn to write. In the vocabulary lists, these core vocabulary words are starred.

Throughout *Chinese Odyssey*, you'll also find the following lists of words in the Vocabulary section.

- Notes: Explain special expression or idioms that appear in the texts. These special expressions are not required for you to learn, but because they are fun and convey something interesting about Chinese culture, most students enjoy learning them.

- Spoken Expressions (口头用语/口頭用語): Part of the required basic vocabulary, these are colloquial expressions that you'll encounter frequently in everyday conversation.

- Featured Vocabulary (词汇注解/詞彙注解): Contains further explanations and examples for the more difficult-to-use or commonly-confused words and phrases.

- Supplementary Vocabulary (补充词汇/補充詞彙): Additional words related to the lesson topic. Not required for you to learn.

Starting in Volume 3 of the second year, we have included a background paragraph as a preface to the opening dialogue, which provides cultural information you need to understand the text. In the third year, the opening passages become more sophisticated as more written language is introduced, and the dialogues are shortened accordingly.

### Phonetics

This section (Lessons 1–8 in Volume 1) teaches you how to pronounce Chinese using pinyin, the standard romanization system. This section includes phonetic presentations along with exercises such as distinguishing tones, distinguishing sounds, pronunciation practice, and sight reading to help you master pinyin.

### Character Writing

This section (Lessons 2–8 in Volume 1) presents Chinese character composition, stroke types, stroke order, and radicals along with a Chinese character box for handwriting practice.

### Grammar

This section presents 3–5 grammar points related to the text in each lesson. The structures are introduced progressively from simple to complex and are displayed in chart form with plenty of supporting examples, making them accessible and easy to use for reference or self-study. You will start by learning parts of speech and the basic word order of a Chinese sentence. Gradually, you will begin to form more complex sentences using new grammatical structures, learn more function words (words with no substantial meaning, but specific grammatical roles), and more complex conjunctions unique to the Chinese language. Throughout the gram-mar sections, there are short "Practice" exercises that allow you to apply the grammar points you've just learned.

### Textbook Exercises

In each lesson of the textbook, we have added some classroom-based exercises to give you an opportunity to practice what you have learned with your teacher and your classmates. The textbook exercises focus on grammar and general understanding of the lessons. This allows the teacher to check whether you understand the materials presented in class and give you feedback as you develop your skills.

## Workbook

Each volume of *Chinese Odyssey* includes a workbook that contains four sections: listening, speaking, reading, and writing. Each section has 2–4 tasks, starting at an easy level and gradually becoming more difficult as your skills progress. For example, in the listening section you first might be asked to listen to a set of Chinese phrases and select the corresponding English. Later on, you might hear a short conversation or monologue and be asked to respond to questions based on the text. Speaking exercises emphasize pronunciation, intonation, and conversational skills along with correct grammatical structure. Reading and writing exercises measure your ability to respond to authentic sections of Chinese text or measure interact in a real-life situation you might encounter (writing an e-mail, filling out a form, writing a summary based on web research, etc).

## Multimedia CD-ROM Set

The multimedia CD-ROM is a stand-alone courseware, and includes the same wide range of activities covering listening, speaking, reading, writing, and grammar that you'll find in the textbook and workbook. In addition, the multimedia CD-ROM includes interactive activities and detailed explanations for the practice material, and offers the following technological advantages to help you further improve your language skills:

- A variety of images, video, audio, and readings that incorporate all the basic language skills in a dynamic multimedia environment.

- An interactive platform that allows you to engage in pre-recorded dialogues with the computer.

- Voice-recording capability that allows you to compare your pronunciation with that of a native speaker.

- The flexibility to optimize activities to your own personal skill level, for example by choosing to hear audio clips at different speeds, and choosing to show or hide pinyin.

- Vocabulary lists that feature step-by-step demonstration of character creation and stroke order.

- Immediate feedback on exercise results, with relevant explanations.

- Video clips and authentic materials that help broaden your understanding of life in contemporary China.

- Easy-to-follow navigation and attractive layout.

For more information on the Multimedia CD-ROM, please see "The Chinese Odyssey Multimedia CD-ROM" on p. xiii.

### *Audio CD*

The audio CDs includes all lesson texts and vocabulary in the textbook, as well as all listening exercises and some speaking exercises in the workbook. The audio CDs are designed for those who prefer not to use the multimedia CD-ROMs.

## Using the Materials in *Chinese Odyssey*

There are four major ways to utilize the materials in *Chinese Odyssey*.

### *Multimedia CD-ROM Set*

This is the primary element, and includes all lessons, grammar, vocabulary, and exercises in the program. It can be used as a stand-alone set, or in conjunction with other elements.

### *Textbook + Multimedia CD-ROM Set*

This combination allows you to work away from the computer, and includes all the lessons, grammar, and vocabulary, plus some additional in-class exercises.

### *Textbook + Workbook + Multimedia CD-ROM Set*

The workbook allows you to do listening, reading, writing, and some speaking exercises without a computer. It includes all the workbook exercises on the CD-ROM, with the exception of some speaking exercises that require voice recording and playback.

### *Textbook + Workbook + Audio CD Set*

This combination works well for people who aren't utilizing the multimedia CD-ROMs. The audio CD set contains audio content for all lessons, plus listening exercises and some speaking exercises.

*Chinese Odyssey* is an excellent courseware package, but like any teaching tool, it's only half of the equation. We've provided you with the materials, and now it's up to you to make the best use of them. Remember, the more you practice your Chinese, the better you will become. We wish you the best of luck and hope that you enjoy *Chinese Odyssey*.

# The Chinese Odyssey Multimedia CD-ROM

The Multimedia CD-ROM is the primary element in the Chinese Odyssey courseware, and may either be used as a stand-alone set or, for those who prefer to work with pen and paper, supplemented with the textbook and workbook. Directly correlated with the textbook and workbook, the multimedia CD-ROM allows you to practice listening, speaking, reading, and writing Chinese in an interactive format at your own pace.

## Texts

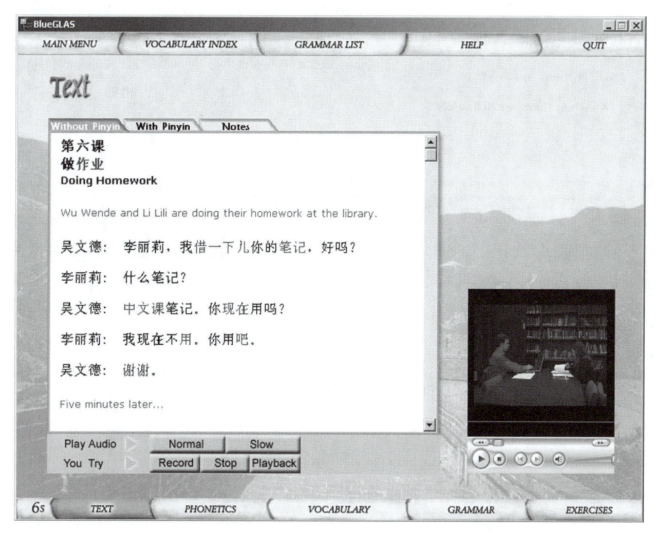

- Read and listen to each lesson's text.

- Show or hide pinyin.

- See a video in which speakers enact the dialogues.

# Phonetics

BlueGLAS

| MAIN MENU | VOCABULARY INDEX | GRAMMAR LIST | HELP | QUIT |

## Phonetics

**Presentation** | Tones | Pinyin Review | All Pinyin

### I. Review of Initials and Finals

The initials and finals selected for review here are based on vocabulary learned in this lesson.  We have included initials and finals from previous lessons in parentheses, to be used with those that we covered in this lesson.

| Initials: | ch | p | (b | zh | sh) | | |
| Finals: | -i | iao | ua | uang | (ao | an | ang) |

### II. Phonetic Spelling Rules

### A. When There are No Initials

iao --> yao    When -iao does not have any initials, i changes to y.

ua --> wa    When -ua does not have any initials, u changes

5s | TEXT | PHONETICS | VOCABULARY | GRAMMAR | EXERCISES

- Learn new sounds and tones.
- See a table containing all sounds in the Chinese language.
- Click on any word to hear its pronunciation.

# Vocabulary

**BlueGLAS**

| MAIN MENU | VOCABULARY INDEX | GRAMMAR LIST | HELP | QUIT |

## *Vocabulary*

| Vocabulary | Practice | Characters | Stroke Type | Stroke Order |

### 词汇 (Cíhuì) Vocabulary

Click the characters for stroke order, and click the pinyin for audio.

1. 作业    zuòyè    n.    homework, assignment

2. 借    jiè    v.    to borrow, lend

3. 一下儿 yíxiàr    phr.    (lit.) "one stroke," often used immediately after the verb.
   一      n.    one
   下儿    m.    stroke

4. 笔记    bǐjì    n.    notes
   笔      n.    pen
   记      v.    to record

| 6s | TEXT | PHONETICS | VOCABULARY | GRAMMAR | EXERCISES |

- View each lesson's vocabulary list.

- Click on any character to see how it's written.

- Click on any pinyin word to hear how it's pronounced.

- Record your voice and compare your pronunciation to that of a native speaker.

# Grammar

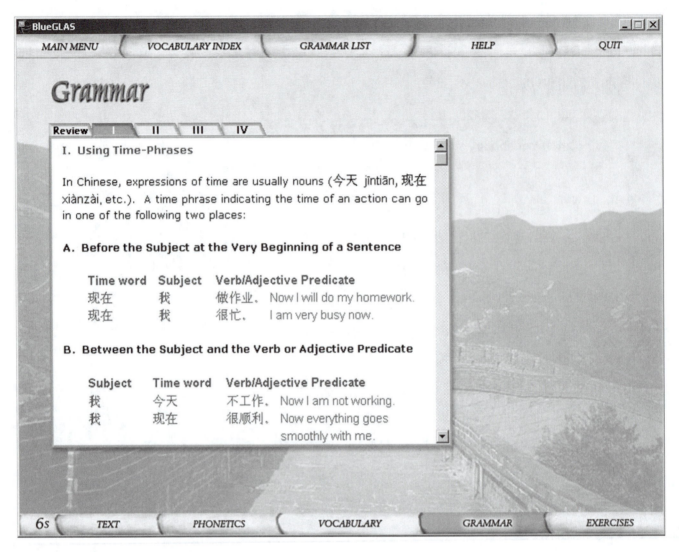

- Review each lesson's grammar points.

# Exercises

## Textbook: Paraphrase Task

Previous Task        Next Task

**Paraphrasing - Task 1: Paraphrasing**

**Exercise 1/2.** Translate the following dialogue into Chinese, using your own words. When you are comfortable with your translation, record yourself speaking. To check your pronunciation, listen to the dialogue between the two speakers.

Exercise 1/2 (Step 1 Oral) ◁ ▷

Record

Stop

Playback

Submit

| Script | Key | Text | Voc | Gram |

**Script 1/2  Returning the notes**

A:    Where are you going?

B:    I am going to return the Chinese notes.

A:    You are not using them now.  Is it okay if I use it for a second?

B:    Sure.

6s | TEXT | PHONETICS | VOCABULARY | GRAMMAR | EXERCISES

- Do exercises in the textbook and workbook.

- See a key with explanations of correct answers.

- Record your voice and compare your pronunciation to that of a native speaker.

- Easily reference the lesson's text, vocabulary list, and grammar notes.

- View your scores.

# List of Abbreviations

## General Abbreviations

| Abbreviation | Full Word |
| --- | --- |
| gram. | grammar |
| lit. | literally |
| sb. | somebody |
| sth. | something |
| voc. | vocabulary |
| vs. | versus |

## Part of Speech Abbreviations

| Abbreviation | Full Word |
| --- | --- |
| adj. | adjective |
| adj. phr. | adjective phrase |
| adv. | adverb |
| aux. | auxiliary |
| b.f. | bound form |
| conj. | conjunction |
| interj. | interjection |
| interrog. | interrogative |
| m.w. | measure word |
| n. | noun |
| n. phr. | noun phrase |
| num. | number |
| part. | particle |
| phr. | phrase |
| pref. | prefix |
| prep. | preposition |
| pron. | pronoun |
| s.e. | spoken expression |
| sent. | sentence |
| suff. | suffix |
| v. | verb |
| v. comp. | verb complement |
| v. obj. | verb object |
| v. phr. | verb phrase |

通向中国

# Chinese Odyssey

*Innovative Chinese Courseware*

SIMPLIFIED Character

## Vol. 1 • TEXTBOOK

Xueying Wang, Li-chuang Chi, and Liping Feng

王学英　　　祁立庄　　　冯力平

 CHENG & TSUI COMPANY Boston

# 1
# Introduction to Chinese Phonetics

***In this lesson you will:***
- Get a brief overview of Chinese phonetics, the Chinese writing system, and spoken Chinese.
- Learn about the pinyin system, including the basics of initials, finals, and tones.

 Overview

Chinese is spoken by more people than any other language except English. It is one of the five official languages of the United Nations. Standard Chinese, or Mandarin, is the form of the language taught throughout the school system of China and is the official medium of communication for the country. Within China, this standard form of the language is known as *putonghua*, or "the common language," to distinguish it from the many other dialects and subdialects of Chinese. One also hears it referred to by the term *Hanyu*, which distinguishes it from the languages of China's fifty-odd minority peoples and from foreign, non-Chinese languages.

In this lesson, you will learn how to pronounce some basic Chinese vocabulary. You will also be introduced — briefly — to the written language, although you won't begin learning how to write until the next lesson.

## Written Chinese

In terms of the written form, Chinese is not an alphabetic language, but is composed of individual characters: each represents a meaningful syllable of the spoken language.

Chinese characters have undergone a long process of evolution. A few characters have developed from pictographs. For example, the drawing ☉ originally represented the sun, and ☽ the moon. Over time, these drawings were gradually formalized into the written characters 日 (*ri* "sun") and 月

1

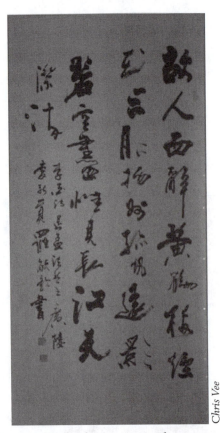

Chris Vee

*Classical poetry by the famous Tang dynasty poet Li Bai.*

(*yue* "moon"). These two "radicals," or root components, were then combined into a single character 明 representing the syllable *ming*, meaning "bright." Many characters — though a relatively small percentage of the total — are thus formed from two or more meaningful components.

The single most prolific principle of character formation is "radical plus phonetic," in which a character is formed from a radical component plus a phonetic component. The radical usually has some connection to the meaning of the compound character, while the phonetic part carries the pronunciation or at least gives a hint at the pronunciation of the character. This principle can be illustrated by the following group of characters, whose pronunciations differ only by tone: 方 *fāng*, 芳 *fāng*, 房 *fáng*, 访 *fǎng*, 放 *fàng*. However, you should note that 方 is an unusually "strong" phonetic. Few "families" of characters that share a common phonetic component will be quite as similar in pronunciation as this group.

## Riddle

Now let's have some fun. Given the meaning of its components, can you guess the identity of the mystery character? The character in question has two top-bottom components: 田 (meaning "field") and 力 (meaning "force"). What does the character 男 mean?

Answer: 男 = man. Sound anachronistic? Maybe. Remember, the Chinese language is thousands of years old. In ancient times, it is likely that men did most of the work in the fields, which probably contributed to the derivation of this character.

    If you guessed correctly, congratulations! If not, don't get discouraged. This is only one of many ways that Chinese characters can be formed. You'll have plenty of opportunities to try again.

## Spoken Chinese

Traditionally, Chinese learned the pronunciation of characters in their regional dialect, while Westerners wanting to learn the Chinese language used one or another of a rather large number of romanization systems that were developed over the past several centuries. Then, in the first half of the twentieth century, the Chinese government began to promote the use of a standard national language, and romanization, as well as other phonetic spelling systems, was used to aid speakers of other dialects in their study of Mandarin. After the official promulgation of *Hanyu* pinyin in 1958, this system became the standard in China and also gradually became the dominant system used outside of China for representing spoken Mandarin. Once you know pinyin, you'll be able to use the Internet, dictionaries, and any other reference with alphanumerical characters. Knowledge of pinyin is also necessary if you want to use many of the Chinese word processors on the market.

# Pinyin

Pinyin, literally "phonetic spelling," uses twenty-five of the twenty-six letters of the Latin alphabet (see how long it will take you to discover which letter

Chris Vee

is not used), plus tone marks and one other diacritic, to represent the sound system of Mandarin.

Linguists discuss the initial and final components of Chinese syllables. The initial is always a consonant, while the final is made up of a vowel nucleus with an optional final consonant and a tone. The only consonants that occur in the final position are -n, -ng, and -r. Thus, in each of the following syllables the first letter is the initial, and the remainder of the syllable is the final: *hao, ri, ming, fang.* (See the following for more detailed information and additional examples.)

## Initials

In the following table the twenty-one initial consonants are arranged in rows and columns to show grouping by place and manner of articulation. Familiarity with this table will help you learn the sounds of Chinese and their spellings in the pinyin system. Most of these sounds are identical or very similar to English sounds spelled with the same letters. However, in several cases, either the sound is different from anything in English, or the spelling itself is likely to be confusing. The Notes section below the table is designed to help with these difficult sounds.

### Table of Initials

| | Stops and Affricates | | | | |
| | Unaspirated | Aspirated | Nasals | Fricatives | Lateral and Retroflex |
|---|---|---|---|---|---|
| Labials | b | p | m | f | |
| Dentals | d | t | n | | l |
| Velars | g | k | | h | |
| Palatals | j | q | | x | |
| Retroflexes | zh | ch | | sh | r |
| Dental sibilants | z | c | | s | |

## Notes

1. The sounds in the first three rows are the same as or very similar to English sounds represented by the same spellings. However, it should be noted that: (a) The unaspirated and aspirated columns of stops and affricates are distinguished *only* by aspiration (the puff of breath that accompanies the *p, t, k,* etc., in column two), because the sounds in columns one and two are unvoiced. (b) In careful articulation, *h* is pronounced with fric-

tion between the back of the tongue and the velum, or soft palate, rather than just the quiet breathiness of an English *h*.

2. The palatals (row four: *j, q, x*) are similar to an English *j, ch,* and *sh* except that the part of the tongue that makes contact with the palate is not the tip but the area a bit further back from the tip.

3. The first three retroflex sounds (row five: *zh, ch, sh*) are also somewhat similar to an English *j, ch,* and *sh*, but they are pronounced with the tip of the tongue turned upward and making contact with the back of the gum ridge or the front part of the palate. In the flow of speech, *r* often sounds much like an initial English *r*, but when articulated carefully, it is very different, with the tip of the tongue curled upward and brought close enough to the front part of the palate so that a local buzzing sound is produced.

4. Row six contains two of the most difficult sounds and one of the easiest. Many beginning students find *z* and *c* difficult, not because English has no similar sounds but because the most similar sounds in English do not occur at the beginning of a word: *z* (unaspirated) is similar to the final sound of "ki**ds**," and *c* (aspirated) is similar to the final sound of "pe**ts**"; *s* is the same as an English *s*.

## Finals

The final of a Chinese syllable can be composed of one, two, or three vowels; or one or two vowels plus one of the final consonants (*-n, -ng,* or *-r*). Linguists usually arrange the finals in four groups — or rows in a table — according to whether the first (or only) sound in the final is: (1) an open vowel, (2) the high front unrounded vowel *i*, (3) the high back rounded vowel *u*, or (4) the high front rounded vowel *ü*. In addition, the very special vowel *-i*, which oc-

*The sidewalk and street that runs along West Lake in Hangzhou.*

curs only after the initials of rows five and six in the table above (*zh, ch, sh, r; z, c, s*), is also placed in row one.

Because the phonetic value — that is, the actual pronunciation — of some of these finals is quite complicated and in a number of cases it is not possible to make useful comparisons with English sounds, we will not attempt to explain the pronunciation at this point. Please be aware that you should pay close attention to the recordings as you learn the sound system of Chinese. Note the spelling rules that follow the table.

### Table of Finals

| -i | a | o | e | ai | ei | ao | ou | an | en | ang | eng | er |
|----|---|---|---|----|----|----|----|----|----|-----|-----|-----|
| i | ia | | ie | | | iao | iu | ian | in | iang | ing | iong |
| u | ua | uo | | uai | ui | | | uan | un | uang | ong | |
| ü | | | üe | | | | | üan | ün | | | |

## Spelling Rules

1.  Note that the first final in row one, which we have written as *-i*, occurs only after the initials *zh, ch, sh, r, z, c,* and *s.* Phonetically, it is entirely different from the *i* in row two. It is pronounced by slightly retracting the tip of the tongue from the position for articulation of the preceding initial consonant.

2.  When a final from row two occurs without an initial consonant, *i* standing alone is written as *yi,* and for the remaining finals, *i* is replaced by *y: ya, ye, yao,* etc.

*A public park in Yangzhou, a city with a rich cultural and historical legacy.*

3. When a final from row three occurs without an initial consonant, *u* standing alone is written as *wu*, and for the remaining finals, *u* is replaced by *w*: *wa, wo, wai*, etc.

4. When a final from row four occurs without an initial consonant, *y* is added in front of the final and the umlaut mark is dropped from the *ü*: *yu, yue, yuan, yun*. When these finals occur after the palatal initials *j, q, x*, the umlaut is dropped: *ju, jue, quan, xun*, etc. When *ü* and *üe* occur after *n* or *l*, the umlaut is kept: *nü, nüe, lü, lüe*. Row four finals do not occur in any environments other than those mentioned here.

## Initial and Final Combinations

Please see the table in the Multimedia CD-ROM in All Pinyin of the Phonetics Section, Lesson 1-8. These are all the syllables in the Chinese language.

As you can see, the total number of Chinese syllables is limited, even when the variations related to all four tones are taken into consideration. On the other hand, the number of characters, when compared to the syllables, is almost limitless — even a small dictionary contains more than 10,000 characters, around 3,000 of which represent words or morphemes used in everyday speech. As a result, there are many homonyms in the Chinese language, because one syllable is usually shared by many characters.

## Tones

Tones are of paramount importance in the Chinese language. Each syllable has up to four main tones, plus a neutral tone. Tones are marked above the main vowel of the pinyin symbols (except for the neutral tone, which has no mark). Listen to the syllable *ma* pronounced in the four different tones.

| Tone | Pinyin | Character | Meaning |
|------|--------|-----------|---------|
| 1st tone | mā | 妈 | mother |
| 2nd tone | má | 麻 | hemp |
| 3rd tone | mǎ | 马 | horse |
| 4th tone | mà | 骂 | to swear, curse |
| Neutral tone | ma | 吗 | particle |

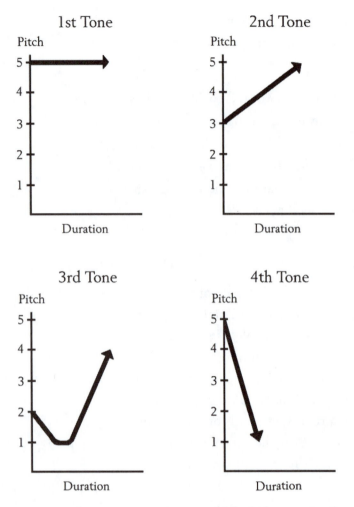

Can you imagine how your mother would feel if you mixed up the first tone with the third? Or with one of the other two tones? Now that we've seen an example, let's learn about the four tones.

The first tone is characterized by a high, steady monotone, without any change in pitch. The second tone is a rising tone that starts lower than the first tone and moves up to a higher pitch. The third tone falls to a very low pitch (even lower than the second tone) and then rises upward. (In everyday conversation, the third tone, unless emphasized, is seldom pronounced fully. It is often truncated into a half-third tone, which stays in the low pitch without much attempt to rise up again.) The fourth tone is a descending tone that starts at a high pitch and then moves down to a lower pitch.

The above is a series of charts that graphs the pitches of the four tones we have just discussed.

The neutral tone is pronounced lightly and quickly, without changing the pitch during pronunciation. However, its pitch varies according to the tones of the preceding, or the preceding and following, syllables.

As the Chinese saying goes, "What is well begun is halfway to success." Seymour, an American college student, never bothered to learn the correct tones. As a result, this was his first experience in China.

## *Joke*

Although Seymour can speak fluent Chinese, he frequently mixes up his tones. After he got off the airplane at the Beijing airport, he didn't know where to get his bags, so he stopped a pretty Chinese girl to ask for directions. Instead of saying, "Xiǎojiě, wǒ xiǎng *wèn wèn* nǐ?" ("Miss, may I ask you a question?"), Seymour asked, "Xiǎojiě, wǒ xiǎng *wén wén* nǐ?" The girl turned around and slapped him! It was only afterwards that the flustered boy realized he had used the second tone instead of the fourth and had actually asked, "May I smell you?" or "May I kiss you?"

This joke highlights the importance of learning proper pronunciation. Remember: It's much easier to learn to speak correctly from the start than to try to correct mistakes later on.

When pronounced correctly, the Chinese language has a unique musical quality to it. When you speak Chinese, try to think of the sentence as a full melodic phrase, rather than getting caught up pausing to check the tone of each syllable. Without further ado, let us begin our journey into this new tonal landscape.

The initials and finals are presented in four parts. Each part of the presentation will be followed by two practices: Distinguishing Tones and Distinguishing Sounds. The Distinguishing Tones exercises are designed to help you distinguish the tones and pronounce them correctly. The Distinguishing Sounds exercises, on the other hand, will teach you to distinguish and pronounce vowels and consonants.

# Part One

## 🎧💻 PRACTICING INITIALS AND FINALS

| Initials: | b | p | m | f | |
| --- | --- | --- | --- | --- | --- |
| | d | t | n | l | |
| Finals: | a | e | o | i | u |
| | ü | ai | ei | ao | ou |

## *Notes*

1. i ➤ y　　When there is no initial, *i* is spelled as *y*.

2. u ➤ w　　When there is no initial, *u* is spelled as *w*.

*Entrance to a teahouse in Shanghai.*

# Distinguishing Tones

Practice saying the tones correctly, making sure that you can recognize the differences among each of the four tones.

| | | | |
|---|---|---|---|
| bō | bó | bǒ | bò |
| pāo | páo | pǎo | pào |
| fū | fú | fǔ | fù |
| duō | duó | duǒ | duò |
| tōu | tóu | tǒu | tòu |
| yū | yú | yǔ | yù |
| lē | dé | měi | hèi |
| pāi | bái | mǎi | nài |

# Distinguishing Sounds

Listen carefully to the following pairs of syllables; note the differences between them, and try to pronounce them correctly.

| Initials: | pó | bó | tāo | lāo |
|---|---|---|---|---|
| | nǐ | lǐ | mǒu | fǒu |

|        |      |      |      |      |
|--------|------|------|------|------|
|        | yì   | lì   | wū   | fū   |
|        | wài  | bài  | nǔ   | lǔ   |
| **Finals:** | mǎi  | měi  | nǎi  | nǎo  |
|        | duō  | dōu  | nú   | nuó  |
|        | là   | lài  | de   | dí   |
|        | lì   | lè   | táo  | tóu  |

# Part Two

## 🎧📖 PRACTICING INITIALS AND FINALS

| **Initials:** | zh  | ch  | sh  | r |
|---------------|-----|-----|-----|---|
|               | z   | c   | s   |   |
| **Finals:**   | -i  | an  | en  |   |
|               | ang | eng | ong |   |

## *Note*

The -i stands for a very special vowel that is articulated by the tip of the tongue at the front of the hard palate (for the *zh-ch-sh-r* series) or behind the upper incisors (for the *z-c-s* series). To prounce this vowel keep the tongue tip in the same position as the preceding consonant, withdrawing it just enough to let air pass through. Since *zh*, *ch*, *sh* and *z*, *c*, *s* are voiceless consonant initials, voicing begins just as the vowel is pronounced. Since *r* is a voiced initial, the syllable *ri* is voiced throughout.

## Distinguishing Tones

Practice saying the tones correctly, making sure that you can recognize the differences among each of the four tones.

|       |       |       |       |
|-------|-------|-------|-------|
| zān   | zán   | zǎn   | zàn   |
| cī    | cí    | cǐ    | cì    |
| zhī   | zhí   | zhǐ   | zhì   |

| | | | |
|---|---|---|---|
| chī | chí | chǐ | chì |
| shī | shí | shǐ | shì |
| sōng | sóng | sǒng | sòng |
| zēng | céng | zhěn | chèn |
| rāng | ráng | zhǎn | chàn |

## Distinguishing Sounds

Listen carefully to the following pairs of syllables. Once you can hear the difference between them, practice saying them correctly.

| Initials: | cēn | sēn | cán | zán |
|---|---|---|---|---|
| | châng | shâng | zhì | chì |
| | róng | chóng | shěng | zhěng |
| | zī | sī | zhè | rè |
| Finals: | rǎn | rǎng | zhěn | zhěng |
| | chán | chéng | shèn | shàng |
| | zēng | zōng | cóng | cáng |
| | sān | sēn | rén | róng |

# Part Three

## 🎧📖 PRACTICING INITIALS AND FINALS

| Initials: | g | k | h | |
|---|---|---|---|---|
| Finals: | ua | uai | ui | uo |
| | uan | un | | |
| | uang | ueng | | |

## *Notes*

1. Initials *g*, *k*, and *h* can never be used with the finals starting with *i* and *ü*.

2. *ui* ➔ *u(e)i*       *ui* is the combination of *u* and *ei*. When there are initials, it is spelled as *-ui*. When there are no initials, it should be written as *wei*.

3. *un ➔ u(e)n*     *un* is the combination of *u* and *en*. When there are initials, it is spelled as *un*. When there are no initials, it should be written as *wen*.

## Distinguishing Tones

Practice saying the tones correctly, making sure that you can recognize the differences among each of the four tones.

| | | | |
|---|---|---|---|
| wā | wá | wǎ | wà |
| huān | huán | huǎn | huàn |
| wāng | wáng | wǎng | wàng |
| wēng | wéng | wěng | wèng |
| kuī | kuí | kuǐ | kuì |
| wēi | wéi | wěi | wèi |
| hūn | hún | hǔn | hùn |
| guāi | huái | kuǎi | kuài |

## Distinguishing Sounds

Listen carefully to the following pairs of syllables; note the differences between them, and try to pronounce them correctly.

| Initials: | guī | kuī | kùn | gùn |
|---|---|---|---|---|
| | huān | kuān | guài | huài |
| | kuā | huā | huǎng | guǎng |
| | wén | hún | gùn | wèn |
| **Finals:** | huán | huáng | guài | guì |
| | wāng | wēng | kuǎ | kuǐ |
| | wēng | wēn | huí | hún |
| | kuò | kùn | gǔn | gǒng |

# Part Four

## 🎧 PRACTICING INITIALS AND FINALS

| Initials: | j | q | x | |
|---|---|---|---|---|
| **Finals:** | ia | iao | ie | iu |

|      |     |      |     |
|------|-----|------|-----|
| ian  | in  | üan  | ün  |
| iang | ing | iong | üe  |

# Notes

1. When *i* follows the initials *j*, *q*, or *x*, it is pronounced like the "i" in the English "ski."

2. *ie* is pronounced like the "ye" in the English "yes."

3. *y* → *i*        When there is no initial, *i* is spelled as *y*.

4. *iu* → *i(o)u*    *iu* is the combination of *i* and *ou*. When there is an initial, it is spelled as -*iu* (e.g., *liu*). When there are no initials, *i* changes to *y* and *u* changes to *ou* (e.g., *you*).

5. Note that the vowel *ü* occurs only: (1) after the initials *j*, *q*, *x* and (in a very few words) *n* and *l*, (2) in syllables with no initial. When it occurs after *j*, *q*, and *x*, the umlaut is omitted: *ju*, *jue*; *qun*, *quan*; *xue*, *xuan*, etc. When it occurs in syllables with no initial, a *y* is added in front of it and the umlaut is omitted: *yu*, *yue*, *yun*, *yuan*. Only when it occurs after *n* or *l* is the umlaut retained: *nü*, *lü*, *nüe*, *lüe*.

# Distinguishing Tones

Practice saying the tones correctly, making sure that you can recognize the differences among each of the four tones.

|      |      |      |      |
|------|------|------|------|
| jiā  | jiá  | jiǎ  | jià  |
| qiāo | qiáo | qiǎo | qiào |
| xiē  | xié  | xiě  | xiè  |
| qīn  | qín  | qǐn  | qìn  |
| xuē  | xué  | xuě  | xuè  |
| yōng | yóng | yǒng | yòng |
| yūn  | yún  | yǔn  | yùn  |
| qiū  | qiú  | jiǔ  | jiù  |

# Distinguishing Sounds

Listen carefully to the following pairs of syllables; note the differences between them, and try to pronounce them correctly.

| Initials: | jiǒng | qióng | quán | xuán |
|-----------|-------|-------|------|------|
|           | xīn   | jǐn   | què  | jué  |
|           | xiāo  | qiǎo  | jǐng | xǐng |
|           | yǒu   | jǒu   | xiè  | yè   |

| Finals: | jiān  | jiǎng | qín  | qíng |
|---------|-------|-------|------|------|
|         | xuān  | xūn   | jué  | jié  |
|         | qiē   | quē   | xiōng| xūn  |
|         | yào   | yà    | yǒu  | yǒng |

## Cast of Characters 人物介绍

李丽莉 and 林笛 are female college students. They are friends and roommates taking Chinese class together.

吴文德 is a male student who attends the same college as 李丽莉 and 林笛. He also studies Chinese and is a close friend of 李丽莉 and 林笛.

高朋 is another male college student who studies Chinese. Initially, he only knows Lin Di, but later on he and 吴文德 become roommates. He is a good student and a good cook.

As time passes, 李丽莉, 林笛, 吴文德 and 高朋 become very close friends.

## Supporting Characters

陈大勇 is a male student, a schoolmate of 李丽莉 and 林笛.

张子倩 is 陈大勇's girlfriend who visits 陈大勇 at his school periodically.

史老师 is one of the instructors who teaches 李丽莉 and 林笛.

胡老师 is 林笛's Chinese teacher.

胡阿姨 is a close family friend of 吴文德.

李叔叔 is 胡阿姨's husband.

高先生 is a long time family friend of 李丽莉.

# 2

# 你早

# Basic Greetings

**In this lesson you will:**

- Review pronunciation, with special emphasis on tones.
- Learn some basic principles of Chinese character composition and rules of phonetic spelling.
- Greet someone in a culturally appropriate way.

It is the first day of school, and Chinese class is about to start.

| | | |
|---|---|---|
| Lǐ Lìlì: | Lín Dí, nǐ zǎo. | |
| 李丽莉： | 林笛，你早。 | |
| Lín Dí: | Zǎo. | |
| 林笛： | 早。 | |
| Lǐ Lìlì : | Shǐ Lǎoshī, nín hǎo! | |
| 李丽莉： | 史老师，您好！ | |
| Shǐ Lǎoshī: | Nǐ hǎo, Lǐ Lìlì! | |
| 史老师： | 你好，李丽莉！ | |
| Lín Dí: | Shǐ Lǎoshī zǎo! | |
| 林笛： | 史老师早！ | |
| Shǐ Lǎoshī: | Nǐ zǎo. | |
| 史老师： | 你早。 | |

 生词表 (Shēngcí Biǎo)

# Vocabulary

| | Character | Pinyin | Part of Speech | English Definition |
|---|---|---|---|---|
| 1. | 你 | nǐ | *pron.* | you (singular) |
| 2. | 早 | zǎo | *adj.* | early |

3. 老师    lǎoshī      *n.*    teacher, professor
   老                  *adj.*  old, respected
   师                  *b.f.*  teacher, master
4. 您      nín         *pron.* you (singular, in formal or polite form)
5. 好      hǎo         *adj.*  good, well

专有名词 **(Zhuānyǒu Míngcí) Proper Nouns**

1. 林笛    Lín Dí                a female's name '
2. 李丽莉  Lǐ Lìlì               a female's name
3. 史老师  Shǐ Lǎoshī            Teacher Shi, Professor Shi

补充词汇 **(Bǔchōng Cíhuì) Supplementary Vocabulary**

1. 先生    xiānsheng   *n.*    gentleman, Mr., Sir, husband
2. 小姐    xiǎojiě     *n.*    young lady, Miss
3. 太太    tàitai      *n.*    Mrs., Madam
4. 早上好。 Zǎoshang hǎo. *sent.* Good morning.
5. 早安。  Zǎoān.      *sent.* Good morning (more formal).
6. 晚安。  Wǎnān.      *sent.* Good night.

语法(Yǔfǎ)

Grammar

## I. Chinese Names

In Chinese, the surname always comes before the given name. Surnames usually consist of one character (i.e., one syllable), although there are a few two-character surnames. Those surnames with one character are called *dān xìng*, or single surnames, while surnames with two characters or more are called *fù xìng*, or compound surnames. No one knows how many unique Chinese surnames there are in total. There are about two hundred common surnames, with Zhang 张(Zhāng), Wang 王(Wáng), Li 李(Lǐ), and Zhao 赵(Zhào) being the most common single surnames and Zhu Ge, Ou Yang, and Si Tu the most common compound surnames.

*Margaret Vee*

*A pagoda in Hangzhou, a city well known for its natural beauty and cultural heritage.*

Chinese given names can have either one or two characters. Given names usually have a very specific meaning. A person's name can state a birthplace or time of birth by using words such as "capital" or "morning." Some names also use words such as "rain," "snow," "winter," and "spring" to express a nature theme. Others include words associated with health or luck, such as *jiàn* (good health), *fú* (good luck), and *shòu* (long life).

Male and female given names have a few key differences. Male names are usually composed of characters that show courage and strength, such as *qiáng* (strong), *hǔ* (tiger), *yǒng* (brave), and *gāng* (steel). Female names are more often composed of characters that emphasize beauty, compassion, and a calm temperament, such as *lì* (beautiful), *yǎ* (elegance), *jìng* (calm), and *shú* (virtuous). On the whole, Chinese people pick names based on the meaning of the characters. The following are the names we have learned in this lesson:

| Surname | Given Name |
|---------|------------|
| 李 | 丽莉 |
| 林 | 笛 |

### *Note*

In addition to a formal name (surname and given name), some people also have a *xiǎo míng*, or nickname, which is usually picked in one's youth. These nicknames are generally used by family members and close friends.

## PRACTICE

Give each student in the class a Chinese name and explain each name's meaning.

## II. Addressing People

In the workplace in China, you should always address a person of higher status by his or her last name followed by the appropriate title to show respect. This also applies in school, when speaking to your professors or other teachers and when dealing with directors, employers, etc. For example:

| Surname | Title | |
|---------|-------|---|
| 史 | 老师 | Professor Shi |

Literally, 史老师 is translated as "Teacher Shi," but it would be awkward to address your instructor this way in standard English. Although the person being addressed may not have the rank of professor, for the purpose of showing respect we will instead translate "老师 + surname" as "Professor + surname" throughout the text.

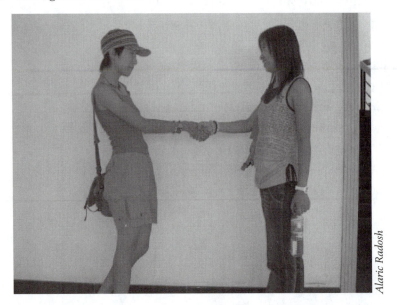

*Alaric Radosh*

## ❀ PRACTICE

Student volunteers play the role of the teacher. As these volunteer "teachers" tell the class their Chinese names, students will address these "teachers" in a culturally correct way.

## III. Greeting People

"Pronoun/Noun + 好(hǎo)/早(zǎo)" is used as a greeting. This structure is NOT a question. The response should be either "你好/早" or "您好/早."

| A. Pronoun | | |
|---|---|---|
| 你 | 好/早。 | Hi/Good morning. |
| 您 | 好/早。 | Hi/Good morning. |

### *Notes*

1. 早     An informal way of greeting people early in the morning.

2. 您好     A more polite way of greeting people who are older or have a higher social status than you. You should use this in situations where you want to show respect or social formality (e.g., when addressing your teacher).

3. 你好     The most common way to greet someone. You can use this at any time of day, in both formal and informal situations.

| B. Surname | Title | |
|---|---|---|
| （史） | 老师 | 好/早。 |

### *Note*

If you are greeting someone and you don't know his or her last name, you can simply greet that person with his or her title (e.g., 老师好 or 老师早).

## ❀ PRACTICE

You are preparing breakfast when you get a phone call from your friend and another from one of your mother's colleagues. Use 好/早 to greet them.

# 语音复习 (Yǔyīn Fùxí)
# Pronunciation Review

## I. Review of Initials and Finals

The initials and finals selected for review are based on vocabulary learned in this lesson.

**Initials:**    h        l        n        sh        z

**Finals:**    i        ao        in        -i

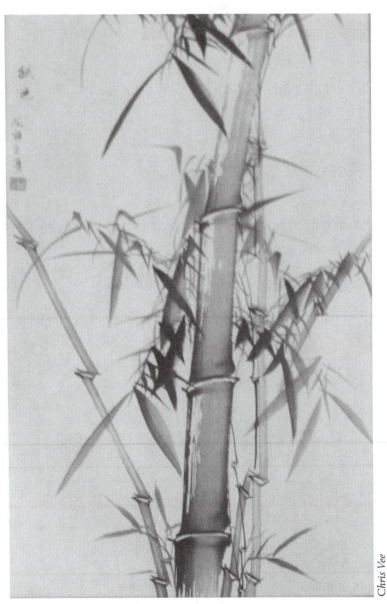

*Chris Vee*

*Chinese brush painting.*

## *Notes*

1. *i* vs. *-i*:    *i* is pronounced "ee" as in the English "leek." It usually follows *b*, *p*, *m*, *n*, *d*, *t*, *l*, *j*, *q*, or *x*. The *-i* stands for a very special vowel that is articulated by the tip of the tongue at the front of the hard palate (for the *zh-ch-sh-r* series) or behind the upper incisors (for the *z-c-s* series). To pronounce this vowel, keep the tongue tip in the same position as the preceding consonant, withdrawing it just enough to let air pass through. Because *zh*, *ch*, *sh*, *z*, *c*, and *s* are voiceless consonant initials, voicing begins just as the vowel is pronounced.

2. *in*:    When there is an initial, *in* is attached directly to that initial (e.g., *lin*). When there is no initial, *y* is added in front of *i* (e.g., *yin*).

## II. Tone Change Rules

The third tone is pronounced as a second tone when it is immediately followed by another third tone. For example:

| | | |
|---|---|---|
| 3rd + 3rd | → | 2nd + 3rd |
| nǐ hǎo | → | ní hǎo |
| nǐ zǎo | → | ní zǎo |
| hǎo lǎoshī | → | háo lǎoshī |

# 写汉字(Xiě Hànzì)
# Character Writing

## I. Character Composition

As you learned in the previous lesson, Chinese is not an alphabetic language. Some of the Chinese characters consist of only one component, while others have multiple components. For example:

| Character | # of Components | Type of Composition |
|---|---|---|
| 史 | One component (史) | Indivisible |
| 好 | Two components (女 and 子) | Left-right |
| 早 | Two components (日 and 十) | Top-bottom |

Please note that some of the characters cannot be divided into different components, so they are called indivisibles. Some can be divided into a left-hand part and a right-hand part (the left-right composition). Others can be divided into a top and a bottom part (the top-bottom composition).

Each Chinese character, simple or complex, is expected to occupy the same amount of space, which is roughly square-shaped.

Therefore, a character with many strokes would have to be squeezed more tightly than one with fewer strokes. For example, although 您 has quite a few more strokes than 好, it must still be compacted into the same amount of space.

## II. Types of Strokes and Stroke Order

All Chinese character components are constructed from a few basic types of strokes. The following are basic strokes used in writing Chinese characters:

Strokes:

Examples: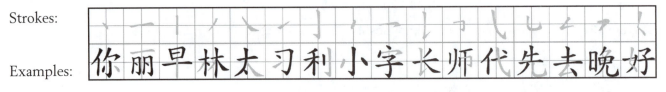

After learning individual strokes, it is also important to understand the basic rules of stroke order used in writing Chinese characters. Each character follows a specific sequence of strokes, or "stroke order." For example, the word 好 is composed like this:

*Rules of Stroke Order*

| Rules | | Examples | Stroke Order |
|---|---|---|---|
| 1. | 一 precedes 丨 | 十 | 一 十 |
| 2. | 丿 precedes 丶 | 八 | 丿 八 |
| 3. | From top to bottom | 吕 | 口 吕 |

| 4. | From left to right | 好 | | 女 | 好 |
| 5. | From outside to inside | 用 | | 冂 | 用 |
| 6. | Inside stroke precedes the sealing stroke | 日 | 冂 | 月 | 日 |
| 7. | Middle stroke precedes the two sides | 小 | 亅 | 小 | 小 |

## III. Key Radical Presentation

Characters with multiple components usually have one part that is a radical. A radical is like a root to which many different components can be attached to form different characters. In Chinese dictionaries and other reference books, words are classified according to these radicals. Some radical names are not intuitive. In each of the lessons throughout this book, we will introduce the names of radicals that will help you write Chinese characters.

1. 你 has the person radical, 亻, which often appears in characters that refer to people.

2. 好 has the female radical, 女, which refers to women and femininity.

3. 您 has the heart radical, 心.

4. 早 has the sun radical, 日.

*Margaret Vee*

*Replica of a classical Chinese residence.*

## IV. Handwriting

Please also note that the printed version of the Chinese characters is not identical to the hand-written version. We have provided both versions for your viewing, along with the space in the Chinese character box for you to practice.

### *Left-Right Composition*

In this group, the left part is proportionally thinner, shorter, or smaller than the right part.

| Character | Practice with Chinese Characters |
|---|---|
| 你<br>好<br>师 | |

### *Top-Bottom Composition*

| Character | Practice with Chinese Characters |
|---|---|
| 您<br>早<br>老 | |

课堂练习 (Kètáng Liànxí)

In-Class Exercises

### 🎧📖 TASK 1. DISTINGUISHING TONES

Your teacher will randomly pronounce the items in each of the following groups. If the first tone you hear is the fourth tone, you should put a fourth tone mark above the first item in a given group. If the second tone you hear is the first tone, put a first tone mark over the second item, and so on (e.g., à á...).

*Sunrise over Huang Shan (Yellow Mountain) in Anhui Province.*

1.  ni        ni        ni        ni

2.  zao       zao       zao       zao

3.  hao       hao       hao       hao

4.  yin       yin       yin       yin

5.  shi       shi       shi       shi

6.  shao      shao      shao      shao

7.  lao       lao       lao       lao

8.  li        li        li        li

## 🎧 TASK 2. DISTINGUISHING SOUNDS

Your teacher will pronounce one of the two syllables in each group. Listen carefully and circle the one you hear.

**Initials**

1. nǐ        lǐ        2. zāo       shāo

3. yì        nì        4. lín       yín

**Finals**

| 1. ní | nín | 2. lǐn | lǐng |
|-------|-----|--------|------|
| 3. shà | shào | 4. zāo | zōu |

## TASK 3. SCRAMBLED WORDS

Rearrange the words and phrases to form grammatically correct and meaningful sentences.

1. 早　　　　你　　　　林笛
2. 好　　　史老师　　　您

## TASK 4. SITUATIONAL DIALOGUE

**Setting:**　　First day of school on campus.
**Cast:**　　　Two students are going to class.
**Situation:**　On the way, you meet some of your classmates and their teachers. Greet them in the culturally acceptable way.

# 3

# 你爸爸妈妈好吗？

# How's Your Family?

***In this lesson you will:***
- Learn to write Chinese characters.
- Use some family-related vocabulary.
- Use Chinese to politely discuss someone's well-being.

Wu Wende runs into a close family friend, Ms. Hu, at the grocery store.

| Hú Āyí: | Wú Wéndé, nǐ hǎo. |
|---|---|
| 胡阿姨： | 吴文德，你好。 |

| Wú Wéndé: | Nín hǎo, Hú Āyí! |
|---|---|
| 吴文德： | 您好，胡阿姨！ |

| Hú Āyí: | Nǐ bàba māma hǎo ma? |
|---|---|
| 胡阿姨： | 你爸爸妈妈好吗？ |

| Wú Wéndé: | Wǒ bàba māma hěn hǎo. |
|---|---|
| 吴文德： | 我爸爸妈妈很好。 |

| Hú Āyí: | Nǐ yéye nǎinai ne? |
|---|---|
| 胡阿姨： | 你爷爷奶奶呢？ |

| Wú Wéndé: | Tāmen yě hěn hǎo. Lǐ Shūshu hǎo ma? |
|---|---|
| 吴文德： | 他们也很好。李叔叔好吗？ |

| Hú Āyí: | Tā yě hěn hǎo. |
|---|---|
| 胡阿姨： | 他也很好。 |

......

| Wú Wéndé: | Hú Āyí, zàijiàn! |
|---|---|
| 吴文德： | 胡阿姨，再见！ |

| Hú Āyí: | Zàijiàn! |
|---|---|
| 胡阿姨： | 再见！ |

# 生词表 (Shēngcí Biǎo)
# Vocabulary

REQUIREMENT: You should be able to use all the vocabulary introduced in each lesson to do your listening, speaking, and reading exercises. For writing characters, you will only be held responsible for the vocabulary words marked with stars.

| Character | Pinyin | Part of Speech | English Definition |
|---|---|---|---|
| 1. 阿姨 | āyí | *n.* | auntie (mother's sister); used to address a woman of one's parents' generation |
| 2. 爸爸 | bàba | *n.* | dad, daddy |
| 3. 妈妈 | māma | *n.* | mom, mommy |
| 4. *吗 | ma | *part.* | an interrogative particle used to form questions |
| 5. *我 | wǒ | *pron.* | I, me |
| 6. *很 | hěn | *adv.* | very |
| 7. 爷爷 | yéye | *n.* | grandpa (father's father) |
| 8. 奶奶 | nǎinai | *n.* | grandma (father's mother) |
| 9. *呢 | ne | *part.* | an interrogative particle used to make up questions (see Grammar III) |
| 10. *他*们 | tāmen | *pron.* | they, them |
| 他 | | *pron.* | he, him |
| *她 | | *pron.* | she, her |
| 们 | | *suff.* | used to pluralize the singular personal pronouns |
| 11. *也 | yě | *adv.* | also, too |
| 12. 叔叔 | shūshu | *n.* | uncle (father's younger brother); used to address a man of one's parents' generation |
| 13. 再见 | zàijiàn | *v. phr.* | "Good-bye," "Farewell," "See you again" |
| 再 | | *adv.* | again |
| 见 | | *v.* | to see; to meet |

*A low bridge crossing in Hangzhou.*

## 专有名词 (Zhuānyǒu Míngcí) **Proper Nouns**

1. 胡阿姨    Hú Āyí                Auntie Hu
2. 吴文德    Wú Wéndé              a male's name
3. 李叔叔    Lǐ Shūshu             Uncle Li

## 补充词汇 (Bǔchōng Cíhuì) **Supplementary Vocabulary**

1. 父亲      fùqin       *n.*    father
2. 母亲      mǔqin       *n.*    mother
3. 父母      fùmǔ        *n.*    parents
4. 哥哥      gēge        *n.*    elder brother
5. 弟弟      dìdi        *n.*    younger brother
6. 姐姐      jiějie      *n.*    elder sister
7. 妹妹      mèimei      *n.*    younger sister
8. 兄弟姐妹  xiōngdì jiěmèi *n.* siblings

# 词汇注解 (Cíhuì Zhùjiě) **Featured Vocabulary**

们 (men): 们 is a plural suffix for pronouns and human nouns. Non-human nouns are in general not pluralized. For example:

Pronouns

　　　你们 you (pl.)　　　我们 we, us　　　他们 they, them

Human Nouns

　　　老师们　　　　　叔叔们　　　　　阿姨们

The use of 们 is complicated. There will be more explanations on 们 in the future lessons.

# 语法 (Yǔfǎ)
# Grammar

## I. Addressing People (Cont'd.)

### A.  Non Family Members

In China, in order to show respect when addressing an older person who is not a family member, you should use the surname + a noun indicating relationship. For example, if your neighbor is about the same age as your parents, you would call him or her "Uncle + Last Name" or "Aunt + Last Name." If she or he is closer to your grandparents' age, you would use "Grandma +Last Name" or "Grandpa+Last Name."

**Noun (indicating relationship)**

| Surname | Title | Pinyin | English |
|---------|-------|--------|---------|
| 胡 | 阿姨 | Hú Āyí | Auntie Hu |
| 李 | 叔叔 | Lǐ Shūshu | Uncle Li |
| 胡 | 奶奶 | Hú Nǎinai | Grandma Hu |
| 李 | 爷爷 | Lǐ Yéye | Grandpa Li |

### B. Family Members

When addressing your own relatives, you don't need to include their last names; just their titles will suffice.

| | | |
|---|---|---|
| 阿姨 | Āyí | Auntie |
| 叔叔 | Shūshu | Uncle |
| 爷爷 | Yéye | Grandpa |
| 奶奶 | Nǎinai | Grandma |

### C.  Husband and Wife

In China, a married woman keeps her own surname instead of taking her husband's surname. For example, when 胡阿姨 (Hú Āyí) married 李叔叔 (Lǐ Shūshu) , she kept her maiden name and was not called 李阿姨 (Lǐ Āyí).

## PRACTICE

Introduce us to at least three people of your grandparents' or parents' ages, using the appropriate titles. Be sure to include people of different genders!

## II. Basic Sentence Structure

Chinese sentences consist of a subject and predicate. They usually come in the following two forms:

    A. Subject + (Adverb) + Predicate Adjective

    B. Subject + (Adverb) + Predicate Verb

  In this lesson, we will focus on sentence structure A, which uses an adjective as the predicate. Here the subject usually precedes the predicate. The subject in Chinese can be a noun such as 爸爸, 老师 (bàba, lǎoshī), or a pronoun such as 你, 您 (nǐ, nín), etc. indicating "who" and "what." Chinese sentences with predicate adjectives are composed of a subject, one or more adverbs, and an adjective. Unlike English, these sentences don't use the verb "to be." For example:

| Subject | | Predicate | |
|---|---|---|---|
| Noun Phrase | Adverbs | Adjective | |
| Statement: 我爸爸妈妈 | 很 | 好。 | My parents are very well. |
| Statement: 李叔叔 | 也很 | 好。 | Uncle Li is also doing okay. |

## *Notes*

1. 很 (hěn): In the "Subject + 很 + Adjective" pattern, 很 cannot be omitted in the positive response. In this pattern, 很 does not serve to intensify the adjective, but is used as a phonetic filler to make the predicate slightly longer.

2. 也 (yě): When 也 and 很 are used together, 也 always comes before 很.

## PRACTICE

Try to make a few sentences using predicate adjectives and make sure that you use 很 and 也 correctly.

## III. The Interrogative Particles 吗 (Ma) and 呢 (Ne)

In general, when a Chinese question is formed, the question's word order stays the same as it was in statement form. The following are two of the many commonly used types of questions in the Chinese language.

*Alaric Radosh*

## A. Questions with Interrogative Particle 吗

This kind of question is formed by adding 吗 to the end of a statement. The pattern is "Statement + 吗." Right now we are only going to briefly introduce its positive responses. We will learn more about this pattern and its responses in the next lesson.

|  | Subject | Predicate Adjective | |  |
|---|---|---|---|---|
|  | **Noun Phrase** | **Adverbs** | **Adjective** |  |
| Question: | 你爸爸妈妈 |  | 好吗？ | How are your dad and mom? |
| Response: | 他们 | 很 | 好。 |  |
| Question: | 李叔叔 |  | 好吗？ | How is Uncle Li? |
| Response: | 他 | 也很 | 好。 |  |

## B. Questions with Interrogative Particle 呢

呢 forms a question as a follow-up to a previous question. It echoes back to something previously mentioned in the conversation, but shifts the attention to a different person or thing. It is similar to "And you?" or "How about you?" in English. For example:

*Previous Question:*

你爷爷好吗？    Is your grandpa well?

*Follow-up Question:*

| Noun/Pronoun | 呢 | |
|---|---|---|
| 你奶奶 | 呢？ | What about your grandma? |

*Typical small Chinese decorative jars.*

Chris Vee

## PRACTICE

You are taking a job at a local nursing home and are concerned about some of the residents. Talk to the staff and ask at least two questions about the residents. Be sure to provide questions which demonstrate that you know how to use 吗 and 呢.

## IV. Brief Introduction to Possessives

In Chinese, the word 的(de) is usually used to indicate possessives. However, with a close relationship, such as family members, the 的 can be omitted. For example:

| Pronoun | Noun |
|---|---|
| 我(的)爸爸妈妈 | my parents |
| 你(的)爷爷奶奶 | your grandparents |

**PRACTICE**

Bring some pictures or photos of your family to class and identify each individual. Feel free to make things up, but demonstrate that you know how to use the "personal pronoun + personal noun" pattern.

# 语音复习(Yǔyīn Fùxí) Pronunciation Review

## I. Review of Initials and Finals

The initials and finals selected for review are based on vocabulary learned in this lesson.

**Initials:**   b   j   m   t   y   w

**Finals:**   a   e   o   u   ai   ei   en   ie   uo   ian

## II. Phonetic Spelling Rules

A.   When a syllable has no initial consonant and the final begins with *i*, the *i* is changed to *y*, unless *i* is the only vowel in the final, in which case *y* is added in front of it. For example:

ie → ye          ian → yan
i → yi            ing → ying

B.   When a syllable has no initial consonant and the final begins with *u*, the *u* is changed to *w*. For example: *uo* → *wo*.

C.   When *u* stands alone, add *w* before *u*. For example: *u* → *wu*.

## III. Neutral Tone

In addition to the four tones already learned in the previous lessons, there is also the neutral tone in Mandarin. The neutral tone is pronounced lightly without any stress and is indicated in pinyin by the absence of any tone mark above the syllable. The following are combinations of each of the four tones with the neutral tone. Try each combination and see if you can pronounce it correctly.

| 1 + neutral: | tāde | māma | lǎoshī ne |
| 2 + neutral: | yéye | pópo | āyí ne |
| 3 + neutral: | nǎinai | shǎzi | zǒuzǒu ba |
| 4 + neutral: | bàba | shàoye | zuòzuò ba |

# 写汉字(Xiě Hànzì)
# Character Writing

## I. Key Radical Presentation

1. 吗 and 呢 share the small mouth radical 口. Many end-of-sentence particles and interjection words also have this radical.

2. 很 has the double-man radical 彳.

## II. Handwriting

### Indivisibles

| Character | Practice with Chinese Characters |
| --- | --- |
| 也 | |

### Left-right Composition

| Character | Practice with Chinese Characters |
| --- | --- |
| 我 | |
| 们 | |
| 他 | |

她
很
吗
呢

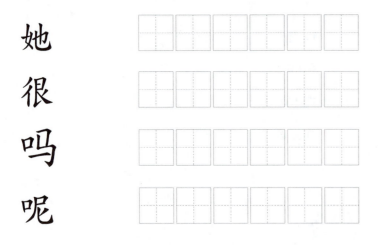

 课堂练习 (Kètáng Liànxí)

# In-Class Exercises

🎧📖 TASK 1. PINYIN EXERCISES

## A. Distinguishing Tones

Listen carefully to the following syllables and mark the correct tones below. Practice saying the tones correctly, making sure that you can recognize the differences among each of the four tones.

1. ye          ye          ye          ye

2. tian        tian        jian        jian

3. bai         bai         mai         mai

4. men         men         ben         ben

5. tuo         tuo         wo          wo

## B. Distinguishing Sounds

Listen carefully to the following pairs of syllables; note the differences between them, and try to pronounce them correctly.

**Initials**

1. jiě        yě           2. tài        dài

3. bèn        pèn          4. mó         fó

**Finals**

1. má         mái          2. biē        bēi

3. wǔ         wǒ           4. jiàn       jiè

## C. Pronunciation Practice

Practice your tones and pronunciation by listening to a native speaker on your audio CD or multimedia CD-ROM.

1. Nǐ hǎo.                2. Wǒ hěn hǎo.        3. Nǐ bàba hǎo ma?

4. Wǒ māma hěn hǎo.      5. Tā yě hěn hǎo.      6. Lǐ Shūshu zài jiàn.

## D. Sight-reading

Read aloud the following phrases. Your sight-reading skills will be measured by your speed and accuracy. (Multimedia CD-ROM only.)

1. zài jiàn                2. zài jiè

3. wǒ men                  4. wú mén

5. jiě jie                 6. zài jiā

7. mèi mei                 8. bù hǎo

## TASK 2. GRAMMATICAL STRUCTURE PRACTICE

Select one of the two choices to correctly complete each of the following dialogues.

1.  A: 你好。

    B: _____。

    a) 我很好              b) 你好

2. A: ＿＿＿＿＿好吗？

   B: 他很好。

   a) 李老师            b) 老师李

3. A: 我爸爸妈妈很好。你爸爸 ＿＿＿＿＿？

   B: 我爸爸也很好。

   a) 吗               b) 呢

4. A: 你爷爷好吗？

   B: 他 ＿＿＿＿＿。

   a) 好               b) 很好

---

## TASK 3. PARAPHRASING

To find out how well you know the grammar and vocabulary covered so far, follow the steps below.

**Step 1.** Translate the following dialogue into Chinese, using your own words. To check your pronunciation, listen to the dialogue on your multimedia CD-ROM.

| | |
|---|---|
| Lǐ Lìlì: | Hello, Auntie Hú. |
| Hú Āyí: | Good morning, Lǐ Lìlì. How are your parents? |
| Lǐ Lìlì: | They are very well. |
| Hú Āyí: | How about your grandparents? |
| Lǐ Lìlì: | They are well, too. Good-bye. |
| Hú Āyí: | Good-bye. |

**Step 2.** Now that you have familiarized yourself with the dialogue, be creative! Think of other words you have learned so far that might work in this dialogue. For example, instead of asking "How are your parents?" you could ask "How are your grandparents?" Try to substitute as many words as possible without disrupting the structure of the dialogue.

---

## TASK 4. PERFORMANCE

Using the grammar and vocabulary you have learned so far, write a short dialogue and perform it for the class. Don't be afraid to set the stage and use costumes or props. Above all, be creative!

# 4

# 好久不见，你怎么样？

# How's It Going?

*In this lesson you will:*
- ▓ Review pronunciation and pinyin spelling rules.
- ▓ Write more Chinese characters.
- ▓ Ask people about their studies, health, and work.

It is early in the morning, and Lin Di is on her way to class.

| | |
|---|---|
| Lín Dí: | Nǐ zǎo, Wú Wéndé. |
| 林笛： | 你早，吴文德。 |
| | |
| Wú Wéndé: | Zǎo. |
| 吴文德： | 早。 |
| | |
| Lín Dí: | Hǎojiǔ bújiàn, nǐ zěnmeyàng? |
| 林笛： | 好久不见，你怎么样？ |
| | |
| Wú Wéndé: | Mǎmǎhūhū. Nǐ ne? |
| 吴文德： | 马马虎虎。你呢？ |
| | |
| Lín Dí: | Wǒ hěn lèi. |
| 林笛： | 我很累。 |
| | |
| Wú Wéndé: | Nǐ xuéxí tài máng, tài jǐnzhāng. |
| 吴文德： | 你学习太忙，太紧张[1]。 |
| | |
| Lín Dí: | Dàjiā dōu hěn jǐnzhāng, nǐ bù jǐnzhāng ma? |
| 林笛： | 大家都很紧张，你不紧张吗？ |
| | |
| Wú Wéndé: | Wǒ bù jǐnzhāng, yě bú lèi. Nǐ tài rènzhēn le. |
| 吴文德： | 我不紧张，也不累。你太认真了[2]。 |
| | |
| Lín Dí: | Shì a. Wǒ kuài chéng shūdāizi le. |
| 林笛： | 是啊。我快成书呆子了[3]。 |

Li Lili meets a long time family friend, Mr. Gao, on the street.

| | |
|---|---|
| Lǐ Lìlì: | Gāo Xiānsheng, nín hǎo. |
| 李丽莉： | 高先生，您好。 |

| Gāo Xiānsheng: | Nǐ hǎo, Lǐ Lìlì. Hǎojiǔ bújiàn, nǐ zěnmeyàng? |
| 高先生： | 你好，李丽莉。好久不见，你怎么样？ |

| Lǐ Lìlì: | Wǒ hěn hǎo. Nín ne? Shēntǐ zěnmeyàng? |
| 李丽莉： | 我很好。您呢？身体怎么样？ |

| Gāo Xiānsheng: | Shēntǐ hái hǎo. |
| 高先生： | 身体还好。 |

| Lǐ Lìlì: | Nín tàitai shēntǐ hǎo ma? |
| 李丽莉： | 您太太身体好吗？ |

| Gāo Xiānsheng: | Tā hái hǎo. Nǐ bàba māma dōu hǎo ma? |
| 高先生： | 她还好。你爸爸妈妈都好吗？ |

| Lǐ Lìlì: | Tāmen dōu hěn hǎo. |
| 李丽莉： | 他们都很好。 |

| Gāo Xiānsheng: | Tāmen gōngzuò shùnlì ma? |
| 高先生： | 他们工作顺利吗？ |

| Lǐ Lìlì: | Gōngzuò dōu hěn shùnlì, dànshì tāmen hěn máng. |
| 李丽莉： | 工作都很顺利， 但是他们很忙。 |

Sentences marked with numbers are explained in the Notes section below. The section provides either cultural information or explanations for the more difficult sentences, which are designed to broaden your knowledge. You do not need to memorize the material in the Notes section. Just read through it and get a general sense of its meaning.

## *Notes*

1. 你学习太紧张。(Nǐ xuéxí tài jǐnzhāng.) This sentence consists of a subject (你) and a sentence providing additional information on the subject (学习太紧张). This kind of sentence is called a "topic-comment" sentence. "您太太身体好吗?" (Nín tàitai shēntǐ hǎo ma?) and "他们工作顺利吗?" (Tāmen gōngzuò shùnlì ma?) all belong to this group. For now, just remember this basic form. You will learn more about this structure in Lesson 9.

2. 你太认真了。(Nǐ tài rènzhēn le.) You are too serious.

3. 我快成书呆子了。(Wǒ kuài chéng shūdāizi le.) I'm turning into a bookworm.

# 生词表 (Shēngcí Biǎo)
## Vocabulary

| Character | Pinyin | Part of Speech | English Definition |
| --- | --- | --- | --- |
| 1. 怎*么样 | zěnmeyàng | *interrog.* | how |
| 2. *还 | hái | *adv.* | still, (not) yet |
| 还好 | | *adj. phr.* | "OK" — not very good, but not very bad either |
| 3. *累 | lèi | *adj.* | tired |
| 4. *学*习 | xuéxí | *n. & v.* | study; to study |
| 5. *太 | tài | *adv.* | too, extremely |
| 6. *忙 | máng | *adj.* | busy |
| 7. 紧张 | jǐnzhāng | *adj.* | tense, stressed, stressful |
| 8. *大*家 | dàjiā | *n.* | everybody |
| 家 | | *n.* | family, home |
| 9. *都 | dōu | *adv.* | all, both |
| 10. *不 | bù | *adv.* | not, no |
| 11. 认真 | rènzhēn | *adj.* | serious, earnest, conscientious |
| 12. 先生 | xiānsheng | *n.* | gentleman, Mr., Sir; husband |
| 13. 身体 | shēntǐ | *n.* | the human body; health condition |
| 14. 太太 | tàitai | *n.* | Mrs., Madam, wife |
| 15. 工*作 | gōngzuò | *n.* | occupation, profession, job |
| | | *v.* | to work |
| 16. 顺利 | shùnlì | *adj.* | smooth (going smoothly) |
| 17. 但是 | dànshì | *conj.* | but, however |

## 专有名词 (Zhuānyǒu Míngcí) Proper Nouns

| 高 | Gāo | a surname, family name |

## 补充词汇 (Bǔchōng Cíhuì) Supplementary Vocabulary

1. 轻松 轻松 qīngsōng    *adj.*    easy
2. 健康 jiànkāng    *adj.*    healthy
3. 可是 kěshì    *adv.*    but

# 口头用语 (Kǒutóu Yòngyǔ) Spoken Expressions

1. **好久不见!**    Hǎojiǔ bújiàn!    Long time no see!

   This is a very commonly used phrase to greet someone you have not seen for awhile.

2. **马马虎虎**    mǎmǎhūhū    neither good nor bad, so-so

   This is commonly used to respond to an inquiry about you or someone you know.

3. **是啊。**    Shì a.    You are right. (indicating agreement)

   This is frequently used to affirm what another person has just said.

## 词汇注解 (Cíhuì Zhùjiě) Featured Vocabulary

### 都不 *(Dōu Bù) vs.* 不都 *(Bù Dōu)*

都不 and 不都 may look similar, but they have different meanings. 都不 can be translated as "none (of them)" or "neither (of the two)." 不都 means "not all of them." 不都 is used less often than 都不.

| | |
|---|---|
| 他们都不忙。 | None of them is busy. |
| 他们不都忙。 | Not all of them are very busy. |

## 语法(Yǔfǎ)
# Grammar

## I. Basic Sentence Structure (Cont'd.)

Of the two common forms of predicates (predicate adjectives and predicate verbs), we will continue to focus exclusively on the sentence pattern "Subject + Predicate Adjective" in this lesson. In predicate adjectives, single-syllable adjectives such as 忙 (máng) should NOT stand alone; usually an adverb, such as 很, or other adverbs, such as 也 (yě), 都 (dōu), 还 (hái), 不 (bù) etc., are required before the single-syllable adjective. In this lesson we have covered:

| Questions | | Answers/Statements | | |
|---|---|---|---|---|
| **Subject** | **Adjective** | **Subject** | **Adverb** | **Adjective** |
| 你爸爸妈妈 | 好吗？ | 他们 | 很 | 好。 |
| Are your parents doing okay? | | They are doing very well. | | |
| | | 他们 | 还 | 好。 |
| | | They are not great, but they are doing OK. | | |
| 你 | 忙吗？ | 我 | 很 | 忙。 |
| Are you busy? | | I am very busy. | | |
| | | 我 | 还 | 好。 |
| | | I'm not too busy; I'm okay. | | |
| 他呢？ | | 他 | 也很 | 忙。 |
| What about him? | | He is also very busy. | | |

## A. Negative Sentences with the Adverb 不 (Bù)

In this lesson, you will learn how to form a negative sentence. The adverb 不 can be placed before an adjective or adverb in order to negate it.

*Chris Vee*

| Subject | Predicate Adjective | |
|---|---|---|
| **Noun/Pronoun** | **Adverb** | **Adjective** |
| 我 | 不 | 忙。 |

I am not busy.

| **Noun/Pronoun** | **Adverbs** | **Adjective** |
|---|---|---|
| 我 | 不很 | 忙。 |

I am not very busy.

## B. Short Responses

A question using 吗 elicits a "yes" or "no" answer. However, Chinese has no equivalent to the English short response "yes" or "no." Usually the adjective itself is repeated to form a positive response, or "不 + adjective" forms the negative response. For additional clarity, a full sentence is often added after the short "yes/no," as in the examples below.

你妈妈忙吗？

忙，她很忙。 or 不忙，她不忙。

## C. Predicate Adjectives without 很 in a Statement

When a single-syllable adjective is used without 很, the sentence is incomplete. This usually indicates that there is a follow-up sentence. For example:

| Sentence 1 | | Sentence 2 | |
|------------|------------|------------|------------|
| Somebody 1 | Adjective 1 | Somebody 2 | Adjective 2 |
| 我妈妈 | 忙， | 我爸爸 | 也 忙。 |

My mom is busy, and so is my dad.

| | | | |
|------------|------------|------------|------------|
| 毛老师 | 忙， | 李老师 | 不 忙。 |

Professor Mao is busy; Professor Li is not.

## II. Using the Adverbs 也 (Yě), 都 (Dōu) and 太 (Tài)

Adverbs such as 也, 都, and 太 (or 很), if they are used in a sentence, always precede adjectives. When these adverbs appear together in the same sentence, they should obey the word order presented below.

| Subject | Predicate Adjective | |
|---------|---------------------|-----------|
| Noun/Pronoun | Adverbs | Adjective |
| 我们 | 也都不太 | 忙。 |

We are not too busy, either.

| | | |
|---------|---------|-----------|
| 我们 | 也都很 | 忙。 |

We are all very busy, too.

### Notes

1. 也 is frequently placed before 都, 很, and 太.

2. 都 is frequently placed before 太 or 很. (太 and 很 cannot be used in the same sentence.)

3. When 也 or 都 modifies 不太, which means "not too," it should be placed before 不太. You should memorize 也都不太 as an adverbial phrase.

---

### 🔲 PRACTICE

Find a partner and use 身体, 学习, and 工作 to create a short dialogue in which one person asks questions using the adjectives and adverbs we have learned so far, and the other provides answers in both positive and negative forms.

## III. Using 怎么样 (Zěnmeyàng)

怎么样 is an interrogative word that means "how." It can be used to make an inquiry about someone's well-being. When used to form a question, 怎么

样 simply replaces the adverb and adjective in the predicate. The sentence structure itself does not change. For example:

|  | Subject | Adverb | Adjective |  |
|---|---|---|---|---|
| Statement: | 他工作 | 很 | 好。 | He is doing fine with his work. |

|  | Subject | 怎么样 |  |  |
|---|---|---|---|---|
| Question: | 他工作 | 怎么样？ |  | How is his work? |

## Compare 怎么样 *with* 好吗

Both "Somebody + 怎么样" and "Somebody + 好吗" are used to inquire about someone's well-being. 怎么样 is more colloquial than 好吗. The negative response to "Somebody + 好吗" or Somebody + 怎么样," 不好, is seldom used. Although grammatically correct, it sounds too blunt. To soften the bluntness, you can use the adverb 太. For example:

More appropriate:    她不太好。  She is not great.

Less appropriate:    他不好。    He is not good.

 **PRACTICE**

Find a partner and have a short dialogue in which one person asks a question using 怎么样 and the other provides both a positive and a negative answer.

# 语音复习(Yǔyīn Fùxí)
# Pronunciation Review

## I. Review of Initials and Finals

The initials and finals selected for review are based on vocabulary learned in this lesson.

**Initials:**  d    g    x    r    zh

**Finals:**  an    ou    un    üe    ia    ang    eng    ong

## II. Tone Change Rule for 不

When 不 is used alone or before the first , second, or third tones, it is pronounced as *bù* (fourth tone). When it is used before a fourth tone syllable or a neutral tone derived from a fourth tone, it is pronounced as *bú* (second tone).

For example:     bù duō   bù máng   bù hǎo   bú gàn   bú kàn

Now it's your turn! Listen carefully to the following sounds. When you are comfortable with the sounds, record your own pronounciation and compare it with the voices on the CD.

A. bú

   1. bú jiàn     2. bú lèi

   3. bú rènzhēn     4. bú shùnlì

B. bù

   1. bù hǎo     2. bù máng

   3. bù jǐnzhāng     4. bù hěnhǎo

# III. Phonetic Spelling Rules

## A. When There Are No Initials

-un ➔ -u(en)     *un* is the combination of *u* and *en*. When there are no initials, *u* changes to *w* and *n* changes to *en* (e.g., *wen*).

-üe ➔ yue     When there are no initials, add *y* before *ue*; *üe* loses the umlaut (e.g., *yue*).

## B. When There Are Initials

-un     Although *-un* is the combination of *u* and *en*, when *-un* has an initial, *e* is dropped so it is spelled as *-un* (e.g., *dun*).

-üe     When *-üe* has initials such as *j, q, x, -üe* is written as *-ue* without the umlaut (e.g., *jue*, *que*, and *xue*). When the initial is *n* or *l*, the umlaut remains (e.g., *lüe, nüe*).

*Sun Zhong Shan (Sun Yat-sen) museum in Nanjing.*

写汉字(Xiě Hànzì)
# Character Writing

## Key Radical Presentation

The running radical: 辶

The heart radical (vertical): 忄

The ear radical: 阝

In this lesson you are going to learn to write ten more Chinese characters. Please pay special attention to their radicals. You can practice writing the characters on a separate piece of paper.

| Character | Practice with Chinese Characters |
|---|---|
| 都 | |
| 忙 | |
| 作 | |
| 累 | |
| 学 | |
| 家 | |
| 还 | |
| 习 | |
| 么 | |
| 大 | |
| 不 | |
| 太 | |

# 课堂练习(Kètáng Liànxí)
# In-Class Exercises

## 🎧💻 TASK 1. PINYIN EXERCISES

### A. Distinguishing Tones

Listen carefully to the following syllables and mark the correct tones below. Practice saying the tones correctly, making sure that you can recognize the differences among each of the four tones.

1. di          di          di          di
2. gu          gu          gu          gu
3. xia         xia         xia         xia
4. rang        rang        rang        rang
5. zhi         zhi         zhi         zhi

### B. Distinguishing Sounds

Listen carefully to the following pairs of syllables; note the differences between them, and try to pronounce them correctly.

**Initials**

1. dān   tān      2. gǒu   kǒu      3. xiá   jiá
4. rǒng  chǒng    5. rì    shì

**Finals**

1. gān   gāng     2. zhàng  zhèng    3. dūn   dōng
4. ròu   ruò      5. xuě    xiě

### C. Pronunciation Practice

Practice your tones and pronunciation by listening to a native speaker on your audio CD or multimedia CD-ROM.

1. xuéxí      jǐnzhāng      wǒmen xuéxí bù jǐnzhāng
2. gōngzuò    shùnlì        dàjiā gōngzuò dōu hěn shùnlì
3. dànshì     rènzhēn       dànshì wǒmen tài rènzhēn

### D. Sight-reading

Read aloud the following phrases. Your sight-reading skills will be measured by your speed and accuracy. (For Multimedia CD-ROM only.)

1. zhīdào       2. Zhōngguó      3. xīn xuésheng
4. Rìběn        5. wèn ān        6. dōu gōngzuò

*Huang Shan in early fall.*

## TASK 2. GRAMMATICAL STRUCTURE PRACTICE

### A. Word Insertion

In each of the following short dialogues, choose the letter (A, B, or C) of the place where the given Chinese character should be inserted to form a grammatically correct sentence.

1. A: 你忙吗？
   B: 我（A）不（B）忙（C）。                                    太

2. A: 李老师、高老师怎么样？
   B: （A）李老师、高老师（B）很好（C）。                          都

3. A: 高先生、高太太身体都好吗？
   B: 高先生身体（A）很好，（B）高太太（C）还好。                  也

4. A: 我爸爸妈妈工作不累。 你爸爸妈妈呢？
   B: 他们工作（A）也（B）都（C）太累。                          不

### B. Word Selection

Select one of the three choices to correctly complete each of the following dialogues.

1. A: 你怎么样？

   B: 我_____，学习工作都很顺利。

   a) 很好      b) 好      c) 都好

2. A: 胡阿姨、李叔叔身体都好吗？

   B: 他们身体 _____。

   a) 不好太    b) 不太好   c) 太不好

3. A: 你叔叔怎么样？

   B: 他很好，工作不忙，学习_____。

      a) 也紧张     b) 也不紧张   c) 不紧张

4. A: 我们不忙。 你们呢？

   B: 我们_____忙。

      a) 也都不太   b) 都也不太   c) 也都太

## C. *Fill in the Blanks*

Fill in the blanks below by selecting the appropriate word for each sentence.
Then translate the sentence into English.

1. 怎么样      忙        紧张

   A: 啊，吴文德，好久不见。你_____?

   B: 我还好，你呢？你学习_____吗？

   A: 很忙。我们大家学习都很_____。

2. 工作        好吗      身体     太认真        吗

   A: 你爸爸工作顺利_____?

   B: 他_____顺利，但是太累。

   A: 你妈妈身体_____?

   B: 她_____还很好。但是她工作太忙了。

   A: 是啊。你妈妈工作_____。

## 🖥 TASK 3. PARAPHRASING

To find out how well you know the grammar and vocabulary covered so far,
follow the steps below.

**Step 1.** Translate the following dialogue into Chinese, using your own words.
To check your pronunciation, listen to the dialogue on your CD.

   A: Uncle Gao, long time no see! How is your health?

   B: My health is so-so. What about you? How is school?

   A: It is okay, but I am very busy.

   B: What about your parents? How is their work?

   A: Their work is going well, but it is too intense.

   B: What about your grandparents?

   A: They are all in very good health. Thanks.

**Step 2.** Now that you have familiarized yourself with the dialogue, be creative! Think of other words you have learned so far that might work in this

dialogue. For example, instead of asking, "Uncle Gao, how is your health?" you could ask, "Auntie Li, how is your work?" Try to substitute as many words as possible without disrupting the structure of the dialogue.

## TASK 4. PICTURE DESCRIPTION

**Topic:** Two students are having lunch together. They have not seen each other for a while and are taking the opportunity to catch up. Write a short conversation in which they talk about their studies. How is the workload affecting their physical and mental health? What is their overall attitude toward their studies?

1.                                          2.

3.

# 5

# 你做什么工作?

# How Do You Make a Living?

> **In this lesson you will:**
> ▨ Do a review of pinyin pronunciation and tones.
> ▨ Learn more character combinations and rules of phonetic spelling.
> ▨ Use basic vocabulary to identify things and people.
> ▨ Ask somebody about his or her profession.

(Note: Starting in this lesson you should focus on recognizing Chinese characters rather than pinyin, so the pinyin has been moved from above the characters to below them.)

Gao Peng and Lin Di are at Gao Peng's house looking at photographs on the wall.

| 林笛: | 这是你妈妈吗? |
|---|---|
| Lín Dí: | Zhè shì nǐ māma ma? |

| 高朋: | 是啊,这是我妈妈,那是我爸爸。 |
|---|---|
| Gāo Péng: | Shì a, zhè shì wǒ māma, nà shì wǒ bàba. |

| 林笛: | 你爸爸妈妈都是老师吗? |
|---|---|
| Lín Dí: | Nǐ bàba māma dōu shì lǎoshī ma? |

| 高朋: | 都不是。我妈妈是护士,我爸爸是医生。 |
|---|---|
| Gāo Péng: | Dōu bú shì. Wǒ māma shì hùshi, wǒ bàba shì yīshēng. |

| 林笛: | 是吗?我爸爸也是医生。 |
|---|---|
| Lín Dí: | Shì ma? Wǒ bàba yě shì yīshēng. |

| 高朋: | 你妈妈呢?她也是护士吗? |
|---|---|
| Gāo Péng: | Nǐ māma ne? Tā yě shi hùshi ma? |

| 林笛: | 不,她做生意。 |
|---|---|
| Lín Dí: | Bù, tā zuò shēngyì. |

......

林笛:　　那是谁？
Lín Dí:　 Nà shì shéi?

高朋:　　那是我哥哥。
Gāo Péng:　Nà shì wǒ gēge.

林笛:　　你哥哥做什么工作？
Lín Dí:　 Nǐ gēge zuò shénme gōng zuò?

高朋:　　他是工程师，那是他的老板。
Gāo Péng:　Tā shì gōngchéngshī, nà shì tā de lǎobǎn.

⋯⋯⋯⋯

林笛:　　这都是你的朋友吗？
Lín Dí:　 Zhè dōu shì nǐ de péngyou ma?

高朋:　　是啊，我朋友很多，这是张子倩，
Gāo Péng:　Shì a, wǒ péngyou hěn duō, zhè shì Zhāng Zǐqiàn,

　　　　那是她哥哥张子文。
　　　　Nà shì tā gēge Zhāng Zǐwén.

林笛:　　这也是你朋友吗？
Lín Dí:　 Zhè yěshì nǐ péngyou ma?

高朋:　　不是，这是张教授，他是我们老师。
Gāo Péng:　Búshì, zhè shì Zhāng Jiàoshòu, tā shì wǒmen lǎoshī.

林笛:　　这都是张教授的书吗？
Lín Dí:　 Zhè dōu shì Zhāng Jiàoshòu de shū ma?

高朋:　　是啊，他的书很多。这是张教授的朋友。
Gāo Péng:　Shì a, tāde shū hěn duō. Zhè shì Zhāng Jiàoshòu de péngyou.

林笛:　　他搞什么？
Lín Dí:　 Tā gǎo shénme?

高朋:　　他搞电脑。林笛，你的问题不少啊？
Gāo Péng:　Tā gǎo diànnǎo. Lín Dí, nǐde wèntí bù shǎo a?

林笛:　　聊聊天嘛[1]。
Lín Dí:　 Liáoliáo tiān ma.

## Note

1. 聊聊天嘛。 (Liáoliáo tiān ma.) Literally, "I don't have anything to talk about, but I am looking for things to say so we can chat." It can be roughly translated as "(I am) just talking for talking's sake."

 ## 生词表 (Shēngcí Biǎo)
# Vocabulary

| Character | Pinyin | Part of Speech | English Definition |
|---|---|---|---|
| 1. *做 | zuò | *v.* | to do |
| 2. *什么 | shénme | *pron.* | what? |
| 3. *这 | zhè | *pron.* | this |
| 4. *是 | shì | *v.* | to be |
| 5. *那 | nà | *pron.* | that |
| 6. 护士 | hùshi | *n.* | nurse |
| 7. 医生 医 医 | yīshēng | *n.* | medical doctor |
| | | *n.* | medicine; medical science |
| 8. 生意 | shēngyì | *n.* | business |
| 9. *谁 | shéi | *pron.* | who, whom |
| 10. 哥哥 | gēge | *n.* | elder brother |
| 11. 工程师 工程 | gōngchéngshī | *n.* | engineer |
| | | *n.* | engineering |
| 12. *的 | de | *part.* | a particle used to indicate possession, similar to the English "apostrophe+s" |
| 13. 老板 | lǎobǎn | *n.* | boss (colloq.) |
| 14. *朋*友 | péngyou | *n.* | friend |
| 15. *多 | duō | *adj.* | many, much (opposite of 少) |
| 16. 教授 | jiàoshòu | *n.* | professor |
| 17. *书 | shū | *n.* | book |

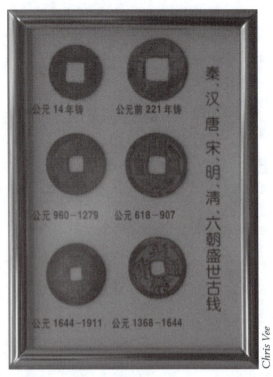

公元 14 年铸    公元前 221 年铸

公元 960 ~ 1279    公元 618 ~ 907

公元 1644 ~ 1911    公元 1368 ~ 1644

秦、汉、唐、宋、明、清、六朝盛世古钱

*Chris Vee*

*Coins from the Qin, Han, Tang, Song, Ming, and Qing dynasties.*

| | | | |
|---|---|---|---|
| 18. 搞*电脑 | gǎo diànnǎo | v. obj. | to specialize in computers (colloq.) |
| 搞 脑 | | v. | to work on, to specialize in, to be engaged in (a certain field) [colloq.] |
| 电 | | n. & adj. | electricity; electronic |
| 脑 | | n. | brain |
| 19. *问题 | wèntí | n. | question, problem, issue |
| 问 | | v. | to ask, to inquire |
| 20. *少 | shǎo | adj. | few, little (opposite of 多) |

## 专有名词 (Zhuānyǒu Míngcí) Proper Nouns

| | | | |
|---|---|---|---|
| 1. 高朋 | Gāo Péng | | a man's name |
| 2. 张子倩 | Zhāng Zǐqiàn | | a woman's name |
| 3. 张子文 | Zhāng Zǐwén | | a man's name |

## 补充词汇 (Bǔchōng Cíhuì) Supplementary Vocabulary

| | | | |
|---|---|---|---|
| 1 大夫 | dàifu | n. | medical doctor |
| 2. 做买卖 | zuò mǎimai | v. obj. | to do business, buy and sell |

| 3. | 上司 | shàngsī | *n.* | boss |
| 4. | 看电视 | kàn diànshì | *v. obj.* | to watch TV |
| 5. | 看电影 | kàn diànyǐng | *v. obj.* | to see a movie |
| 6. | 经理 | jīnglǐ | *n.* | manager |
| 7. | 看书 | kàn shū | *v. obj.* | to read, read a book |
| 8. | 问问题 | wèn wèntí | *v. obj.* | to ask a question |

## 口头用语 (Kǒutóu Yòngyǔ) Spoken Expressions

| 1. | 是吗 | Shì ma? | "Is that true?" or "Really?" |
| | | | This is often used to express surprise or disbelief. |
| 2. | 啊 | a | This is used at the end of a sentence for emphasis. |
| 3. | 嘛 | ma | This is used at the end of the sentence to indicate that something is obvious. |

## 词汇注解 (Cíhuì Zhùjiě) Featured Vocabulary

### 搞电脑 *(Gǎo Diànnǎo)* vs. 做生意 *(Zuò Shēngyì)*

In 搞电脑, 搞 is frequently used to indicate someone's specialization. It is very colloquial. In 做生意, 做 can be used with 生意 or 买卖 to indicate a profession. They should be treated as fixed phrases.

 语法(Yǔfǎ)
Grammar

## I. Sentences Using Action Verbs

In Lessons 2 and 3, you learned the "Subject + Predicate Adjective" structure. This lesson introduces the "Subject +Predicate Verb" structure. There are different kinds of verbs that can function as predicate verbs in the Chinese language. Here, you will learn how to use the action verb as a predicate verb. An action verb describes what the subject does. Look at the examples below:

|  | **Subject** | **Verb** | **Object** |
|---|---|---|---|
| Positive: | 我 | 做 | 生意。 |

I do business.

| | 他们（也）（都） | 做 | 生意。 |
|---|---|---|---|

They (all) do business, (too).

| Negative: | 他 们（也）（都） | 不做 | 生意。 |
|---|---|---|---|

(Lit.) They also not all do business. None of
them do business, either.

| Question: | 你 | 做 | 生意 吗？ |
|---|---|---|---|

Do you do business?

## Notes

1. Questions requiring yes/no answers can be formed by adding 吗 to the
   end of a sentence.

2. A negative sentence is formed by placing 不 before the verb.

3. When modifying action verbs, the adverbs 也 and 都 should be placed
   before the verb and should always be used in that order, just as with
   predicate adjectives.

## PRACTICE

Create a positive sentence using the verb phrases 搞电脑, 做生意, or 问
问题, plus one or more adverbs. Then change that sentence into a question
and provide a negative answer.

## II. Sentences with the Verb 是 (Shì)

In addition to action verbs, the verb 是 can also function as a predicate verb.
In its most general context, the verb 是 means "to be" and can be roughly
translated as "is," "are," or "am." It links the subject of a sentence to a predicate noun. Remember that, as we learned earlier, 是 cannot be used with a
predicate adjective.

| **Subject** | **Adverb** | **Verb** | **Object of Identification** |
|---|---|---|---|
| **Pronoun/Noun** | （也）（都） | **是** | **Pronoun/Noun** |
| Positive: 我妈妈 | | 是 | 老师。 |

My mom is a teacher.

他爸爸妈妈 （也）（都）是 老师。

His dad and mom are both teachers.

Negative: 她妈妈 不是 老师。

Her mom is not a teacher.

她爸爸妈妈 （也）（都）不是 老师。

Her parents aren't teachers, either.

Question: 你妈妈 是 老师 吗？

Is your mom a teacher?

## *Note*

1. When modifying 是, the adverbs 也 and 都 should be placed before 是 if they are used at all.

## PRACTICE

Find a partner and use vocabulary such as 老师，医生，护士，工程师，教授，老板，朋友，高先生，and 李太太 to prepare a short dialogue in which one person asks a question and the other provides responses in both positive and negative forms. Make sure that you are using the verb 是.

## III. Using 这 (Zhè) and 那 (Nà) with the Verb 是 (Shì)

这 and 那 are demonstrative pronouns that are often used with 是 to introduce people or identify people/objects, as in "this is …" or "that is …."

| Demonstrative Pronoun | Verb | Object of Identification |
|---|---|---|
| Subject | 是 | Pronoun/Noun |

Positive: 这/那 是 我朋友。

This is my friend.

Negative: 那 不 是 我朋友。

That is not my friend.

Question: 这/那 是 你朋友吗？

Is this your friend?

## *Notes*

1. In this structure, 这/那 can function only as the subject, NOT the object.

|  |  |
|---|---|
| CORRECT: | 那是他朋友。 |
| xxx INCORRECT: | 他朋友是那。 xxx |

2. When 这 and 那 are used with 都 they are plurals and should be translated as "these all" and "those all" respectively.

3. Without 都, 这/那 can be either plural or singular, depending on the context of the sentence.

---

## PRACTICE

Find a partner and prepare a short dialogue in which one person asks a question using 这/那 and the other answers the question in both positive and negative forms. Example:

Is that your friend?
Yes, that is my friend.
No, that is not my friend.

## IV. Using 的 (De) to Indicate Possession

In Lesson 2, you learned how to use the singular personal pronouns 你/我/他 in a possessive sense to indicate relationship (e.g., 我妈妈, 你弟弟, and 他朋友). In these cases, the possessive particle 的 is omitted because the speaker is referring to a family member. Note, however, that if it is not a family member, 的 must be used to indicate possession. For example: 他的护士. Thus, in Chinese, 的 functions similarly to the possessive "s" in English.

| | Object of Possession | | |
|---|---|---|---|
| **Noun/Pronoun** | 的 | **Noun Phrase** | |
| 电脑 | 的 | 问题 | computer problem |
| 朋友 | 的 | 书 | friend's book |
| 老师 | 的 | 问题 | teacher's question |
| 我们 | 的 | 医生 | our doctor |
| 妈妈 | 的 | 生意 | mother's business |

When plural pronouns such as 我们, 你们, and 他们 are used to modify a noun, 的 is usually used and should be placed between the plural pronouns and the modified noun. The principal exception is when the pronoun is followed by an institution (e.g., our dorm, their school, your company, and our class) or when 我们, 你们, and 他们 are followed by 老师. Then, 的 can also be omitted (e.g., 我们老师).

---

## PRACTICE

Bring a picture of your family or friends to class and identify everyone in the picture using 的. For example: 这是我爸爸。他是医生。那是他的书。

## V. Questions with 谁 (Shéi) / 谁的 (Shéide) / 什么 (Shénme)

In Lesson 3, you learned that when using the interrogative "怎么样" to form a question, the word order remains the same as in a statement. The same rule applies to interrogative pronouns such as 谁, 谁的, 什么, etc. The interrogative pronoun, or "question word," occupies the same position in the sentence as the noun or phrase that will answer the question.

### A. Using 谁 (Shéi)

The word 谁 is equivalent to "who" or "whom" in English. The following are examples of how 谁 can be used to turn a statement into a question.

**谁 *as a Subject***

| Statements | Questions |
|---|---|
| (李丽莉)是他的朋友。 | (谁)是他的朋友? |
| Li Lili is his friend. | Who is his friend? |
| (他朋友)搞电脑。 | (谁)搞电脑? |
| His friend specializes in computers. | Who specializes in computers? |

**谁 *as a Predicate Noun or following the Verb***

| Statements | Questions |
|---|---|
| 那是(我们老师)。 | 那是(谁)? |
| That's your teacher. | Who is that? |
| 他的朋友是(李丽莉)。 | 他的朋友是(谁)? |
| His friend is Li Lili. | Who is his friend? |

## *Notes*

1. 谁是你的朋友? vs 你的朋友是谁? These two sentences, although their basic meanings are the same, have different points of emphasis.

   In 谁是你的朋友?, the speaker is addressing a group of people, asking who among them is the listener's friend. Therefore, you could also say, 他们谁是你的朋友? (Which one of them is your friend?).

   In 你的朋友是谁?, we can assume that the friend is already the focus of conversation and that the speaker wants to clarify exactly whom they have been talking about.

2. In questions, the word order remains the same in both positive and negative forms (e.g., 谁搞电脑? or 谁不搞电脑?).

---

## 🔲 PRACTICE

Find a partner and prepare a short dialogue in which one person asks a question using 谁 as a subject and the other person asks a question using 谁 as an object. Each should provide an answer to the other's question. For example:

> 谁 as a subject: 你们谁搞电脑? 他搞电脑。
> 谁 as an object: 你们老师是谁? 我们老师是史老师。

## B. Using 谁的 (Shéide)

The word 谁的 is equivalent to "whose" in English. The example below demonstrates how to use 谁的 to turn a statement into a question.

*A candy store clerk in Shanghai.*

Alaric Radosh

*Playing the erhu, a traditional Chinese musical instrument.*

### 谁的 *as a Noun Modifier*

| Statements | Questions |
|---|---|
| 那是(他的)电脑。 | 那是(谁的)电脑? |
| That's his computer. | Whose computer is that? |

---

## PRACTICE

Find a partner and have a short conversation in which one person asks a question using 谁的 and the other person responds. For example:

这是谁的书？那是我的书。

## C. Using 什么 (Shénme)

The question word 什么 is equivalent to "what" in English. When used to to turn a statement into a question, 什么 can function either as an object or as a modifier.

### 什么 *as an Object*

| Statements | Questions |
|---|---|
| 他搞(电脑)。 | 他搞(什么)? |
| He specializes in computers. | What does he specialize in? |

什么 *as a Modifier*

| Statements | Questions |
|---|---|
| 我哥哥做（电脑）生意.<br>My older brother specializes in computers. | 你哥哥做（什么）生意？<br>What kind of business does your older brother do? |

## PRACTICE

Find a partner and prepare a short dialogue in which one person asks a question using 什么 as an object and the other person provides an answer. Now reverse the situation, this time using 什么 as a modifer, so that the person who answered is now asking. For example:

什么 as an object: 是什么，搞什么，做什么，问什么
什么 as a modifier: 做什么工作，做什么生意，问什么问题

 语音复习(Yǔyīn Fùxí)
# Pronunciation Review

## I. Review of Initials and Finals

The initials and finals selected for review here are based on vocabulary learned in this lesson. We have included initials and finals from previous lessons in parentheses to be used with those that we cover in this lesson.

**Initials:**    ch    p    (b    zh    sh)

**Finals:**    -i    iao    ua    uang    (ao    an    ang)

## II. Phonetic Spelling Rules

### A. When There Are No Initials

| | |
|---|---|
| *iao* → *yao* | When -*iao* does not have any initials, *i* changes to *y*. |
| *ua* → *wa* | When -*us* does not have any initials, *u* changes to *w*. |
| *uang* → *wang* | When -*uang* does not have any initials, *u* changes to *w*. |

## B. When the Final Is -*i*

The -*i* stands for a very special vowel that is articulated by the tip of the tongue at the front of the hard palate (for the *zh-ch-sh* series). To pronounce this vowel, keep the tongue tip in the same position as for the preceding consonant, withdrawing it just enough to let air pass through. Because *zh-ch-sh* are voiceless consonant initials, voicing begins just as the vowel is pronounced.

## III. Review of Tones

|             | 1st Tone | 2nd Tone | 3rd Tone | 4th Tone |
|-------------|----------|----------|----------|----------|
| 1st Tone:   | tāshuō   | tārén    | tāyě     | tāwèn    |
| 2nd Tone:   | shéishuō | shéimáng | shéigǎo  | shéizuò  |
| 3rd Tone:   | nǐshuō   | nǐwén    | nǐhǎo    | nǐlèi    |
| 4th tone:   | shìtā    | shìshéi  | shìwǒ    | shìshì   |
| Neutral Tone: | gēge   | shénme   | nǐde     | tàitai   |

## *Notes*

1. Remember that a third tone before another third tone is pronounced like a second tone, and a third tone before any other tone is simply a low tone, without the rising contour of the citation form.

*A Chinese health spa in Nanjing.*

2. Note that the pitch of the neutral tone varies according to the tone of the preceding syllable. For example, it carries a noticeably higher pitch after a third tone syllable than after first or fourth tone syllables.

写汉字(Xiě Hànzì)

# Character Writing

## Key Radical Presentation

The speech radical: 讠

The moon radical: 月

The door radical: 门

Today you are going to learn to write ten more Chinese characters. Please pay attention to their radicals. Also, when writing characters that belong to the "left-middle-right" composition group, the left and the middle part need to be squeezed and the right part can take slightly more space than 1/3 the width of the character.

| Character | Practice with Chinese Characters | | | | | |
|---|---|---|---|---|---|---|
| 那 | | | | | | |
| 谁 | | | | | | |
| 什 | | | | | | |
| 的 | | | | | | |
| 朋 | | | | | | |
| 做 | | | | | | |
| 多 | | | | | | |
| 是 | | | | | | |
| 少 | | | | | | |

课堂练习 (Kètáng Liànxí)

## In-Class Exercises

 TASK 1. PINYIN EXERCISES

### A. Distinguishing Tones

Listen carefully to the following syllables and mark the correct tones below. Practice saying the tones correctly, making sure that you can recognize the differences among each of the four tones.

1. ba          ba          ba          ba

2. piao        piao        piao        piao

3. chuang      chuang      chuang      chuang

4. chan        chan        chan        chan

5. wa          wa          wa          wa

### B. Distinguishing Sounds

Listen carefully to the following pairs of syllables; note the differences between them, and try to pronounce them correctly.

**Initials**

1. piāo    biāo      2. bàn    pàn      3. zhǎng  shǎng

4. chuāng  zhuāng    5. shàn   chàn

**Finals**

1. páo      piáo      2. zhuàng  zhàng      3. yāo      yān

4. chuāng  chūn      5. wǎ      wǒ

## C. *Pronunciation Practice*

Practice your tones and pronunciation by listening to a native speaker on your audio CD or multimedia CD-ROM.

1. zhè shì      shéi de          Zhè dōu shì shéi de shū?

2. gēge        zuò shénme       Nǐ gēge zuò shénme gōngzuò?

3. nà shì      jiàoshòu         Nà shì wǒmen jiàoshòu de chē.

4. lǎobǎn      gǎo diànnǎo      Wǒ gēgē de lǎobǎn bù gǎo diànnǎo.

## D. *Sight-reading*

Read aloud the following phrases. Your sight-reading skills will be measured by your speed and accuracy. (For multimedia CD-ROM only.)

1. diànnǎo gōngchéng    2. lǎobǎn bù hǎo

3. jiàoshòu jiāoshū      4. wèntí bù shǎo

5. shēngyì bù hǎo gǎo    6. péngyou bù hǎo zhǎo

## TASK 2. GRAMMATICAL STRUCTURE PRACTICE

Fill in the blanks below by selecting the appropriate word for each sentence.

1. 他朋友是_____？
   a) 谁      b) 谁的      c) 什么
2. 他做_____生意？
   a) 谁      b) 谁的      c) 什么
3. 那是_____电脑。
   a) 我      b) 我的      c) 我们
4. 他的书很多。_____，我的书也不少。
   a) 是啊    b) 是吗      c) 是

## TASK 3. PARAPHRASING

To find out how well you know the grammar and vocabulary covered so far, follow the steps below.

**Step 1.** Translate the following two dialogues into Chinese, using your own words. To check your pronunciation, listen to the dialogues on your CD.

**Dialogue 1.**

F: Who is that?

M: That's my brother.

F: What does your brother specialize in? Is he busy?

M: He is a professor. His work is very intense.

**Dialogue 2.**

F: Whose computers are these?

M: These are my uncle's computers.

F: What work does he do?

M: He is in the computer business. His job is very tiring.

F: Is that right? My brother is also in the computer business. He says it's very stressful.

**Step 2.** Now that you familiarized yourself with the dialogue, be creative! Think of other words you have learned so far that might work in this dialogue. For example, instead of saying "That is my brother," you could say "That is my teacher." Try to substitute as many words as possible without disrupting the structure of the dialogue.

## TASK 4. PICTURE DESCRIPTION

**Topic:** As the two new roommates get to know each other, they spend time looking over their high school photo albums together. The album owner talks about the people in the different pictures, while the other person asks questions. Construct a dialogue between them, using the vocabulary learned in this lesson. Feel free to use the vocabulary from previous lessons as well, such as 累, 忙, 紧张, 认真。

1.

2.

3.

# 6

# 做作业

# Doing Homework

> **In this lesson you will:**
> - Review pronunciation, tones, and pinyin.
> - Learn more about Chinese character composition and the rules of phonetic spelling.
> - Use Chinese to borrow and return items.
> - Talk about schoolwork.

Wu Wende and Li Lili are doing their homework at the library.

| | |
|---|---|
| 吴文德： | 李丽莉，我借一下儿你的笔记，好吗？ |
| Wú Wéndé: | Li Lìlì, wǒ jiè yixiàr nǐde bǐjì, hǎoma? |
| 李丽莉： | 什么笔记？ |
| Lǐ Lìlì: | Shénme bǐjì? |
| 吴文德： | 中文课笔记。你现在用吗？ |
| Wú Wéndé : | Zhōngwén kè bǐjì. Nǐ xiànzài yòng ma? |
| 李丽莉： | 我现在不用。你用吧。 |
| Lǐ Lìlì: | Wǒ xiànzài búyòng. Nǐ yòng ba. |
| 吴文德： | 谢谢。 |
| Wú Wéndé : | Xièxie. |

Five minutes later...

| | |
|---|---|
| 吴文德： | 李丽莉, 还你的笔记。 |
| Wú Wéndé: | Lǐ Lìlì, huán nǐde bǐjì. |
| 李丽莉： | 你现在去哪儿？ |
| Lǐ Lìlì: | Nǐ xiànzài qù nǎr? |
| 吴文德： | 我去休息休息。 |
| Wú Wéndé: | Wǒ qù xiūxi xiūxi. |
| 李丽莉： | 你说什么？你还做作业吗？ |
| Lǐ Lìlì: | Nǐ shuō shénme? Nǐ hái zuò zuòyè ma? |

吴文德：　不做。我今天很糊涂。老师的问题我都不懂。
Wú Wéndé:　Bú zuò. Wǒ jīntiān hěn hútu. Lǎoshī de wèntí wǒ dōu bù dǒng.

　　　　　我快累死了[1]。
　　　　　Wǒ kuài lèi sǐ le.

李丽莉：　今天的作业很难，是吗？你不懂，我来教你。
Lǐ Lìlì:　Jīntiān de zuòyè hěn nán, shìma?　Nǐ bù dǒng, wǒ lái jiāo nǐ.

吴文德：　真的？
Wú Wéndé:　Zhēn de?

李丽莉：　真的。你问问题吧。
Lǐ Lìlì:　Zhēn de. Nǐ wèn wèntí ba.

吴文德：　好，李丽莉老师，您很聪明。你看这是什么意思？
Wú Wéndé:　Hǎo,　Lǐ Lìlì Lǎoshī, nín hěn cōngmíng.　Nǐ kàn zhè shì shénme yìsi?

李丽莉：　我看看。　唉，我也不懂。我们去问问老师吧。
Lǐ Lìlì:　Wǒ kàn kan.　Ài, wǒ yě bù dǒng. Wǒmen qù wèn wen lǎoshī ba.

## Note

我快累死了。 (Wǒ kuài lèi sǐ le.) I am dying of exhaustion.

## 生词表 (Shēngcí Biǎo)

## Vocabulary

| Character | Pinyin | Part of Speech | English Definition |
|---|---|---|---|
| 1. 作业 | zuòyè | *n.* | homework, assignment |
| 2. *借 | jiè | *v.* | to borrow, to lend |
| 借 something: | | | to borrow sth. |
| 借 someone something: | | | to lend somebody (sth.) |
| 3. 一*下儿 | yīxiàr | *phr.* | (lit.) "one stroke," often used immediately after the verb to indicate a short period of time |
| 4. 笔记 | bǐjì | *n.* | notes |

| | | | |
|---|---|---|---|
| 笔 | | *n.* | pen |
| 记 | | *v.* | to record |
| 5. 中*文*课 | Zhōngwén kè | *phr.* | Chinese class |
| 中文 | | *n.* | the Chinese language |
| 课 | | *n.* | class |
| 6. *现*在 | xiànzài | *n.* | now, the present time |
| 7. *用 | yòng | *v.* | to use, need |
| 8. *吧 | ba | *part.* | used at the end of a sentence to indicate uncertainty, to make a suggestion, etc. |
| 9. 谢谢 | xièxie | *v.* | to thank |
| 10. 还 | huán | *v.* | to return (sth. to sb.) |
| | hái | *adv.* | still |
| 11. *去 | qù | *v.* | to go; to be going to (do sth.) |
| 12. *哪儿 | nǎr | *pron.* | which place, where |
| 13. 休息 | xiūxi | *v.* | to rest, to relax |
| 14. *说 | shuō | *v.* | to speak; to say (sth) |
| 15. 今*天 | jīntiān | *n.* | today (see Grammar Section I) |
| 16. 糊涂 | hútu | *adj.* | muddle-headed, confused |
| 17. 懂 | dǒng | *v.* | to understand |
| 18. 难 | nán | *adj.* | difficult, hard |
| 19. *来 | lái | *v.* | to come |
| 20. 教 | jiāo | *v.* | to teach |
| 21. 聪明 | cōngmíng | *adj.* | smart, intelligent |
| 22. *看 | kàn | *v.* | to look, watch, read |
| 23. 意思 | yìsi | *n.* | meaning |

## 补充词汇 (Bǔchōng Cíhuì) Supplementary Vocabulary

| | | | |
|---|---|---|---|
| 1. 功课 | gōngkè | *n.* | assignment |
| 2. 中文班 | Zhōngwén bān | *n.* | Chinese class |

| 3. | 考试 | kǎoshì | *n.* | test, exam |
| | | | *v.* | to take a test or exam |
| 4. | 容易 | róngyì | *adj.* | easy |
| 5. | 词典 | cídiǎn | *n.* | dictionary |
| 6. | 上课 | shàng kè | *v. obj.* | to go to class |
| 7. | 下课 | xià kè | *v. obj.* | to get out of class |
| 8. | 同学 | tóngxué | *n.* | classmate |

## 口头用语 (Kǒutóu Yòngyǔ) Spoken Expressions

| 1. | 唉 | ài | the sound of a sigh |
| 2. | 真的 | zhēn de | Really? |

*A public park in Hangzhou.*

## 词汇注解 (Cíhuì Zhùjiě) Featured Vocabulary

### 1. 吧 *(Ba)*

If you want to make a suggestion, you can simply attach 吧 to the end of a sentence.

| Subject | Verb Phrase | 吧 |
|---|---|---|
| 你 | 用（我的笔记） | 吧。 |

(I suggest that) you use my notes.

| | | |
|---|---|---|
| 我们 | 休息 | 吧。 |

(I suggest that) we rest now.

## 2. 来 (Lái)

The most common use of the verb 来 is "to come." It is also frequently used before the main verb to make a suggestion. For example:

我们来做作业吧。        Let's do homework.

## 3. Different 好 (Hǎo) Phrases

好吗？ (...hǎo ma?) "Is it all right?" or "Is it okay (with you)?" This appears at the end of the statement and is used to ask the other person's opinion or elicit consent. Placing 怎么样 at the end of a sentence serves a similar function.

好吧 (...hǎo ba.) "Okay" or "All right." This generally indicates agreement but not necessarily excitement.

好啊 (...hǎo a!) "Great!" or "Sure!" This is an enthusiastic response.

## 4. Different 看 (Kàn) Phrases

| | | |
|---|---|---|
| 看 | (kàn) | to look |
| 看书 | (kàn shū) | to read |
| 看朋友 | (kàn péngyou) | to visit friends |
| 看医生 | (kàn yīshēng) | to see a doctor |
| 看电视 | (kàn diànshì) | to watch TV |

## 5. 还 (Hái, Huán)

In Chinese, certain characters can have two different sounds; each has its own meaning. The first one we have come across is 还. For example:

| | | | | |
|---|---|---|---|---|
| 还 | huán | verb | to return something | 还你的书。 |
| 还 | hái | adverb | still | 你还做作业吗？ |

# 语法(Yǔfǎ)
# Grammar

## Review

In the previous lessons, you learned how to use many different adverbs and interrogative pronouns. Before you start the new lesson, let's reiterate some basic rules:

A. Adverbs should be placed before adjectives, verbs, or other adverbs. (Lesson 3 Grammar)

B. When an interrogative pronoun is used to form a question, the sentence order remains the same. (Lesson 4 Grammar)

In this lesson, you will learn one more adverb and one more interrogative pronoun.

A. The adverb 还 (hái) in this lesson indicates continuation of action. This is different from 还 in 还好 (Lesson 2).

For example:  你还做作业吗？  Do you still want to do homework?

B. The interrogative pronoun 哪儿 (nǎr) means "where."

For example:  你去哪儿？      Where are you going?

## PRACTICE

Can you make sentences using the adverb 还 and the interrogative pronoun 哪儿? Try it!

## I. Using Time Phrases

In Chinese, expressions of time are usually nouns (今天 jīntiān, 现在 xiànzài, etc.). A time phrase indicating the time of an action can go in one of the following two places:

## A. Before the subject at the very beginning of a sentence

| | | Predicate | |
| Time Word | Subject | Verb/Adjective | |
| --- | --- | --- | --- |
| 今天 | 我 | 做作业。 | I do my homework today. |
| 现在 | 我 | 很忙。 | I am very busy now. |

## B. Between the subject and the predicate verb or adjective

|  |  | Predicate |  |
|---|---|---|---|
| **Subject** | **Time Word** | **Verb/Adjective** |  |
| 我 | 今天 | 不工作。 | Today I do not work. |
| 我 | 现在 | 很紧张。 | I am very tense now. |

As a noun, the time word can also be used to modify a noun. If this is the case, 的 must be placed between the time word and the modified noun. For example: 今天的作业 (today's homework). You will learn more about this in Lesson 7.

---

### 🔲 PRACTICE

Find a partner and have a short dialogue in which one person makes up two questions using the time word 今天 and the other answers the questions using the same time word. Now reverse the roles, so that the person who answered the question earlier now asks a question using 现在 and vice versa.

## II. Sentences with Multiple Verbs

In this lesson, we will learn two different verbs, either of which could be used as the first verb in a multi-verb sentence: 去 (qù, to go) and 来 (lái, to come). The phrase "去/来 + Place + Verb obj." indicates that an action is going to take place soon. The negation word is usually placed before the first verb (e.g., 不去/不来).

| Subject | Verb 1 | Verb 2 (Main Verb) | Object |
|---|---|---|---|
| 你 | 去/来 | 休息休息。 | |

You go and take a break.

| Subject | Verb 1 | Verb 2 (Main Verb) | Object |
|---|---|---|---|
| 我 不 | 去/来 | 做 | 作业。 |

I am not going to do the homework.

## *Compare:*

你现在去/来做作业吗?    Are you going to do (the) homework?

你现在做作业吗?    Are you doing (the) homework right now?

---

## PRACTICE

Find a partner and use verb phrases such as 去借书, 来做作业, 来还你的笔记, 去问一下儿, and 去休息 to create a short dialogue in which one person asks a question that uses multiple verbs and the other answers it in both positive and negative forms.

## III. Verb Repetition and the Verb 一下儿 (Yīxiàr)

There are three ways to lighten the tone of a verb to make the action sound less serious or weighty: 1) by repeating the verb; 2) by repeating the verb with a 一 in between; 3) by attaching 一下儿 to the verb.

### A. Without an Object

| Verb | Repetition | Repetition with 一 | Repetition with 一下儿 |
|---|---|---|---|
| Verb | Verb Verb | Verb 一 Verb | Verb 一下儿 |
| 看<br>to take a look | 看看 | 看一看 | 看一下儿 |
| 休息<br>to take a break | 休息休息 | N/A | 休息一下儿 |

### B. With an Object

| Verb | Repetition | Repetition with 一 | Repetition with 一下儿 |
|---|---|---|---|
| Verb-Obj. | Verb Verb-Obj. | Verb 一 Verb-Obj. | Verb 一下兒-Obj. |
| 看你的作业 | 看看你的作业 | 看一看你的作业 | 看一下你的作业 |

to look at your homework

*Chris Vee*

## *Notes*

1.  Verb 一下儿 must always precede the object if one exists.

    CORRECT:            看一下儿你的作业。

    xxx INCORRECT:      看你的作业一下儿。   xxx

2.  When a single-character verb is repeated, you can insert 一 between the two instances of the verb. When a verb contains two characters, as in the case of 休息, the repetition takes the form of ABAB (休息休息). Do not add 一 in between the repeated verbs.

3.  These forms (repetition of verbs and the "Verb 一下儿") apply only to positive statements and questions. They CANNOT be used in negative sentences.

    CORRECT:            我不看你的作业。

    xxx INCORRECT:      我不看一下儿你的作业。   xxx

4.  When there is more than one verb in a sentence, only the main verb (usually the last verb) is repeated. For example: 我去休息休息。 "I am going to take a break."

---

## PRACTICE

Use the above structures to create your own sentences. How many more verbs can you come up with?

# IV. Tag Questions

A "tag" question is a short question attached to the end of a statement. In this lesson, we will focus on the following two groups.

## A. Using 好吗 (Hǎoma) or 怎么样 (Zenmeyàng)

To make a suggestion or ask about the listener's opinion, use "..., 好吗?" ("..., hǎo ma?")("..., is it all right with you?") or "怎么样?" ("Zěnmeyàng?") ("How is that with you?").

| Statement | Tag Question |
|---|---|
| 我借一下儿你的笔记， | 好吗？ |

I'm going to borrow your notes, okay?

| | |
|---|---|
| 你现在去做作业， | 怎么样？ |

 Now you go and do your homework, how about that?

**Responses:**

Positive: If you agree, you could respond to the above questions with
好啊， 好 or 好吧。

Negative: 不好 sounds very curt and possibly impolite. It might be more diplomatic if you provide an explanation to express disagreement. For example:

> 我们现在去做作业, 好吗？
>
> 我现在很忙。明天(míngtiān; tomorrow), 好吗？

## B. Using 是吗 (Shì ma?)

To confirm information, use 是吗？ (Shì ma?).

| Statement | Tag Question |
|---|---|
| 你不懂， | 是吗？ |

You did not understand, right?

**Responses:**

Positive: 是啊。

Negative: 不是。

## Note

对吗 (Duìma) can also be used as a tag question. For example: 今天的作业很难，对吗？ Today's homework is very difficult, right?

---

## PRACTICE

Find a partner and have a brief conversation in which one person asks a question using one of the tag words and the other provides both positive AND negative responses. The following are suggested phrases for each of the tag questions.

| | | | |
|---|---|---|---|
| 好吗： | 借中文笔记 | 问问题 | 还你的书 |
| 怎么样： | 来说中文 | 去休息 | 教我 |
| 是吗： | 学习太忙 | 工作顺利 | 很糊涂 |

 # 语音复习 (Yǔyīn Fùxí)
# Pronunciation Review

## I. Review of Initials and Finals

The initials and finals selected for review are based on vocabulary learned in this lesson. The initials and finals in parentheses (although reviewed in previous lessons) are used with the initials and finals reviewed in this lesson.

**Initials:** c    k    q    (z    g    j    x)

**Finals:** -i    er/-r    ü    ui    uan    iu    iong    (u)

## II. Phonetic Spelling Rules

### A. When the Final Is *-i*

The *-i* stands for a very special vowel that is articulated by the tip of the tongue behind the upper incisors (for the *z-c-s* series). To prounce this vowel keep the tongue tip in the same position as for the preceding consonant, withdrawing it just enough to let air pass through. Because *z-c-s* are voiceless consonant initials, voicing begins just as the vowel is pronounced.

## B. When There Are No Initials

*ui* → *u(e)i*      *ui* is the combination of *u* and *ei*. In syllables with no initial consonant, *u* changes to *w* and *i* changes to *ei* (e.g., *wei*).

*iu* → *i(o)u*      *iu* is the combination of *i* and *ou*. In syllables with no initial consonant, *i* changes to *y* and *u* changes to *ou* (e.g., *you*).

*iong* → *yong*     When *-iong* is not preceded by an initial consonant, *i* changes to *y*. Therefore, it should be spelled as *yong*.

*uan* → *wan*       When *uan* is not preceded by an initial consonant, *u* changes to *w*. Thus, *uan* will be spelled as *wan*.

*ü* → *yu*          When *ü* is not preceded by an initial consonant, it gains a *y* and loses the umlaut.

## C. When There Are Initials

*ui* → *u(e)i*      Although *ui* is the combination of *u* and *ei*, *e* is dropped if there is an initial and *ui* is directly attached to that initial (e.g., *kui*).

*iu* → *i(o)u*      Although *iu* is the combination of *i* and *ou*, *o* is dropped if there is an initial, and it is directly attached to the initial (e.g., *jiu*).

*ü*                 If the initial is *l* or *n*, *ü* will keep the umlaut (e.g., *lü* or *nü*). However, with any other initials, *ü* loses the umlaut (e.g., *yu, ju, qu*, etc.).

# III. Simple Final *er* and Retroflex *-r*

The *-er* is a full syllable by itself in the following words. See if you can pronounce them correctly.

érzi            érnǚ

ěrduo           ěrchuí

èr shí          èryuán

However, it also functions as a non-syllabic suffix, in which case the *e* is dropped and *r* is simply added to the syllable, or "stem," to which it is suffixed. For example:

yīxià + er          →          yīxiàr

nǎ + er             →          nǎr

| nà + er | → | nàr |
| zhè + er | → | zhèr |
| diǎn + er | → | diǎnr |
| wan + er | → | wanr |

Please note that although the official pinyin spelling rules require that this syllable be written "dianr," it is actually pronounced "diar." The "n" sound is completely dropped when the *-r* suffix is added. Now it is your turn. See if you are able to pronounce the following four tones with zhèr/nàr/nǎr.

| 1st Tone: | tā zhèr | tā nàr | tā nǎr |
| 2nd Tone: | lái zhèr | shéi nàr | huí nǎr |
| 3rd Tone: | wǒ zhèr | wǒ nàr | wǒ nǎr |
| 4th Tone: | zhù zhèr | qù nàr | qù nǎr |

# 写汉字 (Xiě Hànzì)
# Character Writing

## Key Radical Presentation

The hand radical: 扌

The eye radical: 目

| Character | Practice with Chinese Characters |
| --- | --- |
| 借 | |
| 课 | |
| 说 | |
| 吧 | |
| 哪 | |

找现看下在用中文去来天

 课堂练习 (Kètáng Liànxí)

In-Class Exercises

## TASK 1. PINYIN EXERCISES

### A. Distinguishing Tones

Listen carefully to the following syllables and mark the correct tones below. Practice saying the tones correctly, making sure that you can recognize the differences among each of the four tones.

1. ci          ci          ci          ci
2. kui         kui         kui         kui
3. qiu         qiu         qiu         qiu
4. qu          qu          qu          qu
5. huan        huan        huan        huan
6. yong        yong        yong        yong

*Browsing in a Chinese bookstore.*

## B. Distinguishing Sounds

Listen carefully to the following pairs of syllables; note the differences between them, and try to pronounce them correctly.

*Initials*

| | | | | |
|---|---|---|---|---|
| 1. cuì | zuì | 2. kuǎn | guǎn |
| 3. qiū | jiū | 4. xióng | qióng |
| 5. chī | cī | | |

*Finals*

| | | | | |
|---|---|---|---|---|
| 1. yǔ | wǔ | 2. qióng | qiú |
| 3. jū | zhū | 4. yǒu | ǒu |
| 5. kuī | kēi | | |

## C. Pronunciation Practice

Practice your tones and pronunciation by listening to a native speaker on your audio CD or multimedia CD-ROM.

1. huán      bǐjì           nǐ huán wǒ bǐjì, hǎo ma

2. qù        xiūxi yīxiàr    wǒ qù xiūxi yīxiàr, zěnmeyàng

3. xiànzài   lái zuò zuòyè   wǒmen xiànzài lái zuò zuòyè ba

4. jiè yīxiàr  hái yòng      wǒ jiè yīxiàr nǐde bǐjì, nǐ hái yòng ma

*A bridge overlooking the public park in Yangzhou.*

## D. Sight-reading

Read aloud the following phrases. Your sight-reading skills will be measured by your speed and accuracy. (For Multimedia CD-ROM only.)

1.  xuéxí tài lèi, xūyào xiūxi xiūxi
2.  hǎo jiè hǎo huán, zài jiè bù nán
3.  yōngrénzìrǎo, shízài bù cōngmíng

## TASK 2. GRAMMATICAL STRUCTURE PRACTICE

Check your knowledge of grammatical structures with the following exercises.

## A. Scrambled Words

Rearrange the words and phrases to form grammatically correct and meaningful sentences.

1.  我          一下儿          去          笔记          看
2.  书          我          去          现在          看看
3.  做          去          他          现在          作业
4.  休息          去          还          吗          你

## B. *Word Selection*

Select the choice that best completes each sentence.

1. 这都是你的中文书，_____？

   a) 是啊        b) 好吗        c) 对吗

2. 我借你的书看看_____？

   a) 是啊        b) 好吗        c) 对吗

3. 你来看一下儿_____。

   a) 吧          b) 呢          c) 吗

4. _____休息休息吧。

   a) 他们        b) 他          c) 我们

---

## 📖 TASK 3. PARAPHRASING

To find out how well you know the grammar and vocabulary covered so far, follow the steps below.

**Step 1.** Translate the following dialogue into Chinese, using your own words. To check your pronunciation, listen to the dialogue on your CD.

**Dialogue 1.**

   A:     Where are you going?

   B:     I am going to return the Chinese notes.

   A:     You are not using them now. Is it okay if I use them for a second?

   B:     Sure.

**Dialogue 2.**

   A:     Tonight's homework is very difficult, right?

   B:     That's right. How about we do the homework now?

   A:     I am very confused today. I do not understand the teacher's questions. I am going to take a break.

   B:      You are not confused. The homework is very difficult. You do not understand, and neither do I. Let's go and ask the teacher.

**Step 2.** Now that you have familiarized yourself with the dialogue, be creative! Think of other words you have learned so far that might work in this dialogue. For example, instead of asking "Where are you going?" you could ask "Where is he going?" Try to substitute as many words as possible without disrupting the structure of the dialogue.

# ✎ TASK 4. PICTURE DESCRIPTION

**Topic:** Two students are doing homework in the library. One student approaches the other, hoping to borrow something. Construct a dialogue between them, using the pictures as a guide.

1.

2.

3.

# 7

# 欢迎你们常来！
# Welcoming Guests

**In this lesson you will:**

■ Review pronunciation, tones, pinyin, and phonetic spelling rules.

■ Learn to host guests and offer them a choice of drinks.

■ Use Chinese to express gratitude or respond to gratitude.

Li Lili and Lin Di are having a party at their place and have invited some of their family friends. They hear a knock at the door.

| 李丽莉: | 高太太，您好。欢迎，欢迎。 |
|---|---|
| Lǐ Lìlì: | Gāo Tàitai, nín hǎo. Huānyíng, huānyíng. |
| | 高先生，请进，请进。 |
| | Gāo Xiānsheng, qǐng jìn, qǐng jìn. |
| 林笛: | 大家请坐！ |
| Lín Dí: | Dàjiā qǐng zuò! |
| 高太太: | 这是日本茶。 |
| Gāo Tàitai: | Zhè shì Rìběn chá. |
| 高先生: | 这是法国咖啡。 |
| Gāo Xiānsheng: | Zhè shì Fǎguó kāfēi. |
| 林笛: | 哎呀！你们太客气，带这么好的礼物。谢谢。 |
| Lín Dí: | Āiya! Nǐmen tài kèqi, dài zhème hǎo de lǐwù. Xièxie. |
| 高先生: | 谢什么，这是我们的一点儿小意思。 |
| Gāo Xiānsheng: | Xiè shénme, zhè shì wǒmen de yīdiǎnr xiǎo yìsi. |
| 高太太: | 是啊，一点儿小意思。别客气。 |
| Gāo Tàitai: | Shì a, yīdiǎnr xiǎo yìsi. Bié kèqi. |

After dinner, Li Lili and Lin Di begin serving drinks.

| 林笛: | 你们谁喝咖啡？谁喝茶？谁喝酒？谁喝水？ |
|---|---|
| Lín Dí: | Nǐmen shéi hē kāfēi? Shéi hē chá? Shéi hē jiǔ? Shéi hē shuǐ? |

91

高太太：    我喝茶。
Gāo Tàitai:    Wǒ hē chá.

林笛：    您喝什么茶？中国茶，英国茶，还是日本茶？
Lín Dí:    Nín hē shénme chá? Zhōngguó chá, Yīngguó chá, háishì Rìběn chá?

高太太：    我喝中国茶。多谢。
Gāo Tàitai:    Wǒ hē Zhōngguó chá. Duō xiè.

高先生：    你们有什么酒？有白酒吗？
Gāo Xiānsheng:    Nǐmen yǒu shénme jiǔ? Yǒu báijiǔ ma?

林笛：    没有白酒。但是我们有红葡萄酒，有啤酒。
Lín Dí:    Méi yǒu báijiǔ, dànshi wǒmen yǒu hóng pútáojiǔ, yǒu píjiǔ.

    您喝什么酒？
    Nín hē shénme jiǔ?

高先生：    我红葡萄酒，啤酒都不喝。我喝咖啡吧。谢谢。
Gāo Xiānsheng:    Wǒ hóng pútáojiǔ, píjiǔ dōu bù hē. Wǒ hē kāfēi ba. Xièxie.

林笛：    不用谢。你们吃水果，吃点心，还是吃糖？
Lín Dí:    Bú yòng xiè. Nǐmen chī shuǐguǒ, chī diǎnxin, háishì chī táng?

高太太：    我们都不吃糖。我吃水果。
Gāo Tàitai:    Wǒmen dōu bù chī táng. Wǒ chī shuǐguǒ.

高先生：    我吃点心。
Gāo Xiānsheng:    Wǒ chī diǎnxin.

林笛：    高太太，您的茶。高先生，这是您的咖啡。
Lín Dí:    Gāo Tàitai, nín de chá. Gāo Xiānsheng, zhè shì nín de kāfēi.

It's getting late, and everyone starts to leave.

高先生：    谢谢。
Gāo Xiānsheng:    Xièxie.

高太太：    十分感谢！
Gāo Tàitai:    Shífēn gǎnxiè!

李丽莉：    别客气，欢迎你们常来。
Lǐ Lìlì:    Bié kèqi, huānyíng nǐmen cháng lái.

林笛：    谢谢你们的礼物。再见。
Lín Dí:    Xièxie nǐmen de lǐwù. Zàijiàn.

## Note

Whenever you're formally invited to someone's home for a party or a meal, it is customary to bring gifts. It is also common to return the favor and invite the hosts back to your own home for dinner. This practice of returning the favor is called "回请 (huí qǐng)."

# 生词表 (Shēngcí Biǎo)
# Vocabulary

| Character | Pinyin | Part of Speech | English Definition |
|---|---|---|---|
| 1. 欢迎 | huānyíng | *v.* | to welcome (someone's arrival) |
| 2. *常 | cháng | *adv.* | often, frequently |
| 3. *请 | qǐng | *v.* | to politely request, politely ask (sb. to do sth.) |
| 4. *进 | jìn | *v.* | to enter, come in |
| 5. *坐 | zuò | *v.* | to sit |
| 6. *茶 | chá | *n.* | tea |
| 7. 咖啡 | kāfēi | *n.* | coffee |
| 8. *客*气 | kèqi | *adj.* | acting like a guest, courteous |
| 客 | | *n.* | guest(s) |
| 气 | | *n.* | air, atmosphere |
| 9. 带 | dài | *v.* | to carry, bring, take |
| 10. 这么(那么) | zhème (nàme) | *adv.* | such, so this/that (+adj.) |
| 11. 礼物 | lǐwù | *n.* | gift, present |
| 礼 | | *b.f.* | gift, present |
| 物 | | *n.* | object(s) |
| 12. 别 | bié | *adv.* | don't (do sth.); (ask sb.) not to (do sth.) |
| 13. *喝 | hē | *v.* | to drink |
| 14. *酒 | jiǔ | *n.* | wine, liquor, alcoholic drinks in general |
| 葡萄酒 | pútáojiǔ | *n.* | grape wine |
| 啤酒 | píjiǔ | *n.* | beer |

| | | | |
|---|---|---|---|
| 15. *水 | shuǐ | *n.* | water |
| 我喝水。 | báijiǔ | *n.* | a clear distilled liquor; recently also white wine |
| 16. 还是 | háishì | *conj.* | or (used in a question when offering two or more choices) |
| 17. *有 | yǒu | *v.* | to have |
| 18. *没 | méi | *adv.* | no |
| 19. 红 | hóng | *adj.* | red |
| 20. 白 | bái | *adj.* | white |
| 21. *吃 | chī | *v.* | to eat |
| 22. 水果 | shuǐguǒ | *n.* | fruit |
| 果 | | *n.* | fruit |
| 23. 点心 | diǎnxin | *n.* | snacks, light refreshment |
| 24. 糖 | táng | *v.* | candy, sugar |

## 专有名词 (Zhuānyǒu Míngcí) **Proper Nouns**

| | | | |
|---|---|---|---|
| 1. 日本 | Rìběn | | Japan |
| 2. 英国 | Yīngguó | | England |
| 3. 中国 | Zhōngguó | | China |
| 4. 法国 | Fǎguó | | France |

*Alaric Radosh*

*Family and friends gather for dinner in a Chinese home.*

## 补充词汇 (Bǔchōng Cíhuì) Supplementary Vocabulary

| | | | |
|---|---|---|---|
| 1. 冷饮 | lěngyǐn | *n.* | cool drinks |
| 2. 汽水 | qìshuǐ | *n.* | soda |
| 3. 可口可乐 | Kěkǒukělè | *n.* | Coca-Cola |
| 4. 果汁 | guǒzhī | *n.* | juice |
| 5. 客人 | kèrén | *n.* | guest |
| 6. 饼干 | bǐnggān | *n.* | cracker, biscuit |
| 7. 吸烟 | xī yān | *v. obj.* | to smoke (cigarettes, etc.) |
| 8. 吃饭 | chī fàn | *v. obj.* | to eat |
| 9. 好喝 | hǎohē | *adj.* | good, tasty (of drink) |
| 10. 好吃 | hǎochī | *adj.* | good, tasty (of food) |
| 11. 问好 | wènhǎo | *v. phr.* | to send one's best regards |
| 12. 凉水 | liáng shuǐ | *n. phr.* | cold water |

# 口头用语 (Kǒutóu Yòngyǔ) Spoken Expressions

## A. General Terms

| | | |
|---|---|---|
| 1. 哎呀 | Āiya! | a phrase used to express surprise |
| 2. 一点儿小意思 | yīdiǎnr xiǎo yìsi | just a small token |

## B. Expressing Gratitude

The following phrases can be used more or less interchangeably, but note the nuances as indicated by the translations.

| | | |
|---|---|---|
| 1. 谢谢 | Xièxie. | Thanks. |
| 2. 谢谢你/您 | Xièxie nǐ/nín. | Thank you. |
| 3. 多谢 | Duōxiè. | Many thanks. |
| 4. 十分感谢 | Shífēn gǎnxiè. | Thank you very much. |

## C. Responses

The phrases below can be used to respond to an expression of gratitude.

| | | |
|---|---|---|
| 1. 不谢 | Bú xiè. | You are welcome. |
| 2. 别客气 | Bié kèqi. | You don't have to be so polite with me. |
| 3. 谢(我)什么 | Xiè (wǒ) shénme? | What do you need to thank me for? |

4. (你/您)太客气    (Nǐ/nín) tài kèqi.    You are too polite.

5. 不用谢    Bú yòng xiè.    Don't mention it.

## 词汇注解 (Cíhuì Zhùjiě) Featured Vocabulary

### 1. (常)常 (Cháng) Cháng

(常)常 is often used to describe habitual actions. Although 常常 and 常 are almost identical, the single-character "常" tends to attach itself more readily to other single- or double-character words. For example:

他常来我这儿。    He often comes to my place.

他常说汉语。    He frequently speaks Chinese.

The negation of 常 and 常常 is 不常, NOT 不常常.

| CORRECT: | 他不常说汉语。 |
| xxx INCORRECT: | 他常不说汉语。xxx |
| xxx INCORRECT: | 他不常常说汉语。xxx |

### 2. 这么/那么 (Zhème/Nàme)

这么 and 那么 are adverbs that can be translated as "such" or "so." They are frequently used to express the speaker's feelings. Use 这么 (那么) in a similar way to how you would use 很. For example: 这么好的茶！ Such good tea!

### 3. 不 (Bù) vs. 别 (Bié)

不 is placed before an adjective, adverb, or verb to form a negative sentence. It can be translated as "not." For example: 我不去。 (I am not going). 别 is placed before a verb or adjective to request someone not to do something. It can be translated as "Don't." For example: 别去。 (Do not go).

 语法(Yǔfǎ)

## Grammar

## I. Noun Modifiers

Nouns can be modified not only by adjectives but also by other nouns.

### A. Nouns as Noun Modifiers

When a noun is modified by a noun, if the relationship between them is possessive, they are normally linked by the particle 的, as in 老师的书, the

*Chris Vee*

*Chris Vee*

*Chris Vee*

teacher's book(s) (but see Lesson 4 for exceptions to this rule). But when the relationship is simply descriptive, or further specifies a noun's nature or character, the particle 的 is not needed. For example:

| Noun | Modifier | Modified Noun |
|------|----------|---------------|
| 中国 | 茶 | Chinese tea |
| 法国 | 咖啡 | French coffee |
| 中文 | 书 | Chinese book |
| 电脑 | 课 | computer class |

## B. Adjectives as Noun Modifiers

### 1. With Monosyllabic Adjectives

When an adjective is monosyllabic and has NO adverb before it, it attaches directly to the noun.

| Adjective | Noun | |
|-----------|------|---|
| 白 | 酒 | white wine |
| 好 | 朋友 | good friends |
| 红 | 茶 | red tea |

## Note

The adjectives 多 (duō) and 少 (shǎo) are exceptions to the rule especially in spoken language: 多 and 少 usually need an adverb when used to modify a noun and sometimes need 的 before the noun. For example: 很多朋友, many friends; 这么少的礼物, so few gifts.

*Making a toast over a meal.*

Alaric Radosh

## 2. With Disyllabic Adjectives

When a disyllabic adjective is used to modify a noun, the modifier 的 must be placed before the noun to provide descriptive information about the noun. For example: 认真的老师, a serious teacher.

## 3. With Adjectives Preceded by Adverbs

When an adjective has an adverb before it, you should place 的 between the noun and the adjective.

| 很/这么/那么 | Adjective | 的 | Noun | |
|---|---|---|---|---|
| 很 | 好 | 的 | 礼物 | very good gifts |
| 很 | 好 | 的 | 朋友 | very good friends |
| 这么 | 好 | 的 | 礼物 | such good gifts |
| 那么 | 好 | 的 | 朋友 | such good friends |

## *Note*

When the adverb 很 + 多 is used to modify a noun, 的 usually is omitted.
For example: 很多礼物，很多朋友，很多老师。

## PRACTICE

Use the adjectives and nouns below to create as many phrases as possible (e.g., 好老师). Then use the combined phrases with 很/这么/那么 (e.g., 这么好的老师). How many can you create?

**Adjectives:** 好 忙 紧张 认真 顺利 多 少 聪明 糊涂 难

**Nouns:** 老师 学生 工作 老板 朋友 书 问题 电脑 笔记 作业

## II. Using 还是 (Háishi) to Provide Options

When 还是 is used in questions to present multiple options to the listener, 还是 is usually placed before the last choice.

## A. Used to Link Noun Phrases

| | Noun Phrase 1 | Noun Phrase 2 | 還是 | Noun Phrase 3... |
|---|---|---|---|---|
| 你喝 | 中国茶， | 英国茶， | 还是 | 日本茶？ |

Do you want to drink Chinese tea, English tea, or Japanese tea?

| | | | | |
|---|---|---|---|---|
| 你们吃 | 水果， | 点心， | 还是 | 糖？ |

Do you want fruit, cookies, or candy?

## B. Used to Link Verb Phrases

| | Verb Phrase 1 | Verb Phrase 2 | 还是 | Verb Phrase 3... |
|---|---|---|---|---|
| 你 | 喝中国茶， | 喝英国茶， | 还是 | 喝日本茶？ |

Do you want to drink Chinese tea, English tea, or Japanese tea?

| | | | | |
|---|---|---|---|---|
| 你们 | 吃水果， | 吃点心， | 还是 | 吃糖？ |

Do you want fruit, cookies, or candy?

| | | | | |
|---|---|---|---|---|
| 你 | 做作业 | | 还是 | 去休息？ |

Are you going to do the exercises or take a break?

---

### PRACTICE

Come up with two kinds of sentences using 还是 — one linking noun phrases and the other linking verb phrases. (Suggested verbs are 还 借 教 学 吃 喝 看 说 搞 做 and 用.)

## III. Using 都 (Dōu) to Sum Up Objects

You have already learned that the adverb 都 can be used to modify the subject in a sentence. For example: 我们都喝中国茶。 (We all drink Chinese tea.) However, if the items being modified are objects of a sentence, then the objects should either be placed before or after the subject and 都 should still be placed before the verb.

### A. Placing Objects before the Subject

| | Object 1 | Object 2 (...) | Subject | 都 | Verb |
|---|---|---|---|---|---|
| Positive: | 中国茶， | 日本茶 | 我 | 都 | 喝。 |

I drink both Chinese and Japanese tea.

| | | | | | |
|---|---|---|---|---|---|
| Negative: | 中国茶， | 日本茶 | 我 | 都 | 不喝。 |

I drink neither Chinese tea nor Japanese tea.

| | | | | | |
|---|---|---|---|---|---|
| Question: | 中国茶， | 日本茶 | 你 | 都 | 喝吗？ |

Do you drink both Chinese and Japanese tea?

### B. Placing Objects after the Subject

| | Subject | Object 1 | Object 2 (...) | 都 | Verb |
|---|---|---|---|---|---|
| Positive: | 我 | 中国茶， | 日本茶 | | 都喝。 |
| Negative: | 我 | 中国茶， | 日本茶 | | 都不喝。 |
| Question: | 你 | 中国茶， | 日本茶 | 都 | 喝吗？ |

Can you tell what is wrong with the following two sentences?

我都不喝中国茶。　When 都 modifies the subject in this sentence, the subject must be plural, NOT singular.

都我们不喝中国茶。 都 is an adverb and can never be placed before the subject.

---

## ✦ PRACTICE

Find a partner and create a short dialogue in which one person asks a question using one of the 都 patterns above and the other person answers. Then switch roles and do it again. Make sure 都 is placed in the right position! For example:

> A: 你中文书，日文书都看吗？

> B: 我看中文书，不看日文书。or
> 我中文书，日文书都不看。

## IV. Using the Verb 有 (Yǒu)

Up to this point, you have learned two types of verbs: the verb 是 and the action verb. Now we are going to learn the verb 有, which means "to have." 有 is a special verb, because it has its own negation word, 没. In the negative sentence, you can omit 有 entirely or you can say 没有. Do not use 不.

*Enjoying wine and appetizers.*

|  | Subject | 有 | Object |
|---|---|---|---|
| Positive: | 我们 | 有 | 中文书。 |
| | We have Chinese books. | | |
| Negative: | 我们 | 没（有） | 中文书。 |
| | We don't have Chinese books. | | |
| Question: | 你们 | 有 | 中文书 吗？ |
| | Do you have Chinese books? | | |

## PRACTICE

Think of a question using 有, and then answer it in both the positive and negative forms. For extra practice, find a partner and do this question-and-answer exercise in class.

语音复习 (Yǔyīn Fùxí)

# Pronunciation Review

## I. Review of Initials and Finals

The initials and finals selected for review here are those that have not been reviewed in the previous lessons. The initials in parentheses (although reviewed in previous lessons) are used for combination practice with the finals reviewed in this lesson.

**Initials:**   f   s   (p   m   z   c   j   q   x)

**Finals:**   ing   ün   üan   ueng   iang

## II. Phonetic Spelling Rules

### A. Special "Homorganic" Final *-i*

*s(i)*   Remember that the *-i* after the initial *s* represents the homorganic final — "homorganic" because it is articulated in the same position as the preceding consonant. This is the same *-i* as after initials *z* and *c*, similar to *-i* after initials *zh*, *ch*, *sh* and *r*, and very different from *i* after any initials other than these seven.

### B. When There Are No Initials

*-ing → ying*     When *-ing* is not preceded by an initial consonant, add *y: ying*.

| *-iang* → *yang* | When *-iang* is not preceded by an initial consonant, *i* changes to *y: yang.* |
|---|---|
| *ueng* → *weng* | The final *-ueng* does not occur with an initial consonant. Thus it is always spelled "weng." (Of the four tones, *weng* only has characters that take the first, third, and fourth tones — never the second tone.) |
| *ün* → *yun* | When the final *-ün* is not preceded by an initial consonant, add *y: yun.* The umlaut is also omitted, just as it is in all other occurrences of this final. |
| *üan* → *yuan* | When the final *üan* is not preceded by an initial consonant, add *y* and omit the umlaut: *yuan.* |

Note that the umlaut is retained ONLY in the syllables *nü, lü, nüe* and *lüe.* It is written in the BASE FORM finals to indicate the distinction between this high FRONT rounded vowel and the high BACK rounded vowel *u* (with no umlaut). But in the spellings of full syllables, the palatal initials *j, q, x* (see below), and the palatal semivowel *y* indicate this distinction and the umlaut can thus be dropped.

## C. When There Are Initials

| *ün* | The only initial consonants that can precede *-ün* are *j, q* and *x: jun, qun, xun.* |
|---|---|
| *üan* | The only initial consonants that can precede *-üan* are *j, q* and *x: juan, quan, xuan.* |

## III. Tone Combination Review

|  | 1st Tone | 2nd Tone | 3rd Tone | 4th Tone |
|---|---|---|---|---|
| **1st Tone:** | yīngzī | yīngxióng | yīngwǔ | yīngjùn |
| **2nd Tone:** | yuánxiān | yuánxíng | yuánběn | yuánzhuàng |
| **3rd Tone:** | xiǎngtōng | xiǎnglái | xiǎngfǎ | xiǎngyòng |
| **4th Tone:** | sìfāng | sìhuán | sìhǎi | sìyuè |

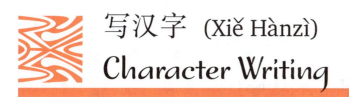

写汉字 (Xiě Hànzì)

# Character Writing

## Key Radical Presentation &#x3002;

The three dot water radical:   氵

The grass radical: 艹

The roof radical: 宀

| Character | Practice with Chinese Characters |
|---|---|
| 欢 | |
| 请 | |
| 啡 | |
| 喝 | |
| 酒 | |
| 咖 | |
| 茶 | |
| 客 | |
| 坐 | |
| 气 | |
| 进 | |
| 迎 | |

课堂练习 (Kètáng Liànxí)

# In-Class Exercises

## 🎧📖 TASK 1. PINYIN EXERCISES

### A. Distinguishing Tones

Listen carefully to the following syllables and mark the correct tones below. Practice saying the tones correctly, making sure that you can recognize the differences among each of the four tones.

*Alaric Radosh*

| | | | |
|---|---|---|---|
| 1. fu | fu | fu | fu |
| 2. ci | ci | ci | ci |
| 3. yuan | yuan | yuan | yuan |
| 4. ying | ying | ying | ying |
| 5. su | su | zu | cu |

## B. Distinguishing Sounds

Listen carefully to the following pairs of syllables; note the differences between them, and try to pronounce them correctly.

### Initials

| | | | | | |
|---|---|---|---|---|---|
| 1. fú | wú | | 2. sī | zī |
| 3. cuō | suō | | 4. pó | fó |
| 5. mó | fó | | | |

### Finals

| | | | | | |
|---|---|---|---|---|---|
| 1. jīng | jīn | | 2. quán | qún |
| 3. xiǎng | xǐng | | 4. xiàn | xiàng |
| 5. wēng | wēn | | | |

## C. Pronunciation Practice

Practice your tones and pronunciation by listening to a native speaker on your audio CD or multimedia CD-ROM.

1. huānyíng    qǐng jìn
   Huānyíng, huānyíng, dàjiā qǐng jìn.

*Making dumplings, a household event.*

2. kèqi         lǐwù

   Nǐmen tài kèqi, dài zhème hǎo de lǐwù.

3. xiè shénme       yìdiǎn xiǎoyìsi

   Xiè shénme, zhè shì wǒmen de yìdiǎn xiǎo yìsi.

4. Yīngguó chá     Rìběn chá

   Yīngguó chá, Rìběn chá, wǒmen dōu yǒu.

## D. Sight-reading

Read aloud the following phrases. Your sight-reading skills will be measured by your speed and accuracy. (For Multimedia CD-ROM only.)

1. Qiānlǐ sòng émáo, lǐ qīng qíngyì zhòng.

2. Fēngshèng de jiǔxí, bu zuì bu sàn.

3. Yīng yǒu jìn yǒu, jìn huān ér sàn.

---

## TASK 2. GRAMMAR STRUCTURE PRACTICE

### A. Error Identification

Can you tell incorrect sentences from correct ones? Circle all the incorrect items and provide explanations for your choices.

1. 我都不喝红酒白酒。
2. 我常常喝茶还是咖啡。
3. 这是很好糖。
4. 您吃什么？点心还是水果？

5. 你们有中国的茶还是日本的茶？

6. 我不常常看书。

## B. *Dialogue Construction*

Use the following three groups of words to construct a dialogue according to the model provided below.

Example:    英文书    法文书    中文书，

A: 你借英文书还是法文书？

B: 英文书，法文书我都不借。你有中文书吗？

A: 我没有中文书。

1. 中国茶    日本茶    英国茶

2. 法国咖啡    英国咖啡    日本咖啡

3. 中文书    中文笔记    英文笔记

4. 水果    点心    水

5. 红糖    白糖    水果糖

## TASK 3. PARAPHRASING

To find out how well you know the grammar and vocabulary covered so far, follow the steps below.

**Step 1.** Translate the following dialogues into Chinese, using your own words. To check your pronunciation, listen to the dialogue on your CD.

**Welcoming Guests**

A:    Grandpa Mao, welcome, welcome! Come in, come in.

B:    How are you? This is your coffee.

A:    You are too polite. You brought such a nice gift. Thank you very much.

B:    No need to thank me; it's just a small token. Don't mention it.

**Entertaining Guests**

A:    Please sit down. What do you want to drink: coffee or tea?

B:    Neither, thank you. Do you have water?

A:    Yes. Please have some water.

B:    Thank you.

A:    You are welcome.

**Step 2.** Now that you have familiarized yourself with the dialogue, be creative! Think of other words you have learned so far that might work in this dialogue. For example, instead of saying, "This is your coffee," you could say, "This is your tea." Try to substitute as many words as possible without disrupting the structure of the dialogue.

## TASK 4. PICTURE DESCRIPTION

**Topic:** A hostess is welcoming her guests, who have just arrived for the weekend. She invites them to come inside and offers them a choice of drinks. The guests give the hostess a small gift and thank her for her hospitality. The hostess has prepared a wonderful feast, and the guests are very appreciative.

1.                                              2.

3.

# 8

# 问姓名
## Asking Someone's Name

**In this lesson you will:**
- Review pinyin combinations and try a few tongue twisters.
- Review strokes and stroke order in writing Chinese characters.
- Learn vocabulary you will need to introduce yourself to others.
- Inquire politely about someone you have just met.

(Note: Starting in this lesson the textbook will not include pinyin for this section. If you would still like to refer to the pinyin, please see your CD-ROM, which will continue to include it.)

Wu Wende goes to a reception organized by the Chinese Department.

吴文德： 请问， 您贵姓？

胡老师： 我姓胡。

吴文德： 您是胡老师？您是林笛的老师，对吗？

胡老师： 对，我教她中文。你呢？你叫什么名字？

吴文德： 我的中文名字叫吴文德。姓吴，叫文德。

我的中国朋友都叫我小吴。

胡老师： 你是我们学校东亚系的学生，是吗？

吴文德： 对，我学汉语，也学日语。

胡老师： 你汉语很不错。

吴文德：　哪里，哪里。我认识很多中国留学生，
　　　　　我常常说汉语。但是，我不懂中国文化，
　　　　　常闹笑话。大家常常开玩笑，
　　　　　叫我小华(笑话)。

胡老师：　你们汉语老师是谁？

吴文德：　是张老师。您认识吗？

胡老师：　老张。认识，认识。

吴文德：　他还不老啊！

胡老师：　(laughs)我知道。但是，他教书经验
　　　　　丰富。所以，我们都叫他老张。

吴文德：　张老师是哪国人？

胡老师：　是中国人。

吴文德：　他是中国哪里人？北京人还是上海人？

胡老师：　北京人，上海人他都不是。他是四川人。
　　　　　你很好奇啊。常常问问题，对吗？

吴文德：　对不起，我的问题太多，是吗？

胡老师：　没关系。

# 生词表 (Shēngcí Biǎo)
# Vocabulary

| Character | Pinyin | Part of Speech | English Definition |
|---|---|---|---|
| 1. 姓名 | xìngmíng | *n.* | name |
| 2. *贵*姓 | guìxìng | *n.* | (formal) (What is) your honorable surname? |
| 贵 | | *adj.* | expensive; honorable |
| 姓 | | *n.* | surname |
| | | *v.* | to be surnamed |
| 3. *对 | duì | *adj.*   correct, right | |
| 4. *叫 | jiào | *v.* | to call; to be called |
| 5. *名*字 | míngzi | *n.* | given name |
| 字 | zì | *n.* | Chinese character; "word" in Western languages |
| 6. 小 | xiǎo | *pref. & adj.* | (placed before a personal *n.*); small, little |
| 7. 学*校 | xuéxiào | *n.* | school |
| 8. 系 | xì | *n.* | department in an academic setting |
| 9. *汉*语 漢 | Hànyǔ | *n.* | the Chinese language |
| 10. 不错 | búcuò | *adj.* | not bad, pretty good, just fine |
| *错 | | *adj.* | wrong |
| 11. 哪里 | nǎlǐ | phr. | where |
| 12. 认*识 認識 | rènshi | *v.* | to be acquainted with, to be familiar with |
| 13. 留学生 | liúxuésheng | *n.* | foreign student (who is studying in a country other than his/her own) |
| 学生 | | *n.* | student |
| 留 | | *v.* | to stay, to stay behind |
| 14. 懂 | dǒng | *v.* | understand, know |
| 15. 文化 | wénhuà | *n.* | culture |

| 16. | 闹笑*话 | nào xiàohua | *v. obj.* | to make a fool of oneself |
| | 闹 | | *v.* | to make noise; to go in for; to do, make |
| | 笑 | | *v.* | to laugh (at) |
| | 话 | | *n.* | word, speech |
| | 笑话 | | *n.* | joke |
| 17. | 开玩笑 | kāi wánxiào | *v. obj.* | to joke, make fun of |
| 18. | *知*道 | zhīdào | *v.* | to know (a fact); to know that… |
| 19. | 经验 验 | jīngyàn | *n.* | experience |
| 20. | 丰富 豐 | fēngfù | *adj.* | rich, abundant |
| 21. | 所以 | suǒyǐ | *conj.* | so, therefore |
| 22. | 哪*国人 | nǎ guó rén | *phr.* | which country |
| | 哪 | | *interrog.* | which |
| | 国 | | *n.* | nation, country |
| | 人 | | *n.* | person, human being |
| 23. | 好奇 | hàoqí | *adj.* | curious/inquisitive |
| 24. | 对不起 | duìbuqǐ | *phr.* | I am sorry, I beg your pardon (lit., unable to "face" someone) |
| 25. | 没关系 關係 | méi guānxi | *phr.* | never mind, it doesn't matter |

## 专有名词 (Zhuānyǒu Míngcí) Proper Nouns

| 1. | 东亚 | Dōngyà | | East Asia |
| 2. | 日语 | Rìyǔ | | the Japanese language |
| 3. | 小华 華 華 | Xiǎo Huá | | a given name |
| 4. | 北京 | Běijīng | | Beijing, the capital of China |
| 5. | 上海 | Shànghǎi | | Shanghai, a large city in east China |
| 6. | 四川 | Sìchuān | | Sichuan, a province in west China |

## 补充词汇 (Bǔchōng Cíhuì) Supplementary Vocabulary

| 1. | 外语 | wàiyǔ | *n.* | foreign language |
| 2. | 美国 | Měiguó | *n.* | U.S.A. |

| | | | |
|---|---|---|---|
| 3. 明白 | míngbai | *v.* | to understand |
| 4. 告诉 | gàosu | *v.* | to tell |
| 5. 讲 講 | jiǎng | *v.* | to speak, to say |
| 6. 有意思 | yǒu yìsi | *phr.* | very interesting |
| 7. 非常抱歉 | fēicháng bàoqiàn | *phr.* | my apologies |

# 口头用语 (Kǒutóu Yòngyǔ) Spoken Expressions

1. 哪里, 哪里     nǎlǐ, nǎlǐ

This phrase is frequently used as a modest response to a compliment.

# 词汇注解 (Cíhuì Zhùjiě) Featured Vocabulary

## 1. 汉语 *(Hànyǔ) vs.* 中文 *(Zhōngwén)*

汉语 is frequently used to describe Chinese in a general sense (usually referring to Chinese as a second language). For example: 学汉语，汉语书.

    中文 has a similar meaning to 汉语 and can be used in any of the same places that 汉语 is used (e. g., 学中文，中文书). It is different in

*Ringing the temple bell brings good fortune.*

Margaret Vee

that it can also be used to describe specific items that involve Chinese writing or language. For example: 中文报（报）(bào) Chinese newspaper

## 2. 知道 *(Zhīdào) vs.* 认识 *(Rènshi)*

Although both 知道 and 认识 can be translated as "to know," in Chinese they have distinct meanings and serve very different functions.

知道: to know a fact; to know of something. It can be followed by either a noun phrase or a clause. It cannot be used to say that you are personally acquainted with someone.

我知道史老师不是美国人。

I know that Professor Shi is not an American citizen.

CORRECT: 我知道小吴这个人。

xxx INCORRECT: 我知道小吴。 xxx

认识: to be acquainted with (someone or something), to know sb./sth. through personal contact. It cannot be followed by a clause.

我认识史老师。        I know Professor Shi personally.

我不认识那个字。      I don't know that word.

xxx INCORRECT: 我认识史老师不是美国人。 xxx

## 3. 意思 *(Yìsi)*

小意思 can be used as one of the responses to someone who thanks you for your gift. "Something 是什么意思" is used to ask for an explanation of a word or phrase or for clarification of a term. The response to the question usually employs the pattern "...就 (jiù) 是...(的意思)"。

这个字是什么意思?    What does this word mean?

## 4. 闹笑话 *(Nào Xiàohua) vs.* 说笑话 *(Shuō Xiàohua) vs.* 开玩笑 *(Kāi Wánxiào)*

These three verb-object phrases may look similar, but they carry different meanings.

闹笑话: to make a fool of someone

开玩笑: to have fun with / kid / tease someone

说笑话: to tell jokes

## 语法 (Yǔfǎ)
## Grammar

## I. Verbs with Two Objects: Direct and Indirect

There are certain Chinese verbs that can take two objects: a direct and an indirect object. Generally, the direct object (referring to something) receives the action of the verb, while the indirect object (referring to someone) tells who or what was affected by the action. This lesson introduces five two-object verbs: 还 (huán), 叫 (jiào), 教 (jiāo), 借 (jiè), and 问 (wèn).

| Subject | Verb<br>叫/还/借/教/问 | Indirect Object<br>Somebody | Direct Object<br>Something |
|---|---|---|---|
| 我朋友 | 叫 | 我 | 小吴。 |
| *My friend calls me "Little Wu."* | | | |
| （我） | 还 | 你 | 笔记。 |
| *I will return your notes to you.* | | | |
| （我） | 借 | 你们 | 我的笔记。 |
| *I lend you my notes.* | | | |
| 我 | 教 | 他 | 中文。 |
| *I teach him Chinese.* | | | |
| 你 | 去问 | 老师 | 问题吗？ |
| *Are you going to ask the teacher a question?* | | | |

## ❂ PRACTICE

Try using 谁 to ask a question concerning an indirect object (e.g., 你借谁 笔记？), using 什么 to ask a question concerning a direct object (e.g., 你 还他什么？), and then using 嗎 to ask a question concerning the entire sentence with direct and indirect object (e.g., 你问老师问题吗？).

## II. Inquiring about Someone's Nationality and Place of Origin

Do you remember the interrogative pronouns we have learned so far? They are 谁, 谁的, 什么, 怎么样, and 哪儿. 哪 cannot be used independently. In 哪儿 ("where"), the addition of the suffix –儿 makes it a whole word. In this lesson you see how 哪 combines with the noun 国 to form a word meaning "what country." We also see how 哪里 combines with (i.e., modifies) the noun 人 to form an expression meaning "a person from where?" Remember that these interrogative expressions, or "question words," occupy the same position in their sentences that the key term does in the answer to the question.

### A. Questions with 哪国 (Nǎ Guó)

Note that 哪国 + Noun serves a dual purpose. If the noun refers to a person, the phrase asks for his or her nationality. If the noun is a product, the phrase asks where it was produced or manufactured.

| Question | | | Response |
|---|---|---|---|
| **Subject** | **是** | **哪国+ Noun** | |
| 他 | 是 | 哪国 人? | 他是中国人。 |
| What country is he from? | | | He is from China./He is Chinese. |
| 他的茶 | 是 | 哪国 茶? | 是(德国)茶。 |
| Which country does his tea come from? | | | It comes from Germany. |

### B. Questions with 哪里 (Nǎli)

哪里+ 人 is used to ask where a person is from.

| Question | | | Response |
|---|---|---|---|
| 你 | 是 | 哪里人? | 我是中国人。 |
| Where are you from? | | | I am from China. |
| 你 | 是 | 中国哪里人? | 我是中国四川人。 |
| Which part of China are you from? | | | I am from Sìchuān, China. |

### *Note*

Some people also use 哪儿的人? when asking where a person is from. For example: 你是中国哪儿的人? instead of 你是中国哪里的人?

*Chris Vee*

## PRACTICE

Talk to the student sitting next to you to find out what city and country they are from, using 哪里 and 哪国, respectively. You may say the city name in English.

## III. Ways of Asking a Person's Name

### A. Asking for Someone's Surname

#### 1. 您贵姓 *(Nín guìxìng?)*

您贵姓 means "What is your honorable surname, please?" and is a very polite way of asking for someone's surname. It is used to address people who are older than you or just simply to show respect. 贵姓 should only be used in this question format; it is NOT appropriate in a response. Moreover, 贵姓 is usually used with the polite second-person pronoun 您. Also, 您 is often omitted, leaving just 请问, 贵姓?

| Question | | Response |
|---|---|---|
| **Subject** | **Verb Object** | |
| (您) | 贵姓 | 我姓胡。 |
| What is your honorable surname, please? | | My surname is Hu. (I am surnamed Hu.) |

#### 2. 姓什么 *(Xìng shénme?)*

For a "third person" one would ask 他姓什么? The phrase 姓什么 can also be used to ask someone's surname in the second person; however, that person should be approximately your age if not younger and /or should have equal or lower social status.

| Question | | | Response |
|---|---|---|---|
| **Subject** | **Verb** | **Object** | |
| 你 | 姓 | 什么？ | 我姓李。 |
| How are you surnamed? | | | I am surnamed Li. |

## B. Asking for Someone's Given Name or Whole Name

1.  叫什么 (Jiào shénme?)
2.  叫什么名字 (Jiào shénme míngzì?)
3.  (Someone) 的名字是什么 (de míngzi shì shénme?)

The above three patterns are commonly used to inquire about either someone's full name or given name.

| Question | | | Response |
|---|---|---|---|
| **Subject** | **Verb** | **Object** | |
| 她 | 叫 | 什么？ | 她叫丽莉。 |
| What is she called? | | | Her first name is Lili. |
| 她 | 叫 | 什么名字？ | 她的名字叫李丽莉。 |
| What is her name? | | | Her name is Li Lili. |
| 她的名字 | 是 | 什么？ | 她的名字是李丽莉。 |
| What is her name? | | | Her name is Li Lili. |

### *Note*
你叫什么？, 她叫什么名字？ or 她的名字叫什么？ are much more casual, friendly, and direct ways of inquiring about someone's name than（您）贵姓.

---

## PRACTICE

Introduce yourself to the class and ask the students next to you for their names and surnames. If you don't know the teacher's name and you ask him or her directly, be sure to ask in a respectful manner.

## IV. Using Polite Language for Communication

The following patterns will come in handy as you start having conversations with Chinese people.

## A. 请问 (May I ask...) is a polite way to ask a question

请问 (qǐngwèn), at the beginning of a sentence, is often used as a polite way to introduce a question. Generally, it is a good idea to use this to get attention, but be careful not to overuse it.

| 请问,　Sentence |  |
|---|---|
| 请问，您是李老师吗？ | May I ask, are you Professor Li? |
| 请问，您贵姓？ | May I ask, what is your honorable surname? |

### 🆒 PRACTICE

In a group of students, use 请问 to ask each other questions.

## B. Responding to a Compliment: 哪里，哪里

The word 哪里 (nǎli) is often doubled to respond to compliments. 哪里 literally means "where?" That is, "Where can the compliment possibly apply in my case?" It is used to show one's modesty and can be translated as "It's nothing," or "You flatter me." Unlike Americans, Chinese people rarely say "Thank you" when flattered or complimented.

For example:

| Compliment | Response |
|---|---|
| 你汉语很不错。 | 哪里，哪里。 |
| Your Chinese is so good! | You flatter me. |

## C. Apologies and Responses

对不起 (duìbùqǐ) literally means "being incapable of facing someone" because you realize you have done something wrong or done something that will cause inconvenience. 没关系 (méi guānxi) is a common response, meaning "never mind" or "it does not matter." For example:

对不起，我问题太多了。　　I am sorry; I ask too many questions.

没关系。　　　　　　　　Never mind (no big deal).

It is NOT used to express sympathy, as one would do with "I am sorry" in English. Therefore, do not use "对不起。" in response to 我身体不太好。

## V. Using Compound Verbs

So far we have learned four compound verbs — 教书(jiāoshū), 看书 (kànshū), 吃饭 (chīfàn), and 喝酒 (hējiǔ) — which consist of a verb and an object. The compound verb in Chinese usually keeps its object. Note that in translation the compounds' English counterparts are usually verbs.

| Verb | English | Example |
|------|---------|---------|
| 教书 | to teach | 他每天教书。 |
| 看书 | to read | 他常常看书。 |
| 吃饭 | to eat | 他去吃饭。 |
| 喝酒 | to drink | 他喝酒。 |

 语音复习 (Yǔyīn Fùxí)
Pronunciation Review

## FINAL REVIEW OF PINYIN

This book has covered a total of twenty-one finals and thirty-eight initials as well as their combinations. The following two sections make up our final review of pinyin.

### I. Challenging Sounds

Each of the following pairs has a very similar sound. As a result, students sometimes have trouble pronouncing them correctly. What about you? Let's make sure you can pronounce them like a native speaker.

| | | | |
|------|------|------|------|
| de | te | lin | ling |
| dou | duo | chen | cheng |
| zun | cun | zhou | jiu |
| chi | che | shan | san |
| shao | xiao | xian | xiang |
| nin | lin | zhao | jiao |

### II. Tongue Twisters

Try the following tongue twisters and see how many you can say correctly on your first try. How long does it take you to perfect them? Have fun!

1. Māma mài mǎ bú mài má,       妈妈卖马不卖麻，

   mǎ màn mā mà, mǎ kuài mā kuā。   马慢妈骂，马快妈夸。

*Outside a bus station in Shanghai.*

2. Zhāng Lǎoshī bù zāng,

　　chéng lǎoshī bù chén,

　　bù zāng lǎoshī bù rènshi bù chén

　　lǎoshī.

张老师不脏，

程老师不沉，

不脏老师不认识不沉

老师。

3. Zi ci si jiùshì zi ci si,

　　zhi chi shi jiùshì zhi chi shi,

　　zi ci si búshì zhi chi shi,

　　zhi chi shi yě búshì zi ci si.

Zi ci si 就是 zi ci si,

zhi chi shi 就是 zhi chi shi,

zi ci si 不是 zhi chi shi,

zhi chi shi 也不是 zi ci si.

4. Sì zhī shī shīzi shì sì zhī

　　shī shīzi,

　　shí zhī shí shīzi shì shí zhī

　　shí shīzi,

　　shí sì zhī sǐ shīzi shì shí

　　sì zhī sǐ shīzi,

　　sì shí sì zhī cí shīzi shì

　　sì shí sì zhī cí shīzi.

四只湿狮子是四只

湿狮子，

十只石狮子是十只

石狮子，

十四只死狮子是十

四只死狮子，

四十四只瓷狮子是

四十四只瓷狮子。

写汉字(Xiě Hànzì)
# Character Writing

## Key Radical Presentation

The closure radical: 口

The wood radical: 木

| Character | Practice with Chinese Characters |
|---|---|
| 贵 | |
| 姓 | |
| 汉 | |
| 语 | |
| 教 | |
| 叫 | |
| 名 | |
| 字 | |
| 认 | |
| 识 | |
| 懂 | |
| 知 | |
| 道 | |
| 国 | |

校
就

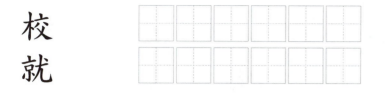

 课堂练习(Kètáng Liànxí)

# In-Class Exercises

## 🎧💻 TASK 1. QUESTIONS AND ANSWERS

How well did you understand the text? Check your comprehension by answering the following questions.

1. 林笛的汉语老师姓什么？

2. 吴文德姓什么，叫什么？他的中国朋友都叫他什么？

3. 吴文德的汉语老师姓什么？他的老师认识胡老师吗？

## 💻 TASK 2. GRAMMATICAL STRUCTURE PRACTICE

### A. Matching

Read the following sentences carefully and then match sentences from the left column with those in the right column.

1. 请问，您是胡先生，对吗？    (a) 不对，她是我们老师！

2. 你们叫我小吴，好吗？    (b) 他不姓林，他姓史。

3. 她也是这儿的学生，对吗？    (c) 不，我是李老师。

4. 你叫什么名字？    (d) 好啊。

5. 你们老师姓林吗？    (e) 姓吴，叫文德。你呢？

## B. Word Selection

Select the choice that best completes each sentence.

1. 我不_____ 他。

    a) 知道          b) 认识        c) 懂

2. 我们老师_____ 。

    a) 叫史          b) 姓史        c) 姓史小英

3. 我不_____你朋友是哪里人。

    a) 知道          b) 认识        c) 懂

4. 请问，他老师的_____是什么？

    a) 贵姓          b) 叫          c) 名字

## C. Scrambled Words

Rearrange the words and phrases to form grammatically correct and meaningful sentences.

**1.** 茶      是      哪国      他的茶

2. 是      人      你      中国      哪里

3. 的      叫      名字      什么      你朋友

4. 人      是      他      我不      哪里            知道

*Chinese brush painting with flowers and birds.*

## 📖 TASK 3. PARAPHRASING

How well do you remember the grammar and vocabulary we've covered so far? Test yourself by translating the following sentences into Chinese.

1. A: What is your name?

   B: My Chinese name is Li Wen, (my) surname is Li. My friends call me Xiao Li.

2. A: Excuse me — may I ask what your honorable surname is, please?

   B: My last name is Hu. You may call me Hu Laoshi.

3. A: Where is he from?

   B: I know he is from China, but I don't know which part.

4. A: Your Chinese is very good now.

   B: You flatter me. I know lots of Chinese students, and we frequently speak Chinese.

5. A: Do you often ask your teachers questions?

   B: No, I don't ask questions very often.

6. A: Thank you for teaching me Chinese. But I have too many questions — my apologies.

   B: It is okay.

## 📖 TASK 4. SITUATIONAL DIALOGUE

**Setting:**    Outside an office building

**Cast:**    Two business associates

**Situation:**    Mr. 李 has just started working as an engineer in a computer company and meets one of his business associates, Ms. 张. The two introduce themselves, exchange surnames, and then talk a bit about themselves, their positions, and the company.

# 9
# 找人
# Looking for Someone

*In this lesson you will:*
- Learn to use Chinese numbers.
- Inquire about a person's whereabouts.
- Ask for and write Chinese addresses.

Li Lili sits in her dorm room. She hears someone knock at the door.

| | |
|---|---|
| 李丽莉： | 请问，你找谁？ |
| 高朋： | 我找林笛，她住这儿，对吗？ |
| 李丽莉： | 对，她住这儿。你好，我叫李丽莉，<br>是林笛的室友。 |
| 高朋： | 你好，我是林笛的同学。我姓高，叫朋。 |
| 李丽莉： | 高朋？久闻大名[1]。林笛说你中文很好！ |
| 高朋： | 哪里，你太客气了。林笛在吗？ |
| 李丽莉： | 她现在不在。她在吴文德那儿做作业。 |
| 高朋： | 吴文德住哪儿？ |
| 李丽莉： | 他住学生宿舍九二五楼。 |
| 高朋： | 他住几层，多少号？ |
| 李丽莉： | 二层二〇九号。 |
| 高朋： | 吴文德的电话号码是多少？ |
| 李丽莉： | 他的电话是二八六一九五七三。<br>我们的电话在那儿，你用吧。 |
| 高朋： | 谢谢。 |

After the phone call:

高朋：　　　林笛还在吴文德那儿，我现在去找她。
　　　　　　麻烦你了。欢迎你以后去我那儿玩儿。

李丽莉：　　好啊，多一个朋友，多一条路[2]。
　　　　　　你住哪儿？

高朋：　　　我住学生宿舍七五六楼，三层三一二号。
　　　　　　以后你一定来玩儿啊！

李丽莉：　　一定。

Forty-five minutes later, Gao Peng returns.

高朋：　　　真不好意思。我去学生宿舍九二五楼
　　　　　　三层找吴文德，但是他不住那儿。

李丽莉：　　吴文德不住那层楼，他的地址是九二
　　　　　　五楼，二层，二〇九号。我们一起去找他吧。

高朋：　　　好啊。我的车在楼下。

Li Lili and Gao Peng are standing in the parking lot.

李丽莉：　　这是你的车吗？这么漂亮的德国车。

高朋：　　　不是。我的车是美国车，你看，在那儿。

Chris Vee

## Notes

1. 久闻大名。(Jiǔ wén dà míng.) Literally, "I heard your name long ago."
   In other words, "Although we have not met, I know who you are."

2. 多一个朋友，多一条路。(Duō yī gè péngyou, duō yī tiáo lù.)
   Literally, "one more friend, one more road," which means "The more friends you have, the better."

 生词表 (Shēngcí Biǎo)

# Vocabulary

| Character | Pinyin | Part of Speech | English Definition |
|---|---|---|---|
| 1.\*找 | zhǎo | *v.* | to look for; to call on, visit (someone) |
| 2.\*住 | zhù | *v.* | to stay at/in; to dwell in/at |
| 3.这儿 | zhèr | *n.* | here, this place |
| 4.\*室友 | shìyǒu | *n.* | roommate |
| 室 | | *n.* | room |
| 5.\*同学 | tóngxué | *n.* | classmate |
| 同 | | *adj.* | same, similar; together with |
| 6.在 | zài | *prep.* | to be located (in, on, at) |
| 7.那儿 | nàr | *pron.* | that place |
| 8.\*宿\*舍 | sùshè | *n.* | dormitory |
| 9.\*楼 樓 | lóu | *n.* | multi-storied building |
| 10.\*几 | jǐ | *num.* | several, a few; how many (used mostly when the estimated response is less than 10) |
| 11.层 | céng | *m.w.* | floor, story (in a building), (lit.) layer |
| 12.多少 | duōshǎo | *adj.* | how many, how much (esp. when the estimated response is greater than 10) |
| 13.\*号 號 | hào | *m.w.* | number in a series |
| 14.电话 | diànhuà | *n.* | telephone |
| 15.号码 | hàomǎ | *n.* | number |
| 16.麻烦 | máfan | *v.* | to bother |
| | | *adj.* | trouble |

| 17. | *以*后 | yǐhòu | n. | later on, in the future |
|-----|--------|-------|-----|-------------------------|
| 18. | *玩儿 | wánr | v. | to have fun; to play; to relax and enjoy oneself |
| 19. | 一*定 | yídìng | adv. | surely, certainly |
| 20. | *地址 | dìzhǐ | n. | address |
|     | 地 | | n. | ground, floor |
| 21. | 一*起 | yìqǐ | adv. | together |
| 22. | *车 | chē | n. | car, vehicles in general |
| 23. | 楼下 | lóu xià | n. | downstairs |
| 24. | 漂亮 | piàoliang | adj. | good-looking, beautiful |
| 25. | *个 | gè | m.w. | general classifier |

## 专有名词 (Zhuānyǒu Míngcí) Proper Nouns

| 1. | 高朋 | Gāo Péng | | a person's name |
|----|------|----------|---|----------------|
| 2. | 德国 | Déguó | | Germany |
| 3. | 美国 | Měiguó | | U. S. A. |

## 补充词汇 (Bǔchōng Cíhuì) Supplementary Vocabulary

| 1. | 同屋 | tóngwū | n. | roommate |
|----|------|--------|-----|----------|
| 2 | 同事 | tóngshì | n. | colleague |
| 3. | 宾馆 | bīnguǎn | n. | hotel |
| 4. | 饭店 | fàndiàn | n. | hotel |
| 5. | 房间 | fángjiān | n. | room |
| 6. | 楼上 | lóu shàng | n. | upstairs |
| 7. | 打电话 | dǎ diànhuà | v. | to make a phone call |

## 口头用语 (Kǒutóu Yòngyǔ) Spoken Expressions

1. 麻烦你了(Máfan nǐ le.) This is used to apologize for bothering someone or to express thanks when someone has done you a favor.

2. 不好意思 (Bù hǎo yìsi.) (I am) embarrassed (to put you to all the trouble).

## 词汇注解 (Cíhuì Zhùjiě) Featured Vocabulary

### 1. The Verb 住 (Zhù)

The verb 住 means "to live, reside, stay at." It has many different usages.
For example:

住 + Specific Location: (more colloquial)

| | | | |
|---|---|---|---|
| 住哪儿 | live where? | 住那儿 | live there |
| 住哪个楼 | live in which building? | 住那个楼 | live in that building |
| 住多少号 | live in which room? | | |

住 + 在 + Place (country, city, institution or dorm): (more formal)

| | | | |
|---|---|---|---|
| 住在中国 | live in China | 住在北京 | live in Beijing |
| 住在学校 | live at school | 住在宿舍 | live in a dorm |

The short form of 住在学校 is 住校.

住在 + 一起 live together

林笛和李丽莉住在一起。 Lin Di and Li Lili live together.

### 2. 几层 (Jǐcéng) vs. 哪层 (Nǎcéng)

几层 and 哪层 ask questions with different meanings; thus, their responses
are different.

| Questions | Responses |
|---|---|
| 几层 How many floors? | 两 (liǎng) 层 There are two floors. |
| 哪层 Which floor? | 二层 Second floor. |

## Numerals 0–10

Chinese uses a decimal counting system. For the first eleven digits (0-10),
each number has its own character. For example:

| 零 | 一 | 二(两) | 三 | 四 | 五 | 六 | 七 | 八 | 九 | 十 |
|---|---|---|---|---|---|---|---|---|---|---|
| líng | yī | èr (liǎng) | sān | sì | wǔ | liù | qī | bā | jiǔ | shí |
| zero | one | two | three | four | five | six | seven | eight | nine | ten |

# *Notes*

1. The Chinese number 一 has two different pronounciations: yī and yāo. Yī is more commonly used, while yāo is used by people from Northern China.

2. When two is used before a measure word, use 两, NOT 二.

# Numerals 11–99

For numbers between 11 and 19, there are two characters each. The first character is simply 十, and the second fills the ones position (see Row 1 in the table on page 130 for more examples).

The 10s (20, 30, 40, etc.) also consist of two characters: The first character stands in the tens position, and the second is 十 itself (see Column 1 in the table on page 130 for more examples).

For all other numbers greater than 20 but less than 100, there are three characters: The first character expresses the number of tens, the second character is 十 itself, and the third character expresses the number of ones.

## *Numbers*

|        | X+1   | X+2   | X+3   | X+4   | X+5   | X+6   | X+7   | X+8   | X+9   |
|--------|-------|-------|-------|-------|-------|-------|-------|-------|-------|
|        | 十一  | 十二  | 十三  | 十四  | 十五  | 十六  | 十七  | 十八  | 十九  |
| 20 二十 | 二十一 | 二十二 | 二十三 | 二十四 | 二十五 | 二十六 | 二十七 | 二十八 | 二十九 |
| 30 三十 | 三十一 | 三十二 | 三十三 | 三十四 | 三十五 | 三十六 | 三十七 | 三十八 | 三十九 |
| 40 四十 | 四十一 | 四十二 | 四十三 | 四十四 | 四十五 | 四十六 | 四十七 | 四十八 | 四十九 |
| 50 五十 | 五十一 | 五十二 | 五十三 | 五十四 | 五十五 | 五十六 | 五十七 | 五十八 | 五十九 |
| 60 六十 | 六十一 | 六十二 | 六十三 | 六十四 | 六十五 | 六十六 | 六十七 | 六十八 | 六十九 |
| 70 七十 | 七十一 | 七十二 | 七十三 | 七十四 | 七十五 | 七十六 | 七十七 | 七十八 | 七十九 |
| 80 八十 | 八十一 | 八十二 | 八十三 | 八十四 | 八十五 | 八十六 | 八十七 | 八十八 | 八十九 |
| 90 九十 | 九十一 | 九十二 | 九十三 | 九十四 | 九十五 | 九十六 | 九十七 | 九十八 | 九十九 |

# 语法(Yǔfǎ)
# Grammar

## I. Location Words

In this lesson, we will learn how to use the location words 这儿 "here" and 那儿 "there."

## A. Using the Noun/Pronoun + 这儿/那儿 (Zhèr/Nàr)

这儿 and 那儿 frequently follow nouns or pronouns to indicate a location.

| Noun/Pronoun | 这儿/那儿 | |
|---|---|---|
| 她 | 这儿 | (Here at) her place... |
| 我 | 这儿 | My place over here... |
| 史老师 | 这儿 | (Here at) Professor Shi's place... |
| 我 | 那儿 | My place over there... |
| 你哥哥 | 那儿 | Your brother's place over there... |
| 谁 | 那儿 | Whose place |

## B. Using the Interrogative Pronoun 哪儿 (Nǎr)

In Lesson 6, you learned that 哪儿 means "which place/what place" or "where." Like all the other question words covered so far (谁, 什么, etc.), it replaces the missing information in a sentence WITHOUT changing the word order. This lesson will focus on "Verb + 哪儿 + Verb Phrase" and its responses.

| | Subject | Verb | Place | Verb Phrase |
|---|---|---|---|---|
| Question: | 她 | 去 | 哪儿？ | |
| | Where is she going? | | | |
| Response: | 她 | 去 | 史老师那儿。 | |
| | She is going to Professor Shi's place. | | | |
| Question: | 你 | 去 | 哪儿 | 喝咖啡？ |
| | Where do you go for coffee? | | | |
| Response: | 我 | 去 | 我哥哥那儿 | 喝咖啡。 |
| | I am going to my brother's place to drink coffee. | | | |

*Morning mist dissipating over Huang Shan.*

Margaret Vee

## PRACTICE

Can you think of any more phrases using "Noun/Pronoun + 这儿/那儿?"
Take a few minutes in class to work with the student sitting next to you. Ask
and respond to each other's questions using the 哪儿 and 这儿 or 那儿
patterns above. For example:

Q: 你去哪儿做作业?          A: 我去同学那儿做作业。

Q: 你来我这儿做作业吗?       A: 我去你那儿做作业。

For your convenience, we have provided below two groups of words for this
practice.

Location:    朋友   奶奶   室友   医生   他的老板
Action:     借笔记   找工作   吃点心   休息   玩儿

## II. Ways to Use the Location Verb 在 (Zài)

在 can function as a verb or a preposition, and it has various meanings.

### A. As a Verb
When used with an object, it means "to be located at/in a certain place." The
subject is a person or a thing.

|  | Subject | 在 | Place |  |
|---|---|---|---|---|
| Question: | 你的车 | 在 | 哪儿? | Where is your car? |
| Response: | 我的车 | 在 | 楼下。 | My car is downstairs. |

| Question: | 林笛 | 在 | 哪儿？ | Where is Lin Di? |
| Question: | 她 | 在 | 吴文德那儿吗？ | Is she at Wu Wende's place (over there)? |
| Response: | 她 | 在 | 吴文德那儿。 | She is at Wu Wende's place (over there). |
| Negative: | 她朋友 | 不在 | 吴文德那儿。 | Her friend is not at Wu Wende's place (over there). |

| | **Subject** | 在 | 吗？ | |
| --- | --- | --- | --- | --- |
| Question: | 林笛 | 在 | 吗？ | Is Lin Di in? |
| Response: | 她 | 在。 | | She is at home. |
| Negative: | 她朋友 | 不在。 | | Her friend is not at home. |

When used without an object, it means "to be in, to be at home." The subject is usually a person.

## B. As a Preposition

In the structure below, 在 is a preposition. You will learn more about prepositional phrases in the next lesson; for now, all you need to know is that "在 + Location" must be placed before the verb.

| | **Subject** | **在 + Place** | **Verb Phrase** |
| --- | --- | --- | --- |
| Question: | 林笛 | 在哪儿 | 做作业？ |
| | Where is Lin Di doing her homework? | | |
| Response: | 她 | 在吴文德那儿 | 做作业。 |
| | She is at Wu Wende's place, doing her homework. | | |

## ◪ PRACTICE

Use the words given below with 在 (both as a verb or a preposition) to ask a question, and then provide a positive and a negative response.

Location: 宿舍, 楼下, 中国, 朋友 家, 老师那儿

Action: 用电话, 问问题, 搞电脑, 做生意, 喝酒

## III. Brief Introduction to Measure Words

In Chinese, numbers or demonstrative pronouns such as 这 and 那, and interrogative pronouns such as 哪, 几, and 多少, cannot be used directly to quantify people or things; you always need to use a measure word. Measure words function as a unit to qualify nouns. Measure words are placed after

*Chinese brush painting on eggshells.*

the number or the demonstrative pronoun. Please keep in mind that different nouns take different measure words. In this lesson, you have learned 个 (gè), 号 (hào), and 层 (céng).

个: 个 is the most commonly used measure word. For example: 一个工作, 两个朋友, 三个老板, 四个护士, 五个电脑, 六个问题, 七个水果, and so on. Or 这/那/哪/几个工作, 这/那/哪/几个朋友, 这/那/哪/几个老板, 这/那/哪/几个电脑, and so on.

号: 号 is frequently used with rooms. For example: 一号教室 Classroom No. 1.

层: 层 is frequently used with 楼. For example: 一层楼 the first floor, or 这/那/哪/几层楼 (this / that / which / how many floors).

You will learn more about measure words in Lesson 12.

## IV. The Interrogative Words 多少 (Duōshǎo) and 几 (Jǐ)

When used interrogatively, 多少 and 几 mean "how many/much." 多少 is used when the number is expected to exceed ten; 几 is used when the number is expected to be under ten. Remember that when using interrogative words to form questions, the word order remains the same as in a statement.

### A. Estimated Number >10

| Subject | Verb | 多少 | Measure Word | |
|---------|------|------|--------------|---|
| 你 | 住 | 多少 | 号？ | What is your room number? |
| 我 | 住 | 209 | 号。 | I live in room 209. |

## B. Estimated Number <10

| Subject | Verb | 几 | Measure Word | |
|---|---|---|---|---|
| 你 | 住 | 几 | 层？ | On which floor do you live? |
| 我 | 住 | 五 | 层。 | I live on the fifth floor. |

### *Note*

The interrogative pronoun 几 must be followed by a measure word. As for the interrogative pronoun 多少, sometimes the measure word can be omitted.

---

### PRACTICE

With a partner, create a short dialogue in which one person asks a question with 几 or 多少 and the other answers. When you're done, switch roles and do it again! Here are some words you can use to create your own questions:
几层 几号 几个医生 几个电脑 多少号
多少朋友 多少学生 多少问题

## V. Chinese Addresses

In Chinese addresses, the largest unit comes first and the other units follow in descending order, with the smallest unit at the end. For example:

Largest ——————————————————————————> Smallest

| Largest Unit | 2nd Largest | 3rd ... | 4th... | Smallest Unit |
|---|---|---|---|---|
| 北京大学 | 学生宿舍 | 七五六楼 | 三层 | 三〇一五号。 |

---

### PRACTICE

Practice saying your own address aloud — first on your own, and then for the whole class. If your address is too difficult to say, make up one in Chinese.

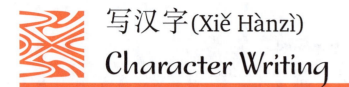

写汉字(Xiě Hànzì)

# Character Writing

## Key Radical Presentation

The hand radical: 扌

The field radical: 丰

| Character | Practice with Chinese Characters |
|---|---|
| 找 | |
| 住 | |
| 室 | |
| 同 | |
| 宿 | |
| 舍 | |
| 楼 | |
| 几 | |
| 号 | |
| 话 | |
| 以 | |
| 后 | |
| 玩 | |
| 定 | |

# 课堂练习(Kètáng Liànxí)

# In-Class Exercises

## 🎧 💻 TASK 1. QUESTIONS AND ANSWERS

How well did you understand the text? Test your comprehension by answering the following questions.

1. 李丽莉认识不认识高朋？你怎么知道？

2. 林笛在哪儿？她的宿舍有人吗？有电话吗？

3. 吴文德是不是高朋的室友？你怎么知道？

## 💻 TASK 2. GRAMMATICAL STRUCTURE PRACTICE

### A. Matching

Read the following sentences carefully and then match sentences from the left column with those in the right column.

**Part 1.**

| | |
|---|---|
| 1. 我的笔记在哪儿？ | a) 我住三二五号。 |
| 2. 李太太，请问，林林在吗？ | b) 我不住学生宿舍。 |
| 3. 你住多少号？ | c) 在我那儿。 |
| 4. 你住学生宿舍吗？ | d) 她不在。 |

**Part 2.**

| | |
|---|---|
| 1. 她住哪层？ | a) 不住，他住学生宿舍。 |
| 2. 你哥哥住你爸爸妈妈那儿吗？ | b) 不，他住四层。 |
| 3. 你弟弟也住三层吗？ | c) 不在，我们这儿的四二九号在三层。 |
| 4. 四二九号不在四层吗？ | d) 六层，六零九号。 |

*A stone statue of a well-known Chinese hero.*

## B. Word Selection

Select the choice that best completes each sentence.

1. 我奶奶不_____。

   a) 住        b) 在        c) 那儿        d) 这儿

2. 你的电话号码是_____?

   a) 几        b) 几号        c) 多少        d) 多少号

3. 我朋友的笔记在_____?

   a) 谁哪儿    b) 谁那儿    c) 你哪儿        d) 你那儿

4. 你住我_____, 好吗?

   a) 的这儿    b) 这儿        c) 这儿宿舍    d) 的这儿宿舍

5. 他住学生_____。

   a) 的宿舍四层十四号四十四楼

   b) 的宿舍四十四楼十四号四层

   c) 宿舍四十四楼十四号四层

   d) 宿舍四十四楼四层十四号

---

## 🔖 TASK 3. PARAPHRASING

How well do you remember the grammar and vocabulary we've covered so far? Test yourself by translating the following sentences into Chinese.

*Nanjing Normal University.*

1. A: Is Wu Wende in?
   B: Sorry, Wu Wende is not in right now. He is still at his friend's place.

2. A: Where is his friend? Do you know the floor and the room number
        of where his friend lives?
   B: Sorry, I don't know. But I have his friend's phone number. It is 536-3295.

3. A: Where do you live now?
   B: I live in the student dorm, building 845, second floor, number 201.

4. A: Can I use your phone for a second?
   B: It's over there. Go ahead.

---

## 📕 TASK 4. SITUATIONAL DIALOGUE

**Setting:**      Outside a residential building

**Cast:**         A student and a resident

**Situation:**   The student goes to return a book to a friend but knocks on
                someone else's door by mistake. The student must provide an
                explanation to the resident and ask for directions to the cor-
                rect apartment.

# 10

# 介绍朋友
# Introducing Friends

*In this lesson you will:*
- Learn to make introductions.
- Set up a date and time to meet someone.
- Politely accept and decline invitations.

Li Lili and Wu Wende walk across campus. They see a female student standing next to a car.

| | |
|---|---|
| 吴文德： | 李丽莉，你看，那是谁？ |
| 李丽莉： | 怎么？你不认识她？她是我的老朋友，姓张，叫子倩。 |
| 吴文德： | 她名字好听，车也那么漂亮。她是不是我们学校的学生？ |
| 李丽莉： | 不是。她的男朋友陈大勇是我们学校的学生。她常常来这儿看陈大勇。 |
| 吴文德： | 噢，她是陈大勇的女朋友。陈大勇说她很聪明。 |
| 李丽莉： | 张子倩，好久不见，你最近怎么样？ |
| 张子倩： | 我还好。李丽莉，你呢？ |
| 李丽莉： | 马马虎虎。（to 吴文德 and 张子倩）你们不认识吧。来，我给你们介绍一下儿。这是吴文德。这是张子倩。 |
| 吴文德： | 你好，张子倩。 |

| 张子倩： | 你好。你们现在去哪儿？ |
|---|---|
| 李丽莉： | 我和吴文德现在去咖啡馆，你去不去？ |
| 张子倩： | 以后吧。[1] 我现在去商店买东西。对了，今天晚上你们忙不忙？陈大勇的同学跟我们一起去中国饭馆儿吃晚饭，你们有没有时间来？ |
| 李丽莉： | 对不起，我今天晚上很忙，没有时间。 |
| 张子倩： | 明天呢？我们一起去看电影，放松一下儿，好不好？ |
| 李丽莉： | 我明天上午、下午都有课，非常忙。后天行不行？ |
| 张子倩： | 行，没问题。吴文德你来不来？ |
| 吴文德： | 来，我一定来。 |
| 张子倩： | 好，后天见。 |

After 张子倩 leaves:

| 李丽莉： | 吴文德，你不是后天下午很忙吗？ |
|---|---|
|  | 你是不是不好意思跟张子倩说"不"？ |
| 吴文德： | 不是。跟大家一起去看电影， |
|  | 放松放松，我当然去啦。[2] |

## Notes

1. 以后吧。 Yǐhòu ba. 以后 means in the future. 吧 indicates suggestion.

2. 我当然去啦。 Wǒ dāngrán qù la. 啦 is placed at the end of the sentence for emphasis.

# 生词表 (Shēngcí Biǎo)
# Vocabulary

| Character | Pinyin | Part of Speech | English Definition |
|---|---|---|---|
| 1.*介*绍 | jièshào | *v.* | to introduce |
| 2.好听 | hǎotīng | *adj.* | (lit.) pretty to listen to |
| 听 | | *v.* | to listen |
| 3.*男 | nán | *adj. & n.* | male |
| 4.*女 | nǚ | *adj. & n.* | female |
| 5.最近 | zuìjìn | *adv.* | recently, lately |
| 6.*给 | gěi | *v.* | to give |
| | | *prep.* | to, for, towards |
| 7.*和 | hé | *conj.* | and, with |
| 8.咖啡*馆 | kāfēiguǎn | *n.* | coffee shop |
| 馆 | | *n.* | (originally) guesthouse, hotel; (now) a place for eating, gathering, etc. |
| 9.*商*店 | shāngdiàn | *n.* | store, department store |
| 商 | | *n.* | commerce |
| 店 | | *n.* | shop, store |
| 10.*买*东*西 | mǎi dōngxi | *v. obj.* | to buy things, to go shopping |
| 买 | | *v.* | to buy, purchase |
| 东西 | | *n.* | object, thing |
| 11.*晚上 | wǎnshang | *n.* | evening |
| 晚 | | *adj.* | late (in time) |
| 上 | | *suff.* | suffix commonly found in nouns |

| 12. | *跟 | gēn | *prep.* | with, together with |
|---|---|---|---|---|
| 13. | *饭馆 | fànguǎn(r) | *n.* | restaurant |
| | 饭 | | *n.* | cooked rice; meal |
| 14. | 晚饭 | wǎnfàn | *n.* | the evening meal, supper, dinner |
| 15. | *时*间 | shíjiān | *n.* | time |
| 16. | *明天 | míngtiān | *n.* | tomorrow |
| 17. | 电影 | diànyǐng | *n.* | movie |
| 18. | 放松 | fàngsōng | *v. comp.* | to relax, loosen |
| 19. | 上午 | shàngwǔ | *n.* | morning |
| 20. | 下午 | xiàwǔ | *n.* | afternoon |
| 21. | *非常 | fēicháng | *adv.* | very, extremely |
| 22. | 后天 | hòutiān | *n.* | the day after tomorrow |
| 23. | 行 | xíng | *adj.* | to be okay, permissible, feasible |
| 24. | 当然 | dāngrán | *adv.* | of course, certainly |

## 专有名词 (Zhuānyǒu Míngcí) Proper Nouns

| 1. | 张子倩 | Zhāng Zǐqiàn | a woman's name |
|---|---|---|---|
| 2. | 陈大勇 | Chén Dàyǒng | a man's name |

## 补充词汇 (Bǔchōng Cíhuì) Supplementary Vocabulary

| 1. | 图书馆 | túshūguǎn | *n.* | library |
|---|---|---|---|---|
| 2. | 书店 | shūdiàn | *n.* | bookstore |
| 3. | 早饭 | zǎofàn | *n.* | breakfast |
| 4. | 午饭 | wǔfàn | *n.* | lunch |
| 5. | 昨天 | zuótiān | *n.* | yesterday |
| 6. | 前天 | qiántiān | *n.* | the day before yesterday |
| 7. | 以前 | yǐqián | *n* | before, ago |
| 8. | 中午 | zhōngwǔ | *n.* | noon |

## 口头用语 (Kǒutóu Yòngyǔ) Spoken Expressions

| | | |
|---|---|---|
| 1. 噢 | ō | Oh! (used when someone realizes something) |
| 2. 怎么 | zěnme | What! What? |
| 3. 老朋友 | lǎo péngyou | (lit.) old friend (i.e., someone who has been a friend for a long time) |
| 4. 对了 | Duì le! | Oh, right! By the way… |
| 5. 没问题 | Méi wèntí. | No problem. |

## 词汇注解 (Cíhuì Zhùjiě) Featured Vocabulary

### 看(Kàn) Someone vs. 去看(Qù Kàn) / 来看 (Lái Kàn) Someone

看 someone and 去/来看 someone look very similar in Chinese, but they have very different meanings:

1. 看 **Someone** = to watch somebody; to look at somebody
   她的男朋友常常看她。
   Her boyfriend often stares at her.
2. 去/来 **(Place)** 看 **Someone** = to go/come to visit someone
   她的男朋友常常来（这儿）看她。
   Her boyfriend often comes (here) to see her.

## 语法(Yǔfǎ)
## Grammar

## Review

In Lesson 6, you learned that time phrases in Chinese are nouns and that they can be placed either before or right after the subject. This lesson introduces five more time words: 后天，下午，上午，明天, and 晚上.

## I. Affirmative-Negative Questions

In this lesson, you are going to learn the affirmative-negative question pattern, which is formed by an affirmative predicate plus a negative predicate without 吗 at the end. This structure requires a positive/negative response (literally "yes/no"), much like the 吗 questions in Lessons 3 and 4. But Chinese has no literal "yes/no" response. You simply repeat the main verb or the main adjective in a sentence if you agree and negate the main verb/adjective if you disagree. See the examples below.

## A. With Predicate Verbs

### 1. Verb 是

| Subject | Verb | 不 | Verb | Object |
|---|---|---|---|---|
| 她 | 是 | 不 | 是 | 学生? |

Literally: "Is she a student or not?"

Positive response: 是 or 她是学生。

Negative response: 不是 or 她不是学生。

### 2. Verb 有

| Subject | Verb | 没 | Verb | Object |
|---|---|---|---|---|
| 她 | 有 | 没 | 有 | 课? |

Literally: "Does she have class or not?"

Positive response: 有 or 她有 课。

Negative response: 没有 or 她没有课。

### 3. Verb 在

| Subject | Verb | 不 | Verb | Object |
|---|---|---|---|---|
| 她 | 在 | 不 | 在 | 宿舍? |

Literally: "Is she in the dorm or not?"

Positive response: 在 or 她在宿舍。

Negative response: 不在 or 她不在宿舍。

*Classical Chinese architecture in a public park.*

### 4. Action Verb

| Subject | Verb | 不 | Verb | Object |
|---------|------|------|------|--------|
| 她 | 去 | 不 | 去 | 商店？ |

Literally: "Is she going to the store or not?"

Positive response: 去 or 她去商店。

Negative response: 不去 or 她不去商店。

In addition, the object in each of the preceding four affirmative-negative questions could also be placed between the positive and negative predicate, which is a little more colloquial.

| Subject | Verb | Object | Negative Word | Verb |
|---------|------|--------|---------------|------|
| 她 | 是 | 学生 | 不 | 是？ |
| 她 | 有 | 课 | 没 | 有？ |
| 她 | 在 | 酒吧 | 不 | 在？ |
| 他 | 去 | 商店 | 不 | 去？ |

## Notes

1. When several verbs are used in the same sentence, the affirmative-negative change usually applies to the first verb, unless you want to emphasize the second verb. For example:

   她去不去商店买东西？
   Emphasizing whether or not she is going to the store.

   她去商店买不买东西？
   Emphasizing whether or not she is going to buy anything.

2. 是不是 can also be used before an action verb to confirm whether or not the subject is going to carry out the action. For example:

   她是不是去商店？ "Is it true that she is going to the shop?"

3. Adverbs like "常," "很," and "也," which are used in the 吗-type question, CANNOT be used in the affirmative-negative question. These adverbs can be used in questions with 是不是.

   CORRECT: 她去不去？ or 他也去吗？ or 她是不是也去？

   xxx INCORRECT: 她也去不去？ xxx

## B. With Predicate Adjectives

| Subject | Adjective | 不 | Adjective |
|---------|-----------|-----|-----------|
| 你们 | 忙 | 不 | 忙? |

Literally: "Are you busy this evening or not?"

Positive response: 忙 or 我们很忙。

Negative response: 不忙 or 我们不忙。

> CORRECT: 你忙不忙? or 你很忙吗? or 你是不是很忙?
>
> xxx INCORRECT: 你很忙不忙? xxx

## C. With Tag Questions

| Main Sentence | | | Tag Question |
|---------------|------|--------|-----------------------|
| **Subject** | **Verb** | **Object** | **Adjective 不 Adjective** |
| 我们现在一起去 | | 咖啡馆 | 好　不　好? |

Literally: "Let's go to a coffee shop right now. Is that all right with you?"

Positive response: 好 or 好啊。

Negative Response: 不好 is too abrupt and is rarely used.

Alternative Response: 以后吧。

---

## PRACTICE

Have a short dialogue in which one person asks an affirmative-negative question and the other provides both positive and negative responses. In your conversation, include the following:

1. Verbs: 做 搞 用 看 吃 喝 学 教 说 来 有
2. Adjectives: 忙 累 难 多 少 认真 漂亮 紧张 麻烦 丰富
3. Tag questions: 好不好 对不对 行不行
4. Adverbs: 常 都 很 也 还 (Using 吗?)

## II. Using the Prepositions 给(Gěi) and 跟(Gēn)

The prepositional phrase consists of the preposition and the noun or noun phrase object of the preposition. In Chinese sentences containing prepositions, a verb phrase usually follows the prepositional phrase. For example, Lesson 9 introduced our first preposition, 在 and its pattern is "在 + Location + Verb + Object (at a place do something)."

In addition, when a sentence contains a prepositional phrase, it is usually the preposition — not the verb — that is negated or otherwise modified by an adverb. For example, 不 is placed before the preposition, not the verb, to form a negative sentence. Likewise, affirmative-negative questions are formed by "Prep + 不 + Prep." This lesson introduces two more prepositions:

A.  跟 means "with (somebody)."

B.  给 introduces the recipient of an action. It means "for (somebody)" or "for the benefit of (somebody)."

## A. Using the Preposition 跟

|  | Subject | Prepositional Phrase | | Verb Phrase |
|---|---|---|---|---|
|  |  | 跟 | Somebody | Verb (Object) |
| Affirm.-neg.: | 他 今天 | 跟不跟 | 我们 | 去吃晚饭？ |

Is he going to have dinner with us or not?

| 吗-question: | 他 今天 | 跟 | 我们 | 去吃晚饭吗？ |
|---|---|---|---|---|

Is he going to have dinner with us or not?

| Positive: | 他 今天 | 跟 | 我们 | 去吃晚饭。 |
|---|---|---|---|---|

He is going to have dinner with us.

| Negative: | 他 今天 | 不跟 | 我们 | 去吃晚饭。 |
|---|---|---|---|---|

He is not going to have dinner with us.

## B. Using the Preposition 给

|  | Subject | Prepositional Phrase | | Verb Phrase |
|---|---|---|---|---|
|  |  | 给 | Somebody | Verb (Object) |
| Affirm.-neg.: | 你 今天 | 给不给 | 我们 | 介绍你的女朋友？ |

Are you going to introduce your girlfriend today or not?

| 吗-question: | 你 今天 | 给 | 我们 | 介绍你的女朋友吗？ |
|---|---|---|---|---|

Are you going to introduce your girlfriend to us today?

| Positive: | 我 来 | 给 | 你们 | 介绍一下儿我的女朋友。 |
|---|---|---|---|---|

Let me introduce my girlfriend to you.

| Negative: | 我 今天　不给　　你们　　介绍我的女朋友。明天吧。 |

I will not introduce my girlfriend to you today. Maybe tomorrow.

---

## 🔲 PRACTICE

Use each of the following prepositions and the given verb phrase to ask a question and provide a positive and negative response to it.

1. 在：工作　上课　做作业
2. 给：介绍　买礼物　做晚饭　打电话
3. 跟：去饭馆　一起玩儿　看电影

## III. Topic-Comment Sentences (Cont'd.)

Lesson 4 briefly discussed a few topic-comment sentences, such as 您太 太身体好吗 and 他们工作顺利吗？Each of these sentences consists of a subject (as a topic) and a sentence that provides more information on the subject (as a comment). The comment can be a simple sentence or a series of sentences. Sentences of this type are called Topic-Comment Sentences. For example:

### A. With One Comment

|  | Subject | Sentence |
|---|---|---|
| Positive: | 他 | 工作很忙。 |

Literally, "He is very busy, in terms of his work."

|  | Subject | Sentence |
|---|---|---|
| Negative: | 他 | 身体不太好。 |

Literally, "He is not very good, in terms of his health."

|  | Subject | Sentence |
|---|---|---|
| Question: | 她 | 人聪明吗？ |

Literally, "Is she, as a person, smart?"

### B. With More Than One Comment

| Subject | Sentence 1 | Sentence 2 | Sentence 3 |
|---|---|---|---|
| 她 | 人聪明， | （她）车也漂亮， | （她）名字也这么好听。 |

Literally, "She is smart, her car is pretty, and her name is also very nice."

*Chris Vee*

## 🔲 PRACTICE

Here are some words you could use as topics when forming a topic-comment sentence: 中文课，我们的，老师，我们学校，我的老板，那个饭馆. Can you add some comments when creating sentences of your own?

A new student has just arrived at your school. Talk to your friends about this person, using the topic-comment construction.

## IV. 和 (Hé) as a Conjunction

The Chinese conjunction 和 is very different from the English conjunction "and." 和 can ONLY be used to link nouns or certain other constructions, while the English "and" can link words belonging to any part of speech and even whole clauses or sentences.

| Nominal 1 | | Nominal 2 | |
|---|---|---|---|
| **Noun/Pronoun 1** | 和 | **Noun/Pronoun 2** | |
| 我 | 和 | 吴文德 | 去喝咖啡。 |

Wu Wende and I are going to get a cup of coffee.

| Nominal 1 | | Nominal 2 | |
|---|---|---|---|
| **Verb-Object 1** | 和 | **Verb-Object 2** | |
| 喝咖啡 | 和 | 吸烟 | 都不好。 |

Drinking coffee and smoking are bad for your health.

## *Note*

1. The verb-object construction can sometimes act as a noun phrase, much like the gerund (-ing) form in English. Take the sentence 喝咖啡和吸烟都不好 for example, where the verb-object constructions 喝咖啡 and 吸烟 function as nominal constructions in the syntax of the larger sentence.

2. Never place 和 between two clauses nor use it to join verbs. It can only join nouns or phrases that function as nominal constructions in a larger sentence.

> xxx INCORRECT::他来美国，和我去中国。xxx
>
> CORRECT: 他来美国，我去中国。
>
> xxx INCORRECT: 他喝咖啡和吸烟。   xxx
>
> CORRECT: 他喝咖啡也吸烟。

In this sentence, 喝咖啡 and 吸烟 are verb phrases functioning as entire predicates.

---

## ◨◪ PRACTICE

Make a sentence with 和 that connects two verb-object phrases.

## V. Rhetorical Questions

A rhetorical question is a statement formulated as a question. It is usually used to make a point or produce a certain effect. 不 / 不是 and the interrogative particle 吗 together make a rhetorical question. For example:

## A. Subject + 不 + Predicate Verb (+ Object) + 吗

你不跟我们一起去酒吧吗？

Aren't you going to the bar with us?

(I thought you were going but now you are not. What is going on?)

## B. Subject + 不是 + Predicate Adjective + 吗

你不是下午很忙吗？

Aren't you supposed to be busy this afternoon?

(I thought you were very busy this afternoon, but you don't seem to be that busy.)

Chris Vee

*A wooden statuette of a Happy Buddha.*

 **PRACTICE**

Try using predicate verbs and adjectives to form at least two of your own rhetorical questions.

## 部首小结(Bùshǒu Xiǎojié)
## Summary of Radicals

Chinese characters have over two hundred radicals. These are useful when you need to look up the words in the dictionary. So far we have covered twenty-five of them. Due to limited space, we will cover only the most commonly used radicals in the following table.

## Table of Key Radicals

| | Radical | Number of Strokes | Definition | Character |
|---|---|---|---|---|
| 1. | 亻 | 2 | man (erect) | 你 |
| 2. | 力 | 2 | strength | 努 |
| 3. | 阝 | 2 | ear | 都 |
| 4. | 讠 | 7 | speech | 认 |
| 5. | 口 | 3 | mouth | 吃 |
| 6. | 土 | 3 | earth | 地 |
| 7. | 大 | 3 | great | 大 |
| 8. | 女 | 3 | female | 好 |
| 9. | 宀 | 3 | roof | 字 |
| 10. | 彳 | 3 | double-man radical | 很 |
| 11. | 忄 | 3 | heart | 忙 |
| 12. | 扌 | 3 | hand | 搞 |
| 13. | 纟 | 6 | silk | 经 |
| 14. | 氵 | 3 | water | 酒 |
| 15. | 艹 | 3 | grass | 茶 |
| 16. | 辶 | 3 | running | 进 |
| 17. | 饣 | 8 | food | 饭 |
| 18. | 马 | 10 | horse | 验 |
| 19. | 门 | 8 | door | 问 |
| 20. | 弓 | 3 | bow | 张 |
| 21. | 日 | 4 | sun | 是 |
| 22. | 木 | 4 | wood, tree | 校 |
| 23. | 月 | 4 | moon, month | 朋 |

| Radical | Number of Strokes | Definition | Character |
|---------|-------------------|------------|-----------|
| 24. 贝 | 7 | cowry shell | 贵 |
| 25. 衤 | 5 | clothing | 衫 |
| 26. 牛 | 4 | ox | 物 |
| 27. 车 | 4 | vehicle | 车 |
| 28. 田 | 5 | field | 男 |
| 29. 目 | 5 | eye | 看 |
| 30. 禾 | 5 | grain | 程 |
| 31. 钅 | 8 | gold, metal | 错 |
| 32. 竹 | 6 | bamboo | 笔 |
| 33. 米 | 6 | rice | 糖 |
| 34. 页 | 9 | page | 顺 |

## 课堂练习 (Kètáng Liànxí)
## In-Class Exercises

### 🎧 TASK 1. QUESTIONS AND ANSWERS

How well did you understand the text? Check your comprehension by answering the following questions.

1. 张子倩是谁？张子倩来学校做什么？
2. 吴文德认识不认识张子倩和她的男朋友？李丽莉呢？
3. 现在他们三个人做什么呢？今天晚上呢？
4. 明天张子倩和李丽莉要做什么？还有谁跟他们一起去？

## TASK 2. GRAMMATICAL STRUCTURE PRACTICE

### A. Fill in the Blanks

Fill in the blanks by taking a word from below and placing it into the appropriate place in the sentence. When you're done, translate the sentence into English.

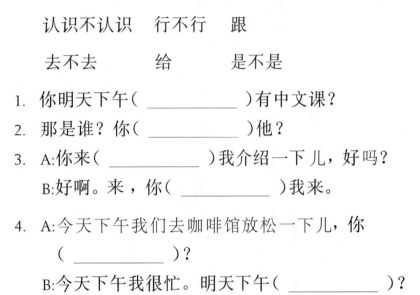

认识不认识    行不行    跟

去不去        给        是不是

1. 你明天下午（ _____ ）有中文课？
2. 那是谁？你（ _____ ）他？
3. A:你来（ _____ ）我介绍一下儿，好吗？

   B:好啊。来，你（ _____ ）我来。

4. A:今天下午我们去咖啡馆放松一下儿，你
   （ _____ ）？

   B:今天下午我很忙。明天下午（ _____ ）？

### B. Error Identification

Can you tell incorrect sentences from correct ones? Circle all the incorrect items and provide explanations for your choices.

1. 你去不去那儿买东西吗？
2. 她常常工作顺利不顺利？
3. 她人聪明，和学习也很好。
4. 他跟我们去不去喝咖啡。
5. 我去饭馆吃饭跟他们。
6. 我介绍你我们老师。他姓张。

## TASK 3. PARAPHRASING

How well do you remember the grammar and vocabulary we've covered so far? Test yourself by translating the following sentences into Chinese. To find out how well you know the grammar and vocabulary covered so far, follow the steps below.

1. A: Do you know each other?
   B: No, we don't. Would you please introduce us?

*Huang Shan in early afternoon.*

2. A: We are going to the store to do some shopping. Are you going?
   B: Maybe later. Right now I'm going to do my homework. I don't have any time.

3. A: This evening I am going to a Chinese restaurant for dinner with some friends. Do you want to come?
   B: With a pretty girl like you? Of course! I'll see you tonight.

4. A: Do you have classes in the morning?
   B: I don't have classes in the morning, but I have classes in the afternoon.

5. A: Are you going to the movie?
   B: Yes, do you want to go with us and relax for a little while?

## TASK 4. SITUATIONAL DIALOGUE

| | |
|---|---|
| **Setting:** | A restaurant |
| **Cast:** | Mr. Li and Ms. Lin |
| **Situation:** | Mr. Li and Ms. Lin are business acquaintances. They are eating dinner at a fancy restaurant when someone stops by to talk to Mr. Li. Mr. Li introduces him as an old friend from China, and they take a moment to talk about his family, his old home, his former profession, etc. |

通向中國

# Chinese
# Odyssey
## Innovative Chinese Courseware

TRADITIONAL Character

Vol. 1 · TEXTBOOK

Xueying Wang, Li-chuang Chi, and Liping Feng

王學英　　祁立莊　　馮力平

CHENG & TSUI COMPANY Boston

# 1

# Introduction to Chinese Phonetics

> **In this lesson you will:**
> - Get a brief overview of Chinese phonetics, the Chinese writing system, and spoken Chinese.
> - Learn about the pinyin system, including the basics of initials, finals, and tones.

## Overview

Chinese is spoken by more people than any other language except English. It is one of the five official languages of the United Nations. Standard Chinese, or Mandarin, is the form of the language taught throughout the school system of China and is the official medium of communication for the country. Within China, this standard form of the language is known as *putonghua*, or "the common language," to distinguish it from the many other dialects and subdialects of Chinese. One also hears it referred to by the term *Hanyu*, which distinguishes it from the languages of China's fifty-odd minority peoples and from foreign, non-Chinese languages.

In this lesson, you will learn how to pronounce some basic Chinese vocabulary. You will also be introduced — briefly — to the written language, although you won't begin learning how to write until the next lesson.

## Written Chinese

In terms of the written form, Chinese is not an alphabetic language, but is composed of individual characters: each represents a meaningful syllable of the spoken language.

Chinese characters have undergone a long process of evolution. A few characters have developed from pictographs. For example, the drawing ☉ originally represented the sun, and ☽ the moon. Over time, these drawings were gradually formalized into the written characters 日 (*ri* "sun") and 月

1

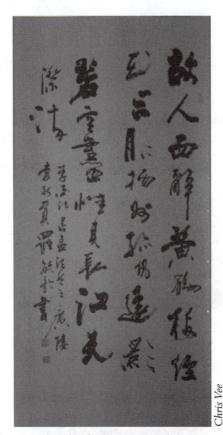

*Chris Vee*

*Classical poetry by the famous Tang dynasty poet Li Bai.*

(*yue* "moon"). These two "radicals," or root components, were then combined into a single character 明 representing the syllable *ming*, meaning "bright." Many characters — though a relatively small percentage of the total — are thus formed from two or more meaningful components.

The single most prolific principle of character formation is "radical plus phonetic," in which a character is formed from a radical component plus a phonetic component. The radical usually has some connection to the meaning of the compound character, while the phonetic part carries the pronunciation or at least gives a hint at the pronunciation of the character. This principle can be illustrated by the following group of characters, whose pronunciations differ only by tone: 方 *fāng*, 芳 *fāng*, 房 *fáng*, 訪 *fǎng*, 放 *fàng*. However, you should note that 方 is an unusually "strong" phonetic. Few "families" of characters that share a common phonetic component will be quite as similar in pronunciation as this group.

## *Riddle*

Now let's have some fun. Given the meaning of its components, can you guess the identity of the mystery character? The character in question has two top-bottom components: 田 (meaning "field") and 力 (meaning "force"). What does the character 男 mean?

Answer: 男 = man. Sound anachronistic? Maybe. Remember, the Chinese language is thousands of years old. In ancient times, it is likely that men did most of the work in the fields, which probably contributed to the derivation of this character.

If you guessed correctly, congratulations! If not, don't get discouraged. This is only one of many ways that Chinese characters can be formed. You'll have plenty of opportunities to try again.

## Spoken Chinese

Traditionally, Chinese learned the pronunciation of characters in their regional dialect, while Westerners wanting to learn the Chinese language used one or another of a rather large number of romanization systems that were developed over the past several centuries. Then, in the first half of the twentieth century, the Chinese government began to promote the use of a standard national language, and romanization, as well as other phonetic spelling systems, was used to aid speakers of other dialects in their study of Mandarin. After the official promulgation of *Hanyu* pinyin in 1958, this system became the standard in China and also gradually became the dominant system used outside of China for representing spoken Mandarin. Once you know pinyin, you'll be able to use the Internet, dictionaries, and any other reference with alphanumerical characters. Knowledge of pinyin is also necessary if you want to use many of the Chinese word processors on the market.

## Pinyin

Pinyin, literally "phonetic spelling," uses twenty-five of the twenty-six letters of the Latin alphabet (see how long it will take you to discover which letter

*Chris Vee*

is not used), plus tone marks and one other diacritic, to represent the sound system of Mandarin.

Linguists discuss the initial and final components of Chinese syllables. The initial is always a consonant, while the final is made up of a vowel nucleus with an optional final consonant and a tone. The only consonants that occur in the final position are *-n*, *-ng*, and *-r*. Thus, in each of the following syllables the first letter is the initial, and the remainder of the syllable is the final: *hao, ri, ming, fang.* (See the following for more detailed information and additional examples.)

# Initials

In the following table the twenty-one initial consonants are arranged in rows and columns to show grouping by place and manner of articulation. Familiarity with this table will help you learn the sounds of Chinese and their spellings in the pinyin system. Most of these sounds are identical or very similar to English sounds spelled with the same letters. However, in several cases, either the sound is different from anything in English, or the spelling itself is likely to be confusing. The Notes section below the table is designed to help with these difficult sounds.

*Table of Initials*

| Stops and Affricates | Lateral and Unaspirated | Aspirated | Nasals | Fricatives | Retroflexive |
|---|---|---|---|---|---|
| Labials | b | p | m | f | |
| Dentals | d | t | n | | l |
| Velars | g | k | | h | |
| Palatals | j | q | | x | |
| Retroflexes | zh | ch | | sh | r |
| Dental sibilants | z | c | | s | |

# Notes

1. The sounds in the first three rows are the same as or very similar to English sounds represented by the same spellings. However, it should be noted that: (a) The unaspirated and aspirated columns of stops and affricates are distinguished *only* by aspiration (the puff of breath that accompanies the *p, t, k*, etc., in column two), because the sounds in columns one and two are unvoiced. (b) In careful articulation, *h* is pronounced with fric-

tion between the back of the tongue and the velum, or soft palate, rather than just the quiet breathiness of an English *h*.

2. The palatals (row four: *j, q, x*) are similar to an English *j, ch,* and *sh* except that the part of the tongue that makes contact with the palate is not the tip but the area a bit further back from the tip.

3. The first three retroflex sounds (row five: *zh, ch, sh*) are also somewhat similar to an English *j, ch,* and *sh*, but they are pronounced with the tip of the tongue turned upward and making contact with the back of the gum ridge or the front part of the palate. In the flow of speech, *r* often sounds much like an initial English *r*, but when articulated carefully, it is very different, with the tip of the tongue curled upward and brought close enough to the front part of the palate so that a local buzzing sound is produced.

4. Row six contains two of the most difficult sounds and one of the easiest. Many beginning students find *z* and *c* difficult, not because English has no similar sounds but because the most similar sounds in English do not occur at the beginning of a word: *z* (unaspirated) is similar to the final sound of "ki**ds**," and *c* (aspirated) is similar to the final sound of "pe**ts**"; *s* is the same as an English *s*.

## Finals

The final of a Chinese syllable can be composed of one, two, or three vowels; or one or two vowels plus one of the final consonants (*-n, -ng,* or *-r*). Linguists usually arrange the finals in four groups — or rows in a table — according to whether the first (or only) sound in the final is: (1) an open vowel, (2) the high front unrounded vowel *i*, (3) the high back rounded vowel *u*, or (4) the high front rounded vowel *ü*. In addition, the very special vowel *-i*, which oc-

*The sidewalk and street that runs along West Lake in Hangzhou.*

curs only after the initials of rows five and six in the table above (*zh, ch, sh, r; z, c, s*), is also placed in row one.

Because the phonetic value — that is, the actual pronunciation — of some of these finals is quite complicated and in a number of cases it is not possible to make useful comparisons with English sounds, we will not attempt to explain the pronunciation at this point. Please be aware that you should pay close attention to the recordings as you learn the sound system of Chinese. Note the spelling rules that follow the table.

### *Table of Finals*

| -i | a | o | e | ai | ei | ao | ou | an | en | ang | eng | er |
|----|----|----|----|----|----|----|----|----|----|----|----|----|
| i | ia | | ie | | | iao | iu | ian | in | iang | ing | iong |
| u | ua | uo | | uai | ui | | | uan | un | uang | ong | |
| ü | | | üe | | | | | üan | ün | | | |

## Spelling Rules

1.  Note that the first final in row one, which we have written as *-i*, occurs only after the initials *zh, ch, sh, r, z, c,* and *s*. Phonetically, it is entirely different from the *i* in row two. It is pronounced by slightly retracting the tip of the tongue from the position for articulation of the preceding initial consonant.

2.  When a final from row two occurs without an initial consonant, *i* standing alone is written as *yi*, and for the remaining finals, *i* is replaced by *y: ya, ye, yao*, etc.

*Margaret Vee*

*A public park in Yangzhou, a city with a rich cultural and historical legacy.*

3. When a final from row three occurs without an initial consonant, *u* standing alone is written as *wu*, and for the remaining finals, *u* is replaced by *w*: *wa, wo, wai*, etc.

4. When a final from row four occurs without an initial consonant, *y* is added in front of the final and the umlaut mark is dropped from the *ü*: *yu, yue, yuan, yun*. When these finals occur after the palatal initials *j, q, x*, the umlaut is dropped: *ju, jue, quan, xun*, etc. When *ü* and *üe* occur after *n* or *l*, the umlaut is kept: *nü, nüe, lü, lüe*. Row four finals do not occur in any environments other than those mentioned here.

## Initial and Final Combinations

Please see the table in the Multimedia CD-ROM in All Pinyin of the Phonetics Section, Lessons 1-8. These are all the syllables in the Chinese language.

As you can see, the total number of Chinese syllables is limited, even when the variations related to all four tones are taken into consideration. On the other hand, the number of characters, when compared to the syllables, is almost limitless — even a small dictionary contains more than 10,000 characters, around 3,000 of which represent words or morphemes used in everyday speech. As a result, there are many homonyms in the Chinese language, because one syllable is usually shared by many characters.

## Tones

Tones are of paramount importance in the Chinese language. Each syllable has up to four main tones, plus a neutral tone. Tones are marked above the main vowel of the pinyin symbols (except for the neutral tone, which has no mark). Listen to the syllable *ma* pronounced in the four different tones.

| Tone | Pinyin | Character | Meaning |
|------|--------|-----------|---------|
| 1st tone | mā | 媽 | mother |
| 2nd tone | má | 麻 | hemp |
| 3rd tone | mǎ | 馬 | horse |
| 4th tone | mà | 罵 | to swear, curse |
| Neutral tone | ma | 嗎 | particle |

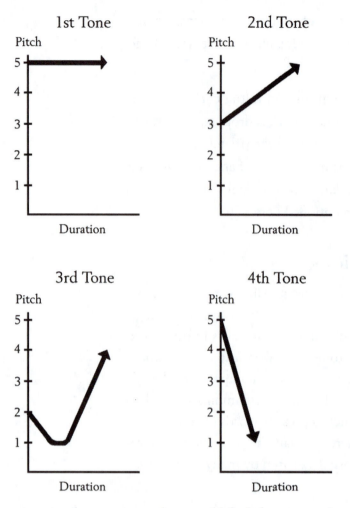

Can you imagine how your mother would feel if you mixed up the first tone with the third? Or with one of the other two tones? Now that we've seen an example, let's learn about the four tones.

The first tone is characterized by a high, steady monotone, without any change in pitch. The second tone is a rising tone that starts lower than the first tone and moves up to a higher pitch. The third tone falls to a very low pitch (even lower than the second tone) and then rises upward. (In everyday conversation, the third tone, unless emphasized, is seldom pronounced fully. It is often truncated into a half-third tone, which stays in the low pitch without much attempt to rise up again.) The fourth tone is a descending tone that starts at a high pitch and then moves down to a lower pitch.

The above is a series of charts that graphs the pitches of the four tones we have just discussed.

The neutral tone is pronounced lightly and quickly, without changing the pitch during pronunciation. However, its pitch varies according to the tones of the preceding, or the preceding and following, syllables.

As the Chinese saying goes, "What is well begun is halfway to success." Seymour, an American college student, never bothered to learn the correct tones. As a result, this was his first experience in China.

## Joke

Although Seymour can speak fluent Chinese, he frequently mixes up his tones. After he got off the airplane at the Beijing airport, he didn't know where to get his bags, so he stopped a pretty Chinese girl to ask for directions. Instead of saying, "Xiǎojiě, wǒ xiǎng *wèn wèn* nǐ?" ("Miss, may I ask you a question?"), Seymour asked, "Xiǎojiě, wǒ xiǎng *wén wén* nǐ?" The girl turned around and slapped him! It was only afterwards that the flustered boy realized he had used the second tone instead of the fourth and had actually asked, "May I smell you?" or "May I kiss you?"

This joke highlights the importance of learning proper pronunciation. Remember: It's much easier to learn to speak correctly from the start than to try to correct mistakes later on.

When pronounced correctly, the Chinese language has a unique musical quality to it. When you speak Chinese, try to think of the sentence as a full melodic phrase, rather than getting caught up pausing to check the tone of each syllable. Without further ado, let us begin our journey into this new tonal landscape.

The initials and finals are presented in four parts. Each part of the presentation will be followed by two practices: Distinguishing Tones and Distinguishing Sounds. The Distinguishing Tones exercises are designed to help you distinguish the tones and pronounce them correctly. The Distinguishing Sounds exercises, on the other hand, will teach you to distinguish and pronounce vowels and consonants.

# Part One

## 🎧💻 PRACTICING INITIALS AND FINALS

| Initials: | b | p | m | f | |
| | d | t | n | l | |
| Finals: | a | e | o | i | u |
| | ü | ai | ei | ao | ou |

## Notes

1. i ➔ y    When there is no initial, *i* is spelled as *y*.

2. u ➔ w    When there is no initial, *u* is spelled as *w*.

*Entrance to a teahouse in Shanghai.*

# Distinguishing Tones

Practice saying the tones correctly, making sure that you can recognize the differences among each of the four tones.

| | | | |
|---|---|---|---|
| bō | bó | bǒ | bò |
| pāo | páo | pǎo | pào |
| fū | fú | fǔ | fù |
| duō | duó | duǒ | duò |
| tōu | tóu | tǒu | tòu |
| yū | yú | yǔ | yù |
| lē | dé | měi | hèi |
| pāi | bái | mǎi | nài |

# Distinguishing Sounds

Listen carefully to the following pairs of syllables; note the differences between them, and try to pronounce them correctly.

| **Initials:** | pó | bó | tāo | lāo |
|---|---|---|---|---|
| | nǐ | lǐ | mǒu | fǒu |

|      |      |      |      |
|------|------|------|------|
| yì   | lì   | wū   | fū   |
| wài  | bài  | nǔ   | lǚ   |

| Finals: | mǎi | měi | nǎi | nǎo |
|---------|-----|-----|-----|-----|
|         | duō | dōu | nú  | nuó |
|         | là  | lài | de  | dí  |
|         | lì  | lè  | táo | tóu |

# Part Two

## 🎧💻 PRACTICING INITIALS AND FINALS

| Initials: | zh  | ch  | sh  | r |
|-----------|-----|-----|-----|---|
|           | z   | c   | s   |   |
| Finals:   | -i  | an  | en  |   |
|           | ang | eng | ong |   |

## Note

The *-i* stands for a very special vowel that is articulated by the tip of the tongue at the front of the hard palate (for the *zh-ch-sh-r* series) or behind the upper incisors (for the *z-c-s* series). To prounce this vowel keep the tongue tip in the same position as the preceding consonant, withdrawing it just enough to let air pass through. Since *zh*, *ch*, *sh* and *z*, *c*, *s* are voiceless consonant initials, voicing begins just as the vowel is pronounced. Since *r* is a voiced initial, the syllable *ri* is voiced throughout.

## Distinguishing Tones

Practice saying the tones correctly, making sure that you can recognize the differences among each of the four tones.

|      |      |      |      |
|------|------|------|------|
| zān  | zán  | zǎn  | zàn  |
| cī   | cí   | cǐ   | cì   |
| zhī  | zhí  | zhǐ  | zhì  |

| | | | |
|---|---|---|---|
| chī | chí | chǐ | chì |
| shī | shí | shǐ | shì |
| sōng | sóng | sǒng | sòng |
| zēng | céng | zhěn | chèn |
| rāng | ráng | zhǎn | chàn |

## Distinguishing Sounds

Listen carefully to the following pairs of syllables. Once you can hear the difference between them, practice saying them correctly.

| | | | | | |
|---|---|---|---|---|---|
| **Initials:** | cēn | sēn | cán | zán |
| | châng | shâng | zhì | chì |
| | róng | chóng | shěng | zhěng |
| | zī | sī | zhè | rè |
| **Finals:** | rǎn | rǎng | zhěn | zhěng |
| | chán | chéng | shèn | shàng |
| | zēng | zōng | cóng | cáng |
| | sān | sēn | rén | róng |

# Part Three

## 🎧💻 PRACTICING INITIALS AND FINALS

| **Initials:** | g | k | h | |
|---|---|---|---|---|
| **Finals:** | ua | uai | ui | uo |
| | uan | un | | |
| | uang | ueng | | |

## *Notes*

1. Initials *g*, *k*, and *h* can never be used with the finals starting with *i* and *ü*.

2. *ui* ➜ *u(e)i*      *ui* is the combination of *u* and *ei*. When there are initials, it is spelled as *-ui*. When there are no initials, it should be written as *wei*.

3.  *un* ➔ *u(e)n*        *un* is the combination of *u* and *en*. When there are initials,
   it is spelled as *un*. When there are no initials, it should be written as *wen*.

## Distinguishing Tones

Practice saying the tones correctly, making sure that you can recognize the
differences among each of the four tones.

| | | | |
|---|---|---|---|
| wā | wá | wǎ | wà |
| huān | huán | huǎn | huàn |
| wāng | wáng | wǎng | wàng |
| wēng | wéng | wěng | wèng |
| kuī | kuí | kuǐ | kuì |
| wēi | wéi | wěi | wèi |
| hūn | hún | hǔn | hùn |
| guāi | huái | kuǎi | kuài |

## Distinguishing Sounds

Listen carefully to the following pairs of syllables; note the differences between them, and try to pronounce them correctly.

| | | | | |
|---|---|---|---|---|
| **Initials:** | guī | kuī | kùn | gùn |
| | huān | kuān | guài | huài |
| | kuā | huā | huǎng | guǎng |
| | wén | hún | gùn | wèn |
| **Finals:** | huán | huáng | guài | guì |
| | wāng | wēng | kuǎ | kuǎi |
| | wēng | wēn | huí | hún |
| | kuò | kùn | gǔn | gǒng |

# Part Four

## 🎧💻 PRACTICING INITIALS AND FINALS

| | | | | |
|---|---|---|---|---|
| **Initials:** | j | q | x | |
| **Finals:** | ia | iao | ie | iu |

| | | | |
|---|---|---|---|
| ian | in | üan | ün |
| iang | ing | iong | üe |

# Notes

1.  When *i* follows the initials *j*, *q*, or *x*, it is pronounced like the "i" in the English "ski."

2.  *ie* is pronounced like the "ye" in the English "yes."

3.  *y → i*          When there is no initial, *i* is spelled as *y*.

4.  *iu → i(o)u*        *iu* is the combination of *i* and *ou*. When there is an initial, it is spelled as *-iu* (e.g., *liu*). When there are no initials, *i* changes to *y* and *u* changes to *ou* (e.g., *you*).

5.  Note that the vowel *ü* occurs only: (1) after the initials *j*, *q*, *x* and (in a very few words) *n* and *l*, (2) in syllables with no initial. When it occurs after *j*, *q*, and *x*, the umlaut is omitted: *ju*, *jue*; *qun*, *quan*; *xue*, *xuan*, etc. When it occurs in syllables with no initial, a *y* is added in front of it and the umlaut is omitted: *yu*, *yue*, *yun*, *yuan*. Only when it occurs after *n* or *l* is the umlaut retained: *nü*, *lü*, *nüe*, *lüe*.

# Distinguishing Tones

Practice saying the tones correctly, making sure that you can recognize the differences among each of the four tones.

| | | | |
|---|---|---|---|
| jiā | jiá | jiǎ | jià |
| qiāo | qiáo | qiǎo | qiào |
| xiē | xié | xiě | xiè |
| qīn | qín | qǐn | qìn |
| xuē | xué | xuě | xuè |
| yōng | yóng | yǒng | yòng |
| yūn | yún | yǔn | yùn |
| qiū | qiú | jiǔ | jiù |

# Distinguishing Sounds

Listen carefully to the following pairs of syllables; note the differences between them, and try to pronounce them correctly.

| Initials: | jiǒng | qióng | quán | xuán |
|---|---|---|---|---|
| | xīn | jǐn | què | jué |
| | xiāo | qiǎo | jǐng | xǐng |
| | yǒu | jǒu | xiè | yè |
| Finals: | jiān | jiǎng | qín | qíng |
| | xuān | xūn | jué | jié |
| | qiē | quē | xiōng | xūn |
| | yào | yà | yǒu | yǒng |

## Cast of Characters 人物介紹

李麗莉 and 林笛 are female college students. They are friends and room-mates taking Chinese class together.

吳文德 is a male student who attends the same college as 李麗莉 and 林笛. He also studies Chinese and is a close friend of 李麗莉 and 林笛.

高朋 is another male college student who studies Chinese. Initially, he only knows Lin Di, but later on he and 吳文德 become roommates. He is a good student and a good cook.

As time passes, 李麗莉, 林笛, 吳文德 and 高朋 become very close friends.

## Supporting Characters

陳大勇 is a male student, a schoolmate of 李麗莉 and 林笛.

張子倩 is 陳大勇's girlfriend who visits 陳大勇 at his school periodically.

史老師 is one of the instructors who teaches 李麗莉 and 林笛.

胡老師 is 林笛's Chinese teacher.

胡阿姨 is a close family friend of 吳文德.

李叔叔 is 胡阿姨's husband.

高先生 is a long time family friend of 李麗莉.

# 2

# 你早

# Basic Greetings

*In this lesson you will:*

▨ Review pronunciation, with special emphasis on tones.

▨ Learn some basic principles of Chinese character composition and rules of phonetic spelling.

▨ Greet someone in a culturally appropriate way.

It is the first day of school, and Chinese class is about to start.

| | |
|---|---|
| Lǐ Lìlì: | Lín Dí, nǐ zǎo. |
| 李麗莉： | 林笛，你早。 |
| Lín Dí: | Zǎo. |
| 林笛： | 早。 |
| Lǐ Lìlì : | Shǐ Lǎoshī, nín hǎo! |
| 李麗莉： | 史老師，您好！ |
| Shǐ Lǎoshī: | Nǐ hǎo, Lǐ Lìlì! |
| 史老師： | 你好，李麗莉！ |
| Lín Dí: | Shǐ Lǎoshī zǎo! |
| 林笛： | 史老師早！ |
| Shǐ Lǎoshī: | Nǐ zǎo. |
| 史老師： | 你早。 |

# 生詞表 (Shēngcí Biǎo)

# Vocabulary

| Character | Pinyin | Part of Speech | English Definition |
|---|---|---|---|
| 1. 你 | nǐ | *pron.* | you (singular) |
| 2. 早 | zǎo | *adj.* | early |

3.  老師   lǎoshī   *n.*   teacher, professor
    老             *adj.*   old, respected
    師             *b.f.*   teacher, master
4.  您     nín     *pron.*  you (singular, in formal or polite form)
5.  好     hǎo     *adj.*   good, well

專有名詞 (Zhuānyǒu Míngcí) **Proper Nouns**

1.  林笛    Lín Dí              a female's name
2.  李麗莉   Lǐ Lìlì             a female's name
3.  史老師   Shǐ Lǎoshī          Teacher Shi, Professor Shi

補充詞彙 (Bǔchōng Cíhuì) **Supplementary Vocabulary**

1.  先生    xiānsheng   *n.*     gentleman, Mr., Sir, husband
2.  小姐    xiǎojiě     *n.*     young lady, Miss
3.  太太    tàitai      *n.*     Mrs., Madam
4.  早上好。  Zǎoshang hǎo. *sent.*  Good morning.
5.  早安。   Zǎoān.      *sent.*  Good morning (more formal).
6.  晚安。   Wǎnān.      *sent.*  Good night.

語法(Yǔfǎ)

# Grammar

## I. Chinese Names

In Chinese, the surname always comes before the given name. Surnames usually consist of one character (i.e., one syllable), although there are a few two-character surnames. Those surnames with one character are called *dān xìng*, or single surnames, while surnames with two characters or more are called *fù xìng*, or compound surnames. No one knows how many unique Chinese surnames there are in total. There are about two hundred common surnames, with Zhang 張(Zhāng), Wang 王(Wáng), Li 李(Lǐ), and Zhao 趙(Zhào) being the most common single surnames and Zhu Ge, Ou Yang, and Si Tu the most common compound surnames.

*Margaret Vee*

*A pagoda in Hangzhou, a city well known for its natural beauty and cultural heritage.*

Chinese given names can have either one or two characters. Given names usually have a very specific meaning. A person's name can state a birthplace or time of birth by using words such as "capital" or "morning." Some names also use words such as "rain," "snow," "winter," and "spring" to express a nature theme. Others include words associated with health or luck, such as *jiàn* (good health), *fú* (good luck), and *shòu* (long life).

Male and female given names have a few key differences. Male names are usually composed of characters that show courage and strength, such as *qiáng* (strong), *hǔ* (tiger), *yǒng* (brave), and *gāng* (steel). Female names are more often composed of characters that emphasize beauty, compassion, and a calm temperament, such as *lì* (beautiful), *yǎ* (elegance), *jìng* (calm), and *shú* (virtuous). On the whole, Chinese people pick names based on the meaning of the characters. The following are the names we have learned in this lesson:

| Surname | Given Name |
|---------|------------|
| 李 | 麗莉 |
| 林 | 笛 |

## *Note*

In addition to a formal name (surname and given name), some people also have a *xiǎo míng*, or nickname, which is usually picked in one's youth. These nicknames are generally used by family members and close friends.

---

## PRACTICE

Give each student in the class a Chinese name and explain each name's meaning.

## II. Addressing People

In the workplace in China, you should always address a person of higher status by his or her last name followed by the appropriate title to show respect. This also applies in school, when speaking to your professors or other teachers and when dealing with directors, employers, etc. For example:

| Surname | Title | |
|---------|-------|--|
| 史 | 老师 | Professor Shi |

Literally, 史老师 is translated as "Teacher Shi," but it would be awkward to address your instructor this way in standard English. Although the person being addressed may not have the rank of professor, for the purpose of showing respect we will instead translate "老师 + surname" as "Professor + surname" throughout the text.

## ▨ PRACTICE

Student volunteers play the role of the teacher. As these volunteer "teachers" tell the class their Chinese names, students will address these "teachers" in a culturally correct way.

## III. Greeting People

"Pronoun/Noun + 好(hǎo)／早(zǎo)" is used as a greeting. This structure is NOT a question. The response should be either "你好／早" or "您好／早."

| A. Pronoun | | |
|---|---|---|
| 你 | 好／早 。 | Hi/Good morning. |
| 您 | 好／早 。 | Hi/Good morning. |

### *Notes*

1. 早    An informal way of greeting people early in the morning.

2. 您好    A more polite way of greeting people who are older or have a higher social status than you. You should use this in situations where you want to show respect or social formality (e.g., when addressing your teacher).

3. 你好    The most common way to greet someone. You can use this at any time of day, in both formal and informal situations.

| B. Surname | Title | |
|---|---|---|
| （史） | 老師 | 好／早 。 |

### *Note*

If you are greeting someone and you don't know his or her last name, you can simply greet that person with his or her title (e.g., 老師好 or 老師早).

## ▨ PRACTICE

You are preparing breakfast when you get a phone call from your friend and another from one of your mother's colleagues. Use 好／早 to greet them.

# 語音複習(Yǔyīn Fùxí)
# Pronunciation Review

## I. Review of Initials and Finals

The initials and finals selected for review are based on vocabulary learned in this lesson.

**Initials:**    h    l    n    sh    z

**Finals:**    i    ao    in    -i

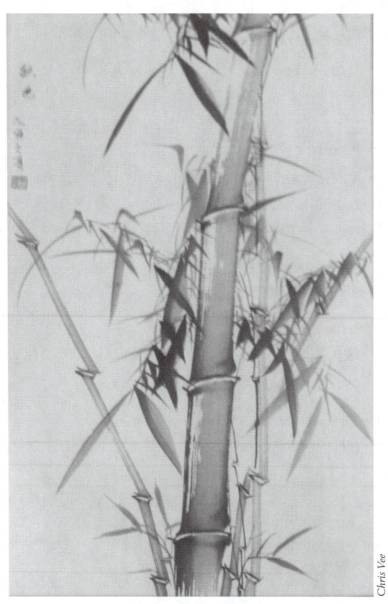

*Chinese brush painting.*

Chris Vee

## Notes

1. *i* vs. *-i*:    *i* is pronounced "ee" as in the English "leek." It usually follows *b, p, m, n, d, t, l, j, q,* or *x*. The *-i* stands for a very special vowel that is articulated by the tip of the tongue at the front of the hard palate (for the *zh-ch-sh-r* series) or behind the upper incisors (for the *z-c-s* series). To pronounce this vowel, keep the tongue tip in the same position as the preceding consonant, withdrawing it just enough to let air pass through. Because *zh, ch, sh, z, c,* and *s* are voiceless consonant initials, voicing begins just as the vowel is pronounced.

2. *in*:    When there is an initial, *in* is attached directly to that initial (e.g., *lin*). When there is no initial, *y* is added in front of *i* (e.g., *yin*).

## II. Tone Change Rules

The third tone is pronounced as a second tone when it is immediately followed by another third tone. For example:

| 3rd + 3rd | → | 2nd + 3rd |
|---|---|---|
| nǐ hǎo | → | ní hǎo |
| nǐ zǎo | → | ní zǎo |
| hǎo lǎoshī | → | háo lǎoshī |

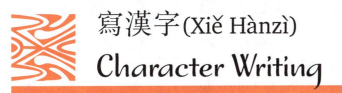

# 寫漢字(Xiě Hànzì)
# Character Writing

## I. Character Composition

As you learned in the previous lesson, Chinese is not an alphabetic language. Some of the Chinese characters consist of only one component, while others have multiple components. For example:

| Character | # of Components | Type of Composition |
|---|---|---|
| 史 | One component (史) | Indivisible |
| 好 | Two components (女 and 子) | Left-right |
| 早 | Two components (日 and 十) | Top-bottom |

Please note that some of the characters cannot be divided into different components, so they are called indivisibles. Some can be divided into a left-hand part and a right-hand part (the left-right composition). Others can be divided into a top and a bottom part (the top-bottom composition).

Each Chinese character, simple or complex, is expected to occupy the same amount of space, which is roughly square-shaped.

Therefore, a character with many strokes would have to be squeezed more tightly than one with fewer strokes. For example, although 您 has quite a few more strokes than 好, it must still be compacted into the same amount of space.

## II. Types of Strokes and Stroke Order

All Chinese character components are constructed from a few basic types of strokes. The following are basic strokes used in writing Chinese characters:

Strokes:

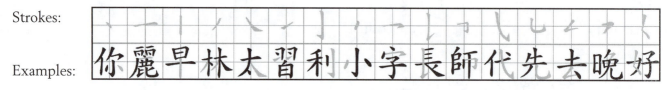

Examples:

After learning individual strokes, it is also important to understand the basic rules of stroke order used in writing Chinese characters. Each character follows a specific sequence of strokes, or "stroke order." For example, the word 好 is composed like this:

***Rules of Stroke Order***

| Rules | | | Examples | Stroke Order |
|---|---|---|---|---|
| 1. | 一 precedes | 丨 | 十 | 一 十 |
| 2. | 丿 precedes | 丶 | 八 | 丿 八 |
| 3. | From top to bottom | | 呂 | 口 呂 |

| 4. | From left to right | 好 | | 女 | 好 |
| 5. | From outside to inside | 用 | | 冂 | 用 |
| 6. | Inside stroke precedes the sealing stroke | 日 | 冂 | 日 | 日 |
| 7. | Middle stroke precedes the two sides | 小 | 亅 | 小 | 小 |

## III. Key Radical Presentation

Characters with multiple components usually have one part that is a radical. A radical is like a root to which many different components can be attached to form different characters. In Chinese dictionaries and other reference books, words are classified according to these radicals. Some radical names are not intuitive. In each of the lessons throughout this book, we will introduce the names of radicals that will help you write Chinese characters.

1. 你 has the person radical, 亻, which often appears in characters that refer to people.

2. 好 has the female radical, 女, which refers to women and femininity.

3. 您 has the heart radical, 心.

4. 早 has the sun radical, 日.

*Margaret Vee*

*Replica of a classical Chinese residence.*

## IV. Handwriting

Please also note that the printed version of the Chinese characters is not identical to the hand-written version. We have provided both versions for your viewing, along with the space in the Chinese character box for you to practice.

### *Left-Right Composition*

In this group, the left part is proportionally thinner, shorter, or smaller than the right part.

| Character | Practice with Chinese Characters |
|---|---|
| 你 好 師 | |

### *Top-Bottom Composition*

| Character | Practice with Chinese Characters |
|---|---|
| 您 早 老 | |

 課堂練習 (Kètáng Liànxí)

## In-Class Exercises

### 🎧📕 TASK 1. DISTINGUISHING TONES

Your teacher will randomly pronounce the items in each of the following groups. If the first tone you hear is the fourth tone, you should put a fourth tone mark above the first item in a given group. If the second tone you hear is the first tone, put a first tone mark over the second item, and so on (e.g., à á...).

*Sunrise over Huang Shan (Yellow Mountain) in Anhui Province.*

1. ni      ni      ni      ni

2. zao      zao      zao      zao

3. hao      hao      hao      hao

4. yin      yin      yin      yin

5. shi      shi      shi      shi

6. shao      shao      shao      shao

7. lao      lao      lao      lao

8. li      li      li      li

## 🎧💻 TASK 2. DISTINGUISHING SOUNDS

Your teacher will pronounce one of the two syllables in each group. Listen carefully and circle the one you hear.

**Initials**

1. nǐ      lǐ      2. zāo      shāo

3. yì      nì      4. lín      yín

**Finals**

1. ní              nín              2. lǐn              lǐng

3. shà            shào            4. zāo            zōu

---

## TASK 3. SCRAMBLED WORDS

Rearrange the words and phrases to form grammatically correct and meaningful sentences.

1. 早          你          林笛

2. 好          史老師        您

---

## TASK 4. SITUATIONAL DIALOGUE

**Setting:**     First day of school on campus.

**Cast:**        Two students are going to class.

**Situation:**   On the way, you meet some of your classmates and their teachers. Greet them in the culturally acceptable way.

# 3

# 你爸爸媽媽好嗎？

# How's Your Family?

**In this lesson you will:**

- ▓ Learn to write Chinese characters.
- ▓ Use some family-related vocabulary.
- ▓ Use Chinese to politely discuss someone's well-being.

Wu Wende runs into a close family friend, Ms. Hu, at the grocery store.

| | | |
|---|---|---|
| Hú Āyí: | Wú Wéndé, nǐ hǎo. | |
| 胡阿姨： | 吳文德，你好。 | |
| | | |
| Wú Wéndé: | Nín hǎo, Hú Āyí! | |
| 吳文德： | 您好，胡阿姨！ | |
| | | |
| Hú Āyí: | Nǐ bàba māma hǎo ma? | |
| 胡阿姨： | 你爸爸媽媽好嗎？ | |
| | | |
| Wú Wéndé: | Wǒ bàba māma hěn hǎo. | |
| 吳文德： | 我爸爸媽媽很好。 | |
| | | |
| Hú Āyí: | Nǐ yéye nǎinai ne? | |
| 胡阿姨： | 你爺爺奶奶呢？ | |
| | | |
| Wú Wéndé: | Tāmen yě hěn hǎo. Lǐ Shūshu hǎo ma? | |
| 吳文德： | 他們也很好。李叔叔好嗎？ | |
| | | |
| Hú Āyí: | Tā yě hěn hǎo. | |
| 胡阿姨： | 他也很好。 | |

......

| | | |
|---|---|---|
| Wú Wéndé: | Hú Āyí, zàijiàn! | |
| 吳文德： | 胡阿姨，再見！ | |
| | | |
| Hú Āyí: | Zàijiàn! | |
| 胡阿姨： | 再見！ | |

# 生詞表 (Shēngcí Biǎo)
# Vocabulary

REQUIREMENT: You should be able to use all the vocabulary introduced in each lesson to do your listening, speaking, and reading exercises. For writing characters, you will only be held responsible for the vocabulary words marked with stars.

| Character | Pinyin | Part of Speech | English Definition |
|---|---|---|---|
| 1. 阿姨 | āyí | *n.* | auntie (mother's sister); used to address a woman of one's parents' generation |
| 2. 爸爸 | bàba | *n.* | dad, daddy |
| 3. 媽媽 | māma | *n.* | mom, mommy |
| 4. *嗎 | ma | *part.* | an interrogative particle used to form questions |
| 5. *我 | wǒ | *pron.* | I, me |
| 6. *很 | hěn | *adv.* | very |
| 7. 爺爺 | yéye | *n.* | grandpa (father's father) |
| 8. 奶奶 | nǎinai | *n.* | grandma (father's mother) |
| 9. *呢 | ne | *part.* | an interrogative particle used to make up questions (see Grammar III) |
| 10. *他們 | tāmen | *pron.* | they, them |
| *他 | | *pron.* | he, him |
| *她 | | *pron.* | she, her |
| 們 | | *suff.* | used to pluralize the singular personal pronouns |
| 11. *也 | yě | *adv.* | also, too |
| 12. 叔叔 | shūshu | *n.* | uncle (father's younger brother); used to address a man of one's parents' generation |
| 13. 再見 | zàijiàn | *v. phr.* | "Good-bye," "Farewell," "See you again" |
| 再 | | *adv.* | again |
| 見 | | *v.* | to see; to meet |

*A low bridge crossing in Hangzhou.*

## 專有名詞 (Zhuānyǒu Míngcí) **Proper Nouns**

| | | | |
|---|---|---|---|
| 1. | 胡阿姨 | Hú Āyí | Auntie Hu |
| 2. | 吳文德 | Wú Wéndé | a male's name |
| 3. | 李叔叔 | Lǐ Shūshu | Uncle Li |

## 補充詞彙 (Bǔchōng Cíhuì) **Supplementary Vocabulary**

| | | | | |
|---|---|---|---|---|
| 1. | 父親 | fùqin | *n.* | father |
| 2. | 母親 | mǔqin | *n.* | mother |
| 3. | 父母 | fùmǔ | *n.* | parents |
| 4. | 哥哥 | gēge | *n.* | elder brother |
| 5. | 弟弟 | dìdi | *n.* | younger brother |
| 6. | 姊姊 | jiějie | *n.* | elder sister |
| 7. | 妹妹 | mèimei | *n.* | younger sister |
| 8. | 兄弟姊妹 | xiōngdì jiěmèi | *n.* | siblings |

## 詞彙注解 (Cíhuì Zhùjiě) **Featured Vocabulary**

們 (men): 們 is a plural suffix for pronouns and human nouns. Non-human nouns are usually not pluralized. For example:

Pronouns

      你們 you (pl.)      我們 we, us      他們 they, them

Human Nouns

      老師們         叔叔們        阿姨們

The use of 們 is complicated. There will be more explanations on 們 in the future lessons.

# 語法 (Yǔfǎ)
# Grammar

## I. Addressing People (Cont'd.)

### A.  Non Family Members

In China, in order to show respect when addressing an older person who is not a family member, you should use the surname + a noun indicating relationship. For example, if your neighbor is about the same age as your parents, you would call him or her "Uncle + Last Name" or "Aunt + Last Name." If she or he is closer to your grandparents' age, you would use "Grandma +Last Name" or "Grandpa+Last Name."

**Noun (indicating relationship)**

| Surname | Title | Pinyin | English |
|---------|-------|--------|---------|
| 胡 | 阿姨 | Hú Āyí | Auntie Hu |
| 李 | 叔叔 | Lǐ Shūshu | Uncle Li |
| 胡 | 奶奶 | Hú Nǎinai | Grandma Hu |
| 李 | 爺爺 | Lǐ Yéye | Grandpa Li |

### B. Family Members

When addressing your own relatives, you don't need to include their last names; just their titles will suffice.

| | | |
|---|---|---|
| 阿姨 | Āyí | Auntie |
| 叔叔 | Shūshu | Uncle |
| 爺爺 | Yéye | Grandpa |
| 奶奶 | Nǎinai | Grandma |

### C.  Husband and Wife

In China, a married woman keeps her own surname instead of taking her husband's surname. For example, when 胡阿姨 (Hú Āyí) married 李叔叔 (Lǐ Shūshu) , she kept her maiden name and was not called 李阿姨 ( Lǐ Āyí).

## ⬚ PRACTICE

Introduce us to at least three people of your grandparents' or parents' ages, using the appropriate titles. Be sure to include people of different genders!

## II. Basic Sentence Structure

Chinese sentences consist of a subject and predicate. They usually come in the following two forms:

     A. Subject + (Adverb) + Predicate Adjective

     B. Subject + (Adverb) + Predicate Verb

  In this lesson, we will focus on sentence structure A, which uses an adjective as the predicate. Here the subject usually precedes the predicate. The subject in Chinese can be a noun such as 爸爸, 老師 (bàba, lǎoshī), or a pronoun such as 你, 您 (nǐ, nín), etc. indicating "who" and "what." Chinese sentences with predicate adjectives are composed of a subject, one or more adverbs, and an adjective. Unlike English, these sentences don't use the verb "to be." For example:

| | Subject<br>Noun Phrase | Adverbs | Predicate<br>Adjective | |
|---|---|---|---|---|
| Statement: | 我爸爸媽媽 | 很 | 好。 | My parents are very well. |
| Statement: | 李叔叔 | 也很 | 好。 | Uncle Li is also doing okay. |

## *Notes*

1. 很 (hěn): In the "Subject + 很 + Adjective" pattern, 很 cannot be omitted in the positive response. In this pattern, 很 does not serve to intensify the adjective, but is used as a phonetic filler to make the predicate slightly longer.

2. 也 (yě): When 也 and 很 are used together, 也 always comes before 很.

## ⬚ PRACTICE

Try to make a few sentences using predicate adjectives and make sure that you use 很 and 也 correctly.

## III. The Interrogative Particles 嗎 (Ma) and 呢 (Ne)

In general, when a Chinese question is formed, the question's word order stays the same as it was in statement form. The following are two of the many commonly used types of questions in the Chinese language.

*Alaric Radosh*

## A. Questions with Interrogative Particle 嗎

This kind of question is formed by adding 嗎 to the end of a statement. The pattern is "Statement + 嗎." Right now we are only going to briefly introduce its positive responses. We will learn more about this pattern and its responses in the next lesson.

|  | Subject | Predicate Adjective | | |
|---|---|---|---|---|
|  | Noun Phrase | Adverbs | Adjective | |
| Question: | 你爸爸媽媽 | | 好嗎？ | How are your dad and mom? |
| Response: | 他們 | 很 | 好。 | |
| Question: | 李叔叔 | | 好嗎？ | How is Uncle Li? |
| Response: | 他 | 也很 | 好。 | |

## B. Questions with Interrogative Particle 呢

呢 forms a question as a follow-up to a previous question. It echoes back to something previously mentioned in the conversation, but shifts the attention to a different person or thing. It is similar to "And you?" or "How about you?" in English. For example:

*Previous Question:*

你爺爺好嗎？              Is your grandpa well?

*Follow-up Question:*

| Noun/Pronoun | 呢 | |
|---|---|---|
| 你奶奶 | 呢？ | What about your grandma? |

*Chris Vee*

*Typical small Chinese decorative jars.*

## PRACTICE

You are taking a job at a local nursing home and are concerned about some of the residents. Talk to the staff and ask at least two questions about the residents. Be sure to provide questions which demonstrate that you know how to use 嗎 and 呢.

## IV. Brief Introduction to Possessives

In Chinese, the word 的(de) is usually used to indicate possessives. However, with a close relationship, such as family members, the 的 can be omitted. For example:

| Pronoun | Noun | |
|---|---|---|
| 我(的)爸爸媽媽 | my parents | |
| 你(的)爺爺奶奶 | your grandparents | |

## PRACTICE

Bring some pictures or photos of your family to class and identify each individual. Feel free to make things up, but demonstrate that you know how to use the "personal pronoun + personal noun" pattern.

# 語音複習 (Yǔyīn Fùxí)
# Pronunciation Review

## I. Review of Initials and Finals

The initials and finals selected for review are based on vocabulary learned in this lesson.

**Initials:**   b   j      m      t      y      w

**Finals:**   a   e   o   u   ai   ei   en   ie   uo   ian

## II. Phonetic Spelling Rules

A.   When a syllable has no initial consonant and the final begins with *i*, the *i* is changed to *y*, unless *i* is the only vowel in the final, in which case *y* is added in front of it. For example:

   *ie* ➔ *ye*        *ian* ➔ *yan*

   *i* ➔ *yi*         *ing* ➔ *ying*

B.   When a syllable has no initial consonant and the final begins with *u*, the *u* is changed to *w*. For example: *uo* ➔ *wo*.

C.   When *u* stands alone, add *w* before *u*. For example: *u* ➔ *wu*.

## III. Neutral Tone

In addition to the four tones already learned in the previous lessons, there is also the neutral tone in Mandarin. The neutral tone is pronounced lightly without any stress and is indicated in pinyin by the absence of any tone mark above the syllable. The following are combinations of each of the four tones with the neutral tone. Try each combination and see if you can pronounce it correctly.

| | | | |
|---|---|---|---|
| 1 + neutral: | tāde | māma | lǎoshī ne |
| 2 + neutral: | yéye | pópo | āyí ne |
| 3 + neutral: | nǎinai | shǎzi | zǒuzǒu ba |
| 4 + neutral: | bàba | shàoye | zuòzuò ba |

 寫漢字(Xiě Hànzì)
# Character Writing

## I. Key Radical Presentation

1. 嗎 and 呢 share the small mouth radical 口. Many end-of-sentence particles and interjection words also have this radical.

2. 很 has the double-man radical 彳.

## II. Handwriting

### Indivisibles

| Character | Practice with Chinese Characters |
|---|---|
| 也 | |

### Left-right Composition

| Character | Practice with Chinese Characters |
|---|---|
| 我 | |
| 們 | |
| 他 | |

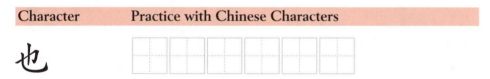

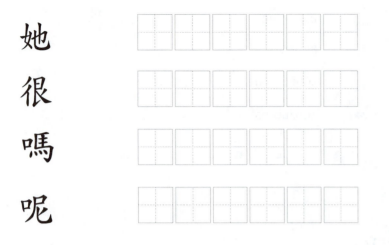

她
很
嗎
呢

課堂練習 (Kètáng Liànxí)

# In-Class Exercises

 **TASK 1. PINYIN EXERCISES**

## A. Distinguishing Tones

Listen carefully to the following syllables and mark the correct tones below. Practice saying the tones correctly, making sure that you can recognize the differences among each of the four tones.

1.  ye        ye        ye        ye

2.  tian      tian      jian      jian

3.  bai       bai       mai       mai

4.  men       men       ben       ben

5.  tuo       tuo       wo        wo

## B. Distinguishing Sounds

Listen carefully to the following pairs of syllables; note the differences between them, and try to pronounce them correctly.

**Initials**

1. jiě       yě        2. tài       dài

3. bèn       pèn       4. mó        fó

**Finals**

1. má        mái       2. biē       bēi

3. wǔ        wǒ        4. jiàn      jiè

## C. *Pronunciation Practice*

Practice your tones and pronunciation by listening to a native speaker on your audio CD or multimedia CD-ROM.

1. Nǐ hǎo.

2. Wǒ hěn hǎo.

3. Nǐ bàba hǎo ma?

4. Wǒ māma hěn hǎo.

5. Tā yě hěn hǎo.

6. Lǐ Shūshu zài jiàn.

## D. *Sight-reading*

Read aloud the following phrases. Your sight-reading skills will be measured by your speed and accuracy. (Multimedia CD-ROM only.)

1. zài jiàn

2. zài jiè

3. wǒ men

4. wú mén

5. jiě jie

6. zài jiā

7. mèi mei

8. bù hǎo

## TASK 2. GRAMMATICAL STRUCTURE PRACTICE

Select one of the two choices to correctly complete each of the following dialogues.

1. A: 你好。

   B: _____。

   a) 我很好          b) 你好

2. A: _____好嗎？

   B: 他很好。

   a) 李老師              b) 老師李

3. A: 我爸爸媽媽很好。你爸爸 _____？

   B: 我爸爸也很好。

   a) 嗎              b) 呢

4. A: 你爺爺好嗎？

   B: 他 _____。

   a) 好              b) 很好

---

## TASK 3. PARAPHRASING

To find out how well you know the grammar and vocabulary covered so far, follow the steps below.

**Step 1.** Translate the following dialogue into Chinese, using your own words. To check your pronunciation, listen to the dialogue on your multimedia CD-ROM.

| | |
|---|---|
| Lǐ Lìlì: | Hello, Auntie Hú. |
| Hú Āyí: | Good morning, Lǐ Lìlì. How are your parents? |
| Lǐ Lìlì: | They are very well. |
| Hú Āyí: | How about your grandparents? |
| Lǐ Lìlì: | They are well, too. Good-bye. |
| Hú Āyí: | Good-bye. |

**Step 2.** Now that you have familiarized yourself with the dialogue, be creative! Think of other words you have learned so far that might work in this dialogue. For example, instead of asking "How are your parents?" you could ask "How are your grandparents?" Try to substitute as many words as possible without disrupting the structure of the dialogue.

---

## TASK 4. PERFORMANCE

Using the grammar and vocabulary you have learned so far, write a short dialogue and perform it for the class. Don't be afraid to set the stage and use costumes or props. Above all, be creative!

# 4

# 好久不見，你怎麼樣？
# How's It Going?

*In this lesson you will:*
- Review pronunciation and pinyin spelling rules.
- Write more Chinese characters.
- Ask people about their studies, health, and work.

It is early in the morning, and Lin Di is on her way to class.

| | |
|---|---|
| Lín Dí: | Nǐ zǎo, Wú Wéndé. |
| 林笛： | 你早，吳文德。 |
| | |
| Wú Wéndé: | Zǎo. |
| 吳文德： | 早。 |
| | |
| Lín Dí: | Hǎojiǔ bújiàn, nǐ zěnmeyàng? |
| 林笛： | 好久不見，你怎麼樣？ |
| | |
| Wú Wéndé: | Mǎmǎhūhū. Nǐ ne? |
| 吳文德： | 馬馬虎虎。你呢？ |
| | |
| Lín Dí: | Wǒ hěn lèi. |
| 林笛： | 我很累。 |
| | |
| Wú Wéndé: | Nǐ xuéxí tài máng, tài jǐnzhāng. |
| 吳文德： | 你學習太忙[1]，太緊張。 |
| | |
| Lín Dí: | Dàjiā dōu hěn jǐnzhāng, nǐ bù jǐnzhāng ma? |
| 林笛： | 大家都很緊張，你不緊張嗎？ |
| | |
| Wú Wéndé: | Wǒ bù jǐnzhāng, yě bú lèi. Nǐ tài rènzhēn le. |
| 吳文德： | 我不緊張，也不累。你太認真了[2]。 |
| | |
| Lín Dí: | Shì a. Wǒ kuài chéng shūdāizi le. |
| 林笛： | 是啊。我快成書呆子了[3]。 |

Li Lili meets a long time family friend, Mr. Gao, on the street.

| | |
|---|---|
| Lǐ Lìlì: | Gāo Xiānsheng, nín hǎo. |
| 李麗莉： | 高先生，您好。 |

| | |
|---|---|
| Gāo Xiānsheng: | Nǐ hǎo, Lǐ Lìlì. Hǎojiǔ bújiàn, nǐ zěnmeyàng? |
| 高先生： | 你好，李麗莉。好久不見，你怎麼樣？ |

| | |
|---|---|
| Lǐ Lìlì: | Wǒ hěn hǎo. Nín ne? Shēntǐ zěnmeyàng? |
| 李麗莉： | 我很好。您呢？身體怎麼樣？ |

| | |
|---|---|
| Gāo Xiānsheng: | Shēntǐ hái hǎo. |
| 高先生： | 身體還好。 |

| | |
|---|---|
| Lǐ Lìlì: | Nín tàitai shēntǐ hǎo ma? |
| 李麗莉： | 您太太身體好嗎？ |

| | |
|---|---|
| Gāo Xiānsheng: | Tā hái hǎo. Nǐ bàba māma dōu hǎo ma? |
| 高先生： | 她還好。你爸爸媽媽都好嗎？ |

| | |
|---|---|
| Lǐ Lìlì: | Tāmen dōu hěn hǎo. |
| 李麗莉： | 他們都很好。 |

| | |
|---|---|
| Gāo Xiānsheng: | Tāmen gōngzuò shùnlì ma? |
| 高先生： | 他們工作順利嗎？ |

| | |
|---|---|
| Lǐ Lìlì: | Gōngzuò dōu hěn shùnlì, dànshì tāmen hěn máng. |
| 李麗莉： | 工作都很順利，但是他們很忙。 |

Sentences marked with numbers are explained in the Notes section below. The section provides either cultural information or explanations for the more difficult sentences, which are designed to broaden your knowledge. You do not need to memorize the material in the Notes section. Just read through it and get a general sense of its meaning.

## *Notes*

1. 你學習太緊張。 (Nǐ xuéxí tài jǐnzhāng.) This sentence consists of a subject（你）and a sentence providing additional information on the subject（學習太緊張）. This kind of sentence is called a "topic-comment" sentence. "您太太身體好嗎？"(Nín tàitai shēntǐ hǎo ma?) and "他們工作順利嗎？" (Tāmen gōngzuò shùnlì ma?) all belong to this group. For now, just remember this basic form. You will learn more about this structure in Lesson 9.

2. 你太認真了。 (Nǐ tài rènzhēn le.) You are too serious.

3. 我快成書呆子了。 (Wǒ kuài chéng shūdāizi le.) I'm turning into a bookworm.

生詞表 (Shēngcí Biǎo)
# Vocabulary

| Character | Pinyin | Part of Speech | English Definition |
|---|---|---|---|
| 1. 怎*麼樣 | zěnmeyàng | *interrog.* | how |
| 2. *還 | hái | *adv.* | still, (not) yet |
| 還好 | | *adj. phr.* | "OK" — not very good, but not very bad either |
| 3. *累 | lèi | *adj.* | tired |
| 4. *學*習 | xuéxí | *n. & v.* | study; to study |
| 5. *太 | tài | *adv.* | too, extremely |
| 6. *忙 | máng | *adj.* | busy |
| 7. 緊張 | jǐnzhāng | *adj.* | tense, stressed, stressful |
| 8. *大*家 | dàjiā | *n.* | everybody |
| 家 | | *n.* | family, home |
| 9. *都 | dōu | *adv.* | all, both |
| 10. *不 | bù | *adv.* | not, no |
| 11. 認真 | rènzhēn | *adj.* | serious, earnest, conscientious |
| 12. 先生 | xiānsheng | *n.* | gentleman, Mr., Sir; husband |
| 13. 身體 | shēntǐ | *n.* | the human body; health condition |
| 14. 太太 | tàitai | *n.* | Mrs., Madam, wife |
| 15. 工*作 | gōngzuò | *n.* | occupation, profession, job |
| | | *v.* | to work |
| 16. 順利 | shùnlì | *adj.* | smooth (going smoothly) |
| 17. 但是 | dànshì | *conj.* | but, however |

## 專有名詞 (Zhuānyǒu Míngcí) **Proper Nouns**

| | | |
|---|---|---|
| 高 | Gāo | a surname, family name |

## 補充詞彙 (Bǔchōng Cíhuì) **Supplementary Vocabulary**

| | | | |
|---|---|---|---|
| 1. 輕鬆 | qīngsōng | *adj.* | easy |
| 2. 健康 | jiànkāng | *adj.* | healthy |
| 3. 可是 | kěshì | *adv.* | but |

# 口頭用語 (Kǒutóu Yòngyǔ) **Spoken Expressions**

1. 好久不見！　Hǎojiǔ bújiàn!　Long time no see!

    This is a very commonly used phrase to greet someone you have not seen for awhile.

2. 馬馬虎虎　mǎmǎhūhū　neither good nor bad, so-so

    This is commonly used to respond to an inquiry about you or someone you know.

3. 是啊。　Shì a.　You are right. (indicating agreement)

    This is frequently used to affirm what another person has just said.

## 詞彙注解 (Cíhuì Zhùjiě) Featured Vocabulary

### 都不 *(Dōu Bù)* vs. 不都 *(Bù Dōu)*

都不 and 不都 may look similar, but they have different meanings. 都不 can be translated as "none (of them)" or "neither (of the two)." 不都 means "not all of them." 不都 is used less often than 都不.

| | |
|---|---|
| 他們都不忙。 | None of them is busy. |
| 他們不都忙。 | Not all of them are very busy. |

## 語法(Yǔfǎ)
# Grammar

## I. Basic Sentence Structure (Cont'd.)

Of the two common forms of predicates (predicate adjectives and predicate verbs), we will continue to focus exclusively on the sentence pattern "Subject + Predicate Adjective" in this lesson. In predicate adjectives, single-syllable adjectives such as 忙 (máng) should NOT stand alone; usually an adverb, such as 很, or other adverbs, such as 也 (yě), 都 (dōu), 還 (hái), 不(bù) etc., are required before the single-syllable adjective. In this lesson we have covered:

| Questions | | Answers/Statements | | |
|---|---|---|---|---|
| **Subject** | **Adjective** | **Subject** | **Adverb** | **Adjective** |
| 你爸爸媽媽 | 好嗎？ | 他們 | 很 | 好。 |
| Are your parents doing okay? | | They are doing very well. | | |
| | | 他們 | 還 | 好。 |
| | | They are not great, but they are doing OK. | | |
| 你 | 忙嗎？ | 我 | 很 | 忙。 |
| Are you busy? | | I am very busy. | | |
| | | 我 | 還 | 好。 |
| | | I'm not too busy; I'm okay. | | |
| 他 | 呢？ | 他 | 也很 | 忙。 |
| What about him? | | He is also very busy. | | |

## A. Negative Sentences with the Adverb 不 (Bù)

In this lesson, you will learn how to form a negative sentence. The adverb 不 can be placed before an adjective or adverb in order to negate it.

*Chris Vee*

| Subject | Predicate Adjective | |
|---|---|---|
| **Noun/Pronoun** | **Adverb** | **Adjective** |
| 我 | 不 | 忙。 |

I am not busy.

| **Noun/Pronoun** | **Adverbs** | **Adjective** |
|---|---|---|
| 我 | 不很 | 忙。 |

I am not very busy.

## B. Short Responses

A question using 嗎 elicits a "yes" or "no" answer. However, Chinese has no equivalent to the English short response "yes" or "no." Usually the adjective itself is repeated to form a positive response, or "不 + adjective" forms the negative response. For additional clarity, a full sentence is often added after the short "yes/no," as in the examples below.

> 你媽媽忙嗎？
> 忙，她很忙。 or 不忙，她不忙。

## C. Predicate Adjectives without 很 in a Statement

When a single-syllable adjective is used without 很, the sentence is incomplete. This usually indicates that there is a follow-up sentence. For example:

| Sentence 1 | | Sentence 2 | |
|---|---|---|---|
| **Somebody 1** | **Adjective 1** | **Somebody 2** | **Adjective 2** |
| 我媽媽 | 忙， | 我爸爸 | 也忙。 |

My mom is busy, and so is my dad.

| | | | |
|---|---|---|---|
| 毛老師 | 忙， | 李老師 | 不忙。 |

Professor Mao is busy; Professor Li is not.

## II. Using the Adverbs 也 (Yě), 都 (Dōu) and 太 (Tài)

Adverbs such as 也, 都, and 太 (or 很), if they are used in a sentence, always precede adjectives. When these adverbs appear together in the same sentence, they should obey the word order presented below.

| Subject | Predicate Adjective | |
|---|---|---|
| **Noun/Pronoun** | **Adverbs** | **Adjective** |
| 我們 | 也都不太 | 忙。 |

We are not too busy, either.

| | | |
|---|---|---|
| 我們 | 也都很 | 忙。 |

We are all very busy, too.

### *Notes*

1. 也 is frequently placed before 都, 很, and 太.

2. 都 is frequently placed before 太 or 很. (太 and 很 cannot be used in the same sentence.)

3. When 也 or 都 modifies 不太, which means "not too," it should be placed before 不太. You should memorize 也都不太 as an adverbial phrase.

---

### ▣ PRACTICE

Find a partner and use 身體, 學習, and 工作 to create a short dialogue in which one person asks questions using the adjectives and adverbs we have learned so far, and the other provides answers in both positive and negative forms.

## III. Using 怎麼樣 (Zěnmeyàng)

怎麼樣 is an interrogative word that means "how." It can be used to make an inquiry about someone's well-being. When used to form a question, 怎麼

樣 simply replaces the adverb and adjective in the predicate. The sentence structure itself does not change. For example:

|  | **Subject** | **Adverb** | **Adjective** |  |
| --- | --- | --- | --- | --- |
| Statement: | 他工作 | 很 | 好。 | He is doing fine with his work. |

|  | **Subject** | 怎麼樣 |  |
| --- | --- | --- | --- |
| Question: | 他工作 | 怎麼樣？ | How is his work? |

### *Compare* 怎麼樣 *with* 好嗎

Both "Somebody + 怎麼樣" and "Somebody + 好嗎" are used to inquire about someone's well-being. 怎麼樣 is more colloquial than 好嗎. The negative response to "Somebody + 好嗎" or Somebody + 怎麼樣," 不好, is seldom used. Although grammatically correct, it sounds too blunt. To soften the bluntness, you can use the adverb 太. For example:

More appropriate:    她不太好。  She is not great.

Less appropriate:    他不好。  He is not good.

 **PRACTICE**

Find a partner and have a short dialogue in which one person asks a question using 怎麼樣 and the other provides both a positive and a negative answer.

# 語音練習 (Yǔyīn Fùxí)
# Pronunciation Review

## I. Review of Initials and Finals

The initials and finals selected for review are based on vocabulary learned in this lesson.

**Initials:**  d    g    x    r    zh

**Finals:**  an    ou    un    üe    ia    ang    eng    ong

## II. Tone Change Rule for 不

When 不 is used alone or before the first , second, or third tones, it is pronounced as *bù* (fourth tone). When it is used before a fourth tone syllable or a neutral tone derived from a fourth tone, it is pronounced as *bú* (second tone).

For example:    bù duō   bù máng   bù hǎo   bú gàn   bú kàn

Now it's your turn! Listen carefully to the following sounds. When you are comfortable with the sounds, record your own pronounciation and compare it with the voices on the CD.

A.  bú

   1. bú jiàn     2. bú lèi

   3. bú rènzhēn     4. bú shùnlì

B.  bù

   1. bù hǎo     2. bù máng

   3. bù jǐnzhāng     4. bù hěnhǎo

# III. Phonetic Spelling Rules

## A. When There Are No Initials

*-un* ➜ *-u(en)*    *un* is the combination of *u* and *en*. When there are no initials, *u* changes to *w* and *n* changes to *en* (e.g., *wen*).

*-üe* ➜ *yue*    When there are no initials, add *y* before *ue*; *üe* loses the umlaut (e.g., *yue*).

## B. When There Are Initials

*-un*    Although *-un* is the combination of *u* and *en*, when *-un* has an initial, *e* is dropped so it is spelled as *-un* (e.g., *dun*).

*-üe*    When *-üe* has initials such as *j, q, x, -üe* is written as *-ue* without the umlaut (e.g., *jue, que,* and *xue*). When the initial is *n* or *l,* the umlaut remains (e.g., *lüe, nüe*).

*Sun Zhong Shan (Sun Yat-sen) museum in Nanjing.*

# 寫漢字(Xiě Hànzì)
# Character Writing

## Key Radical Presentation

The running radical: 辶

The heart radical (vertical): 忄

The ear radical: 阝

In this lesson you are going to learn to write ten more Chinese characters. Please pay special attention to their radicals. You can practice writing the characters on a separate piece of paper.

| Character | Practice with Chinese Characters |
|---|---|
| 作 | |
| 都 | |
| 忙 | |
| 家 | |
| 學 | |
| 累 | |
| 還 | |
| 大 | |
| 習 | |
| 麼 | |
| 不 | |
| 太 | |

# 課堂練習(Kètáng Liànxí)
# In-Class Exercises

## 🎧💻 TASK 1. PINYIN EXERCISES

### A. Distinguishing Tones

Listen carefully to the following syllables and mark the correct tones below. Practice saying the tones correctly, making sure that you can recognize the differences among each of the four tones.

1. di        di        di        di
2. gu        gu        gu        gu
3. xia       xia       xia       xia
4. rang      rang      rang      rang
5. zhi       zhi       zhi       zhi

### B. Distinguishing Sounds

Listen carefully to the following pairs of syllables; note the differences between them, and try to pronounce them correctly.

**Initials**

1. dān  tān      2. gǒu  kǒu      3. xiá  jiá
4. rǒng  chǒng   5. rì  shì

**Finals**

1. gān  gāng     2. zhàng  zhèng  3. dūn  dōng
4. ròu  ruò      5. xuě  xiě

### C. Pronunciation Practice

Practice your tones and pronunciation by listening to a native speaker on your audio CD or multimedia CD-ROM.

1. xuéxí      jǐnzhāng      wǒmen xuéxí bù jǐnzhāng
2. gōngzuò    shùnlì        dàjiā gōngzuò dōu hěn shùnlì
3. dànshì     rènzhēn       dànshì wǒmen tài rènzhēn

### D. Sight-reading

Read aloud the following phrases. Your sight-reading skills will be measured by your speed and accuracy. (For Multimedia CD-ROM only.)

1. zhīdào        2. Zhōngguó       3. xīn xuésheng
4. Rìběn         5. wèn ān         6. dōu gōngzuò

*Huang Shan in early fall.*

## TASK 2. GRAMMATICAL STRUCTURE PRACTICE

### A. Word Insertion

In each of the following short dialogues, choose the letter (A, B, or C) of the place where the given Chinese character should be inserted to form a grammatically correct sentence.

1. A:    你忙嗎？
   B:    我（A）不（B）忙（C）。                                    太

2. A:    李老師、高老師怎麼樣？
   B:    （A）李老師、高老師（B）很好（C）。                    都

3. A:    高先生高太太身體都好嗎？
   B:    高先生身體（A）很好，（B）高太太（C）還好。        也

4. A:    我爸爸媽媽工作不累。 你爸爸媽媽呢？
   B:    他們工作（A）也（B）都（C）太累。                    不

### B. Word Selection

Select one of the three choices to correctly complete each of the following dialogues.

1. A:    你怎麼樣？

   B:    我_____，學習工作都很順利。

        a) 很好        b) 好        c) 都好

2. A:    胡阿姨、李叔叔身體都好嗎？

   B:    他們身體 _____。

        a) 不好太     b) 不太好   c) 太不好

3. A:　你叔叔怎麼樣？

　　B:　他很好，工作不忙，學習_____。

　　　　a) 也緊張　　b) 也不緊張　c) 不緊張

4. A:　我們不忙。你們呢？

　　B:　我們_____忙。

　　　　a) 也都不太　b) 都也不太　c) 也都太

## C. *Fill in the Blanks*

Fill in the blanks below by selecting the appropriate word for each sentence.
Then translate the sentence into English.

1. 怎麼樣　　　忙　　　緊張

　　A:　啊，吳文德，好久不見。你_____？

　　B:　我還好，你呢？你學習_____嗎？

　　A:　很忙。我們大家學習都很_____。

2. 工作　　　好嗎　　身體　　太認真　　嗎

　　A:　你爸爸工作順利_____？

　　B:　他_____順利，但是太累。

　　A:　你媽媽身體_____？

　　B:　她_____還很好。但是她工作太忙了。

　　A:　是啊。你媽媽工作_____。

---

## 🖳 TASK 3. PARAPHRASING

To find out how well you know the grammar and vocabulary covered so far,
follow the steps below.

**Step 1.** Translate the following dialogue into Chinese, using your own words.
To check your pronunciation, listen to the dialogue on your CD.

　　A:　Uncle Gao, long time no see! How is your health?

　　B:　My health is so-so. What about you? How is school?

　　A:　It is okay, but I am very busy.

　　B:　What about your parents? How is their work?

　　A:　Their work is going well, but it is too intense.

　　B:　What about your grandparents?

　　A:　They are all in very good health. Thanks.

**Step 2.** Now that you have familiarized yourself with the dialogue, be creative! Think of other words you have learned so far that might work in this dialogue. For example, instead of asking, "Uncle Gao, how is your health?" you could ask, "Auntie Li, how is your work?" Try to substitute as many words as possible without disrupting the structure of the dialogue.

# TASK 4. PICTURE DESCRIPTION

**Topic:** Two students are having lunch together. They have not seen each other for a while and are taking the opportunity to catch up. Write a short conversation in which they talk about their studies. How is the workload affecting their physical and mental health? What is their overall attitude toward their studies?

1.                                                           2.

3.

# 5
# 你做什麼工作？
# How Do You Make a Living?

***In this lesson you will:***

■ Do a review of pinyin pronunciation and tones.

■ Learn more character combinations and rules of phonetic spelling.

■ Use basic vocabulary to identify things and people.

■ Ask somebody about his or her profession.

(Note: Starting in this lesson you should focus on recognizing Chinese characters rather than pinyin, so the pinyin has been moved from above the characters to below them.)

Gao Peng and Lin Di are at Gao Peng's house looking at photographs on the wall.

林笛：　　這是你媽媽嗎？
Lín Dí:　　Zhè shì nǐ māma ma?

高朋：　　是啊，這是我媽媽，那是我爸爸。
Gāo Péng:　Shì a, zhè shì wǒ māma, nà shì wǒ bàba.

林笛：　　你爸爸媽媽都是老師嗎？
Lín Dí:　　Nǐ bàba māma dōu shì lǎoshī ma?

高朋：　　都不是。我媽媽是護士，我爸爸是醫生。
Gāo Péng:　Dōu bú shì. Wǒ māma shì hùshi, wǒ bàba shì yīshēng.

林笛：　　是嗎？媽媽也是醫生。
Lín Dí:　　Shì ma? Wǒ bàba yě shì yīshēng.

高朋：　　你媽媽呢？她也是護士嗎？
Gāo Péng:　Nǐ māma ne? Tā yě shi hùshi ma?

林笛：　　不，她做生意。
Lín Dí:　　Bù, tā zuò shēngyì.

......

林笛：　　　那是誰？
Lín Dí:　　 Nà shì shéi?

高朋：　　　那是我哥哥。
Gāo Péng:　Nà shì wǒ gēge.

林笛：　　　你哥哥做什麼工作？
Lín Dí:　　 Nǐ gēge zuò shénme gōng zuò?

高朋：　　　他是工程師，那是他的老闆。
Gāo Péng:　Tā shì gōngchéngshī, nà shì tā de lǎobǎn.

......

林笛：　　　這都是你的朋友嗎？
Lín Dí:　　 Zhè dōu shì nǐ de péngyou ma?

高朋：　　　是啊，我朋友很多，這是張子倩，
Gāo Péng:　Shì a, wǒ péngyou hěn duō, zhè shì Zhāng Zǐqiàn,

　　　　　　那是她哥哥張子文。
　　　　　　Nà shì tā gēge Zhāng Zǐwén.

林笛：　　　這也是你朋友嗎？
Lín Dí:　　 Zhè yěshì nǐ péngyou ma?

高朋：　　　不是，這是張教授，他是我們老師。
Gāo Péng:　Búshì, zhè shì Zhāng Jiàoshòu, tā shì wǒmen lǎoshī.

林笛：　　　這都是張教授的書嗎？
Lín Dí:　　 Zhè dōu shì Zhāng Jiàoshòu de shū ma?

高朋：　　　是啊，他的書很多。這是張教授的朋友。
Gāo Péng:　Shì a, tāde shū hěn duō. Zhè shì Zhāng Jiàoshòu de
　　　　　　péngyou.

林笛：　　　他搞什麼？
Lín Dí:　　 Tā gǎo shénme?

高朋：　　　他搞電腦。林笛，你的問題不少啊？
Gāo Péng:　Tā gǎo diànnǎo. Lín Dí, nǐde wèntí bù shǎo a?

林笛：　　　聊聊天嘛[1]。
Lín Dí:　　 Liáoliáo tiān ma.

## *Note*

1.     聊聊天嘛。 (Liáoliáo tiān ma.) Literally, "I don't have anything to talk about, but I am looking for things to say so we can chat." It can be roughly translated as "(I am) just talking for talking's sake."

 生詞表 (Shēngcí Biǎo)
# Vocabulary

| Character | Pinyin | Part of Speech | English Definition |
|---|---|---|---|
| 1.*做 | zuò | *v.* | to do |
| 2.*什麼 | shénme | *pron.* | what? |
| 3.*這 | zhè | *pron.* | this |
| 4.*是 | shì | *v.* | to be |
| 5.*那 | nà | *pron.* | that |
| 6. 護士 | hùshi | *n.* | nurse |
| 7. 醫生 | yīshēng | *n.* | medical doctor |
|    醫 | | *n.* | medicine; medical science |
| 8. 生意 | shēngyì | *n.* | business |
| 9.*誰 | shéi | *pron.* | who, whom |
| 10. 哥哥 | gēge | *n.* | elder brother |
| 11. 工程師 | gōngchéngshī | *n.* | engineer |
|    工程 | | *n.* | engineering |
| 12.*的 | de | *part.* | a particle used to indicate possession, similar to the English "apostrophe+s" |
| 13. 老闆 | lǎobǎn | *n.* | boss (colloq.) |
| 14.*朋*友 | péngyou | *n.* | friend |
| 15.*多 | duō | *adj.* | many, much (opposite of 少) |
| 16. 教授 | jiàoshòu | *n.* | professor |
| 17.*書 | shū | *n.* | book |

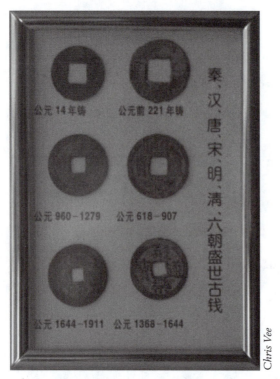

秦、汉、唐、宋、明、清、六朝盛世古钱

公元 14 年铸    公元前 221 年铸

公元 960－1279    公元 618－907

公元 1644－1911    公元 1368－1644

*Chris Vee*

*Coins from the Qin, Han, Tang, Song, Ming, and Qing dynasties.*

| 18. 搞*電腦 | gǎo diànnǎo | v. obj. | to specialize in computers (colloq.) |
|---|---|---|---|
| 搞 | | v. | to work on, to specialize in, to be engaged in (a certain field) [colloq.] |
| 電 | | n. & adj. | electricity; electronic |
| 腦 | | n. | brain |
| 19. *問題 | wèntí | n. | question, problem, issue |
| 問 | | v. | to ask, to inquire |
| 20. *少 | shǎo | adj. | few, little (opposite of 多) |

## 專有名詞 (Zhuānyǒu Míngcí) Proper Nouns

| 1. 高朋 | Gāo Péng | a man's name |
|---|---|---|
| 2. 張子倩 | Zhāng Zǐqiàn | a woman's name |
| 3. 張子文 | Zhāng Zǐwén | a man's name |

## 補充詞彙 (Bǔchōng Cíhuì) Supplementary Vocabulary

| 1 大夫 | dàifu | n. | medical doctor |
|---|---|---|---|
| 2. 做買賣 | zuò mǎimai | v. obj. | to do business, buy and sell |

| 3. 上司 | shàngsī | *n.* | boss |
| 4. 看電視 | kàn diànshì | *v. obj.* | to watch TV |
| 5. 看電影 | kàn diànyǐng | *v. obj.* | to see a movie |
| 6. 經理 | jīnglǐ | *n.* | manager |
| 7. 看書 | kàn shū | *v. obj.* | to read, read a book |
| 8. 問問題 | wèn wèntí | *v. obj.* | to ask a question |

## 口頭用語 (Kǒutóu Yòngyǔ) Spoken Expressions

| 1. 是嗎 | Shì ma? | "Is that true?" or "Really?" |
| | | This is often used to express surprise or disbelief. |
| 2. 啊 | a | This is used at the end of a sentence for emphasis. |
| 3. 嘛 | ma | This is used at the end of the sentence to indicate that something is obvious. |

## 詞彙注解 (Cíhuì Zhùjiě) Featured Vocabulary

### 搞電腦 *(Gǎo Diànnǎo)* vs. 做生意 *(Zuò Shēngyì)*

In 搞電腦, 搞 is frequently used to indicate someone's specialization. It is very colloquial. In 做生意, 做 can be used with 生意 or 買賣 to indicate a profession. They should be treated as fixed phrases.

 語法(Yǔfǎ)

# Grammar

## I. Sentences Using Action Verbs

In Lessons 2 and 3, you learned the "Subject + Predicate Adjective" structure. This lesson introduces the "Subject +Predicate Verb" structure. There are different kinds of verbs that can function as predicate verbs in the Chinese language. Here, you will learn how to use the action verb as a predicate verb. An action verb describes what the subject does. Look at the examples below:

|  | Subject | Verb | Object |
|---|---|---|---|
| Positive: | 我 | 做 | 生意。 |

I do business.

|  | 他們（也）（都） | 做 | 生意。 |
|---|---|---|---|

They (all) do business, (too).

| Negative: | 他們（也）（都） | 不做 | 生意。 |
|---|---|---|---|

(Lit.) They also not all do business. None of
them do business, either.

| Question: | 你 | 做 | 生意 嗎？ |
|---|---|---|---|

Do you do business?

## Notes

1. Questions requiring yes/no answers can be formed by adding 嗎 to the
   end of a sentence.

2. A negative sentence is formed by placing 不 before the verb.

3. When modifying action verbs, the adverbs 也 and 都 should be placed
   before the verb and should always be used in that order, just as with
   predicate adjectives.

## ⊞ PRACTICE

Create a positive sentence using the verb phrases 搞電腦, 做生意, or 問
問題, plus one or more adverbs. Then change that sentence into a question
and provide a negative answer.

## II. Sentences with the Verb 是 (Shì)

In addition to action verbs, the verb 是 can also function as a predicate verb.
In its most general context, the verb 是 means "to be" and can be roughly
translated as "is," "are," or "am." It links the subject of a sentence to a predicate noun. Remember that, as we learned earlier, 是 cannot be used with a
predicate adjective.

| Subject | Adverb | Verb | Object of Identification |
|---|---|---|---|
| Pronoun/Noun | （也）（都） | 是 | Pronoun/Noun |
| Positive: 我媽媽 |  | 是 | 老師。 |

My mom is a teacher.

他爸爸媽媽　　（也）（都）　是　　老師。

His dad and mom are both teachers.

Negative:　她媽媽　　　　　　　　　不是　老師。

Her mom is not a teacher.

她爸爸媽媽　　（也）（都）　不是　老師。

Her parents aren't teachers, either.

Question:　你媽媽　　　　　　　　　是　　老師　嗎？

Is your mom a teacher?

## *Note*

1. When modifying 是, the adverbs 也 and 都 should be placed before 是 if they are used at all.

---

## 🔲 PRACTICE

Find a partner and use vocabulary such as 老師，醫生，護士，工程師，教授，老闆，朋友，高先生， and 李太太 to prepare a short dialogue in which one person asks a question and the other provides responses in both positive and negative forms. Make sure that you are using the verb 是.

## III. Using 這 (Zhè) and 那 (Nà) with the Verb 是 (Shì)

這 and 那 are demonstrative pronouns that are often used with 是 to introduce people or identify people/objects, as in "this is …" or "that is …."

| Demonstrative Pronoun Subject | Verb 是 | Object of Identification Pronoun/Noun |
|---|---|---|
| Positive: 這/那 | 是 | 我朋友。 |

This is my friend.

Negative:　那 不　　　是　　　我朋友。

That is not my friend.

Question:　這/那　　　是　　　你朋友嗎？

Is this your friend?

## *Notes*

1. In this structure, 這/那 can function only as the subject, NOT the object.

| CORRECT: | 那是他朋友。 |
|---|---|
| xxx INCORRECT: | 他朋友是那。xxx |

2. When 這 and 那 are used with 都, they are plurals and should be translated as "these all" and "those all" respectively.

3. Without 都, 這/那 can be either plural or singular, depending on the context of the sentence.

---

## ⚙ PRACTICE

Find a partner and prepare a short dialogue in which one person asks a question using 這/那 and the other answers the question in both positive and negative forms. Example:

> Is that your friend?
> Yes, that is my friend.
> No, that is not my friend.

## IV. Using 的 (De) to Indicate Possession

In Lesson 2, you learned how to use the singular personal pronouns 你/我/他 in a possessive sense to indicate relationship (e.g., 我媽媽, 你弟弟, and 他朋友). In these cases, the possessive particle 的 is omitted because the speaker is referring to a family member. Note, however, that if it is not a family member, 的 must be used to indicate possession. For example: 他的護士. Thus in Chinese, 的 functions similarly to the possessive "s" in English.

| | | **Object of Possession** | |
|---|---|---|---|
| **Noun/Pronoun** | **的** | **Noun Phrase** | |
| 電腦 | 的 | 問題 | computer problem |
| 朋友 | 的 | 書 | friend's book |
| 老師 | 的 | 問題 | teacher's question |
| 我們 | 的 | 醫生 | our doctor |
| 媽媽 | 的 | 生意 | mother's business |

When plural pronouns such as 我們, 你們, and 他們 are used to modify a noun, 的 is usually used and should be placed between the plural pronouns and the modified noun. The principal exception is when the pronoun is followed by an institution (e.g., our dorm, their school, your company, and our class) or when 我們, 你們, and 他們 are followed by 老師. Then, 的 can also be omitted (e.g., 我們老師).

---

## ⚇ PRACTICE

Bring a picture of your family or friends to class and identify everyone in the picture using 的. For example: 這是我爸爸。他是醫生。那是他的書。

## V. Questions with 誰 (Shéi) / 誰的 (Shéide) / 什麼 (Shénme)

In Lesson 3, you learned that when using the interrogative "怎麼樣" to form a question, the word order remains the same as in a statement. The same rule applies to interrogative pronouns such as 誰, 誰的, 什麼, etc. The interrogative pronoun, or "question word," occupies the same position in the sentence as the noun or phrase that will answer the question.

### A. Using 誰 (Shéi)

The word 誰 is equivalent to "who" or "whom" in English. The following are examples of how 誰 can be used to turn a statement into a question.

#### 誰 as a Subject

| Statements | Questions |
|---|---|
| (李麗莉)是他的朋友。 | (誰)是他的朋友? |
| Li Lili is his friend. | Who is his friend? |
| (他朋友)搞電腦。 | (誰)搞电脑? |
| His friend specializes in computers. | Who specializes in computers? |

#### 誰 as a Predicate Noun or following the Verb

| Statements | Questions |
|---|---|
| 那是(我們老師)。 | 那是(誰)? |
| That's your teacher. | Who is that? |
| 他的朋友是(李麗莉)。 | 他的朋友是(誰)? |
| His friend is Li Lili. | Who is his friend? |

## *Notes*

1. 誰是你的朋友？vs 你的朋友是誰？These two sentences, although their basic meanings are the same, have different points of emphasis.

   In 誰是你的朋友？, the speaker is addressing a group of people, asking who among them is the listener's friend. Therefore, you could also say, 他們誰是你的朋友？ (Which one of them is your friend?).

   In 你的朋友是誰？, we can assume that the friend is already the focus of conversation and that the speaker wants to clarify exactly whom they have been talking about.

2. In questions, the word order remains the same in both positive and negative forms (e.g., 誰搞電腦？or 誰不搞電腦？).

---

## ⊡ PRACTICE

Find a partner and prepare a short dialogue in which one person asks a question using 誰 as a subject and the other person asks a question using 誰 as an object. Each should provide an answer to the other's question. For example:

    誰 as a subject: 你們誰搞電腦？ 他搞電腦。
    誰 as an object: 你們老師是誰？ 我們老師是史老師。

## B. Using 誰的 (Shéide)

The word 誰的 is equivalent to "whose" in English. The example below demonstrates how to use 誰的 to turn a statement into a question.

*A candy store clerk in Shanghai.*

Alaric Radosh

*Playing the erhu, a traditional Chinese musical instrument.*

### 誰的 *as a Noun Modifier*

| Statements | Questions |
|---|---|
| 那是（他的）電腦。 | 那是（誰的）電腦？ |
| That's his computer. | Whose computer is that? |

---

## PRACTICE

Find a partner and have a short conversation in which one person asks a
question using 誰的 and the other person responds. For example:

這是誰的書？那是我的書。

## C. Using 什麼 (Shénme)

The question word 什麼 is equivalent to "what" in English. When used to
to turn a statement into a question, 什麼 can function either as an object
or as a modifier.

### 什麼 *as an Object*

| Statements | Questions |
|---|---|
| 他搞（電腦）。 | 他搞（什麼）？ |
| He specializes in computers. | What does he specialize in? |

## 什麼 *as a Modifier*

| Statements | Questions |
|---|---|
| 我哥哥做（電腦）生意. | 你哥哥做（什麼）生意？ |
| My older brother specializes in computers. | What kind of business does your older brother do? |

## PRACTICE

Find a partner and prepare a short dialogue in which one person asks a question using 什麼 as an object and the other person provides an answer. Now reverse the situation, this time using 什麼 as a modifer, so that the person who answered is now asking. For example:

什麼 as an object: 是什麼，搞什麼，做什麼，問什麼
什麼 as a modifier: 做什麼工作，做什麼生意，問什麼問題

# 語音複習 (Yǔyīn Fùxí)
# Pronunciation Review

## I. Review of Initials and Finals

The initials and finals selected for review here are based on vocabulary learned in this lesson. We have included initials and finals from previous lessons in parentheses to be used with those that we cover in this lesson.

| Initials: | ch | p | (b | zh | sh) |
|---|---|---|---|---|---|

| Finals: | -i | iao | ua | uang | (ao | an | ang) |
|---|---|---|---|---|---|---|---|

## II. Phonetic Spelling Rules

### A. When There Are No Initials

iao → yao　　　When *-iao* does not have any initials, *i* changes to *y*.

ua → wa　　　When *-us* does not have any initials, *u* changes to *w*.

uang → wang　　　When *-uang* does not have any initials, *u* changes to *w*.

## B. When the Final Is -*i*

The -*i* stands for a very special vowel that is articulated by the tip of the tongue at the front of the hard palate (for the *zh-ch-sh* series). To pronounce this vowel, keep the tongue tip in the same position as for the preceding consonant, withdrawing it just enough to let air pass through. Because *zh-ch-sh* are voiceless consonant initials, voicing begins just as the vowel is pronounced.

## III. Review of Tones

|            | 1st Tone | 2nd Tone | 3rd Tone | 4th Tone |
|------------|----------|----------|----------|----------|
| 1st Tone:  | tāshuō   | tārén    | tāyě     | tāwèn    |
| 2nd Tone:  | shéishuō | shéimáng | shéigǎo  | shéizuò  |
| 3rd Tone:  | nǐshuō   | nǐwén    | nǐhǎo    | nǐlèi    |
| 4th tone:  | shìtā    | shìshéi  | shìwǒ    | shìshì   |
| Neutral Tone: | gēge  | shénme   | nǐde     | tàitai   |

## *Notes*

1.  Remember that a third tone before another third tone is pronounced like a second tone, and a third tone before any other tone is simply a low tone, without the rising contour of the citation form.

*A Chinese health spa in Nanjing.*

2. Note that the pitch of the neutral tone varies according to the tone of the preceding syllable. For example, it carries a noticeably higher pitch after a third tone syllable than after first or fourth tone syllables.

# 寫漢字(Xiě Hànzì)
# Character Writing

## Key Radical Presentation

The speech radical: 言

The moon radical: 月

The door radical: 門

Today you are going to learn to write ten more Chinese characters. Please pay attention to their radicals. Also, when writing characters that belong to the "left-middle-right" composition group, the left and the middle part need to be squeezed and the right part can take slightly more space than 1/3 the width of the character.

| Character | Practice with Chinese Characters |
|---|---|
| 那 | |
| 誰 | |
| 甚 | |
| 的 | |
| 朋 | |
| 做 | |
| 多 | |
| 是 | |
| 少 | |

電 書 這 友 問

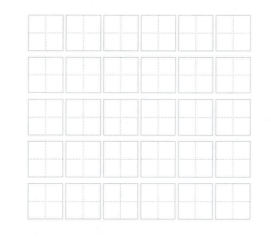

 課堂練習 (Kètáng Liànxí)

# In-Class Exercises

## 📖 TASK 1. PINYIN EXERCISES

### A. Distinguishing Tones

Listen carefully to the following syllables and mark the correct tones below. Practice saying the tones correctly, making sure that you can recognize the differences among each of the four tones.

1. ba        ba        ba        ba

2. piao      piao      piao      piao

3. chuang    chuang    chuang    chuang

4. chan      chan      chan      chan

5. wa        wa        wa        wa

### B. Distinguishing Sounds

Listen carefully to the following pairs of syllables; note the differences between them, and try to pronounce them correctly.

**Initials**

1. piāo      biāo      2. bàn     pàn      3. zhǎng   shǎng

4. chuāng    zhuāng    5. shàn    chàn

**Finals**

1. páo       piáo       2. zhuàng zhàng     3. yāo      yān

4. chuāng    chūn       5. wǎ      wǒ

## C. *Pronunciation Practice*

Practice your tones and pronunciation by listening to a native speaker on your audio CD or multimedia CD-ROM.

1. zhè shì      shéi de            Zhè dōu shì shéi de shū?

2. gēge         zuò shénme         Ň gēge zuò shénme gōngzuò?

3. nà shì       jiàoshòu           Nà shì wǒmen jiàoshòu de chē.

4. lǎobǎn       gǎo diànnǎo        Wǒ gēgē de lǎobǎn bù gǎo diànnǎo.

## D. *Sight-reading*

Read aloud the following phrases. Your sight-reading skills will be measured by your speed and accuracy. (For multimedia CD-ROM only.)

1. diànnǎo gōngchéng    2. lǎobǎn bù hǎo

3. jiàoshòu jiāoshū      4. wèntí bù shǎo

5. shēngyì bù hǎo gǎo    6. péngyou bù hǎo zhǎo

## 🔖 TASK 2. GRAMMATICAL STRUCTURE PRACTICE

Fill in the blanks below by selecting the appropriate word for each sentence.

1. 他朋友是_____？
   a) 誰      b) 誰的      c) 什麼

2. 他做_____生意？
   a) 誰      b) 誰的      c) 什麼

3. 那是_____電腦。
   a) 我      b) 我的      c) 我們

4. 他的書很多。_____，我的書也不少。
   a) 是啊      b) 是嗎      c) 是

## TASK 3. PARAPHRASING

To find out how well you know the grammar and vocabulary covered so far, follow the steps below.

**Step 1.** Translate the following two dialogues into Chinese, using your own words. To check your pronunciation, listen to the dialogues on your CD.

**Dialogue 1.**

> F:      Who is that?
>
> M:      That's my brother.
>
> F:      What does your brother specialize in? Is he busy?
>
> M:      He is a professor. His work is very intense.

**Dialogue 2.**

> F:      Whose computers are these?
>
> M:      These are my uncle's computers.
>
> F:      What work does he do?
>
> M:      He is in the computer business. His job is very tiring.
>
> F:      Is that right? My brother is also in the computer business. He says it's very stressful.

**Step 2.** Now that you familiarized yourself with the dialogue, be creative! Think of other words you have learned so far that might work in this dialogue. For example, instead of saying "That is my brother," you could say "That is my teacher." Try to substitute as many words as possible without disrupting the structure of the dialogue.

## TASK 4. PICTURE DESCRIPTION

**Topic:** As the two new roommates get to know each other, they spend time looking over their high school photo albums together. The album owner talks about the people in the different pictures, while the other person asks questions. Construct a dialogue between them, using the vocabulary learned in this lesson. Feel free to use the vocabulary from previous lessons as well, such as 累, 忙, 緊張, 認真。

1.

2.

3.

# 6

# 做作業

# Doing Homework

**In this lesson you will:**
- Review pronunciation, tones, and pinyin.
- Learn more about Chinese character composition and the rules of phonetic spelling.
- Use Chinese to borrow and return items.
- Talk about schoolwork.

Wu Wende and Li Lili are doing their homework at the library.

吳文德 ： 李麗莉，我借一下兒你的筆記，好嗎？
Wú Wéndé: Li Lìlì, wǒ jiè yixiàr nǐde bǐjì, hǎoma?

李麗莉 ： 什麼筆記？
Lǐ Lìlì: Shénme bǐjì?

吳文德 ： 中文課筆記。你現在用嗎？
Wú Wéndé: Zhōngwén kè bǐjì. Nǐ xiànzài yòng ma?

李麗莉 ： 我現在不用。你用吧。
Lǐ Lìlì: Wǒ xiànzài búyòng. Nǐ yòng ba.

吳文德 ： 謝謝。
Wú Wéndé: Xièxie.

Five minutes later...

吳文德 ： 李麗莉，還你的筆記。
Wú Wéndé: Lǐ Lìlì, huán nǐde bǐjì.

李麗莉 ： 你現在去哪兒？
Lǐ Lìlì: Nǐ xiànzài qù nǎr?

吳文德 ： 我去休息休息。
Wú Wéndé: Wǒ qù xiūxi xiūxi.

李麗莉 ： 你說什麼？你還做作業嗎？
Lǐ Lìlì: Nǐ shuō shénme? Nǐ hái zuò zuòyè ma?

| | | |
|---|---|---|
| 吳文德： | 不做。我今天很糊塗。 老師的問題我都不懂。 | |
| Wú Wéndé: | Bú zuò. Wǒ jīntiān hěn hútu. Lǎoshī de wèntí wǒ dōu bù dǒng. | |

我快累死了[1]。
Wǒ kuài lèi sǐ le.

| | |
|---|---|
| 李麗莉： | 今天的作業很難，是嗎？你不懂，我來教你。 |
| Lǐ Lìlì: | Jīntiān de zuòyè hěn nán, shìma? Nǐ bù dǒng, wǒ lái jiāo nǐ. |

| | |
|---|---|
| 吳文德： | 真的？ |
| Wú Wéndé: | Zhēn de? |

| | |
|---|---|
| 李麗莉： | 真的。你問問題吧。 |
| Lǐ Lìlì: | Zhēn de. Nǐ wèn wèntí ba. |

| | |
|---|---|
| 吳文德： | 好李麗莉老師，您很聰明。你看這是什麼意思？ |
| Wú Wéndé: | Hǎo Lǐ Lìlì Lǎoshī, nín hěn cōngmíng. Nǐ kàn zhè shì shénme yìsi? |

| | |
|---|---|
| 李麗莉： | 我看看。唉，我也不懂。我們去問問老師吧。 |
| Lǐ Lìlì: | Wǒ kàn kan. Ài, wǒ yě bù dǒng. Wǒmen qù wèn wen lǎoshī ba. |

## Note

我快累死了。 (Wǒ kuài lèi sǐ le.) I am dying of exhaustion.

## 生詞表 (Shēngcí Biǎo)

# Vocabulary

| | Character | Pinyin | Part of Speech | English Definition |
|---|---|---|---|---|
| 1. | 作業 | zuòyè | n. | homework, assignment |
| 2. | *借 | jiè | v. | to borrow, to lend |
| | 借 something: | | | to borrow sth. |
| | 借 someone something: | | | to lend somebody (sth.) |
| 3. | 一*下兒 | yīxiàr | phr. | (lit.) "one stroke," often used immediately after the verb to indicate a short period of time |
| 4. | 筆記 | bǐjì | n. | notes |

| | | | |
|---|---|---|---|
| 筆 | | *n.* | pen |
| 記 | | *v.* | to record |
| 5. 中*文*課 | Zhōngwén kè | *phr.* | Chinese class |
| 中文 | | *n.* | the Chinese language |
| 課 | | *n.* | class |
| 6. *現*在 | xiànzài | *n.* | now, the present time |
| 7. *用 | yòng | *v.* | to use, need |
| 8. *吧 | ba | *part.* | used at the end of a sentence to indicate uncertainty, to make a suggestion, etc. |
| 9. 謝謝 | xièxie | *v.* | to thank |
| 10. 還 | huán | *v.* | to return (sth. to sb.) |
| | hái | *adv.* | still |
| 11. *去 | qù | *v.* | to go; to be going to (do sth.) |
| 12. *哪兒 | nǎr | *pron.* | which place, where |
| 13. 休息 | xiūxi | *v.* | to rest, to relax |
| 14. *說 | shuō | *v.* | to speak; to say (sth) |
| 15. 今*天 | jīntiān | *n.* | today (see Grammar Section I) |
| 16. 糊塗 | hútu | *adj.* | muddle-headed, confused |
| 17. 懂 | dǒng | *v.* | to understand |
| 18. 難 | nán | *adj.* | difficult, hard |
| 19. *來 | lái | *v.* | to come |
| 20. 教 | jiāo | *v.* | to teach |
| 21. 聰明 | cōngmíng | *adj.* | smart, intelligent |
| 22. *看 | kàn | *v.* | to look, watch, read |
| 23. 意思 | yìsi | *n.* | meaning |

補充詞彙 (Bǔchōng Cíhuì) **Supplementary Vocabulary**

| | | | |
|---|---|---|---|
| 1. 功課 | gōngkè | *n.* | assignment |
| 2. 中文班 | Zhōngwén bān | *n.* | Chinese class |

| 3. | 考試 | kǎoshì | n. | test, exam |
| | | | v. | to take a test or exam |
| 4. | 容易 | róngyì | adj. | easy |
| 5. | 詞典 | cídiǎn | n. | dictionary |
| 6. | 上課 | shàng kè | v. obj. | to go to class |
| 7. | 下課 | xià kè | v. obj. | to get out of class |
| 8. | 同學 | tóngxué | n. | classmate |

## 口頭用語 (Kǒutóu Yòngyǔ) Spoken Expressions

| 1. | 唉 | ài | the sound of a sigh |
| 2. | 真的 | zhēn de | Really? |

*A public park in Hangzhou.*

## 詞彙注解 (Cíhuì Zhùjiě) Featured Vocabulary

### 1. 吧 (Ba)

If you want to make a suggestion, you can simply attach 吧 to the end of a sentence.

| Subject | Verb Phrase | 吧 |
|---|---|---|
| 你 | 用（我的筆記） | 吧。 |

(I suggest that) you use my notes.

| 我們 | 休息 | 吧。 |
|---|---|---|

(I suggest that) we rest now.

## 2. 來 *(Lái)*

The most common use of the verb 來 is "to come." It is also frequently used before the main verb to make a suggestion. For example:

我們來做作業吧。　　　　　Let's do homework.

## 3. *Different* 好 *(Hǎo) Phrases*

好嗎？ (...hǎo ma?) "Is it all right?" or "Is it okay (with you)?" This appears at the end of the statement and is used to ask the other person's opinion or elicit consent. Placing 怎麼樣 at the end of a sentence serves a similar function.

好吧 (...hǎo ba.) "Okay" or "All right." This generally indicates agreement but not necessarily excitement.

好啊！(...hǎo a!) "Great!" or "Sure!" This is an enthusiastic response.

## 4. *Different* 看 *(Kàn) Phrases*

| 看 | (kàn) | to look |
|---|---|---|
| 看書 | (kàn shū) | to read |
| 看朋友 | (kàn péngyou) | to visit friends |
| 看醫生 | (kàn yīshēng) | to see a doctor |
| 看電視 | (kàn diànshì) | to watch TV |

## 5. 還 *(Hái, Huán)*

In Chinese, certain characters can have two different sounds; each has its own meaning. The first one we have come across is 還. For example:

| 還 | huán | verb | to return something | 還你的書。 |
|---|---|---|---|---|
| 還 | hái | adverb | still | 你還做作業嗎？ |

 語法(Yǔfǎ)
# Grammar

## Review

In the previous lessons, you learned how to use many different adverbs and interrogative pronouns. Before you start the new lesson, let's reiterate some basic rules:

A.  Adverbs should be placed before adjectives, verbs, or other adverbs. (Lesson 3 Grammar)

B.  When an interrogative pronoun is used to form a question, the sentence order remains the same. (Lesson 4 Grammar)

In this lesson, you will learn one more adverb and one more interrogative pronoun.

A.  The adverb 還 (hái) in this lesson indicates continuation of action. This is different from 還 in 還好 (Lesson 2).

    For example:  你還做作業嗎？  Do you still want to do homework?

B.  The interrogative pronoun 哪兒 (nǎr) means "where."

    For example:  你去哪儿？        Where are you going?

## ◑ PRACTICE

Can you make sentences using the adverb 还 and the interrogative pronoun 哪兒？ Try it!

## I. Using Time Phrases

In Chinese, expressions of time are usually nouns (今天 jīntiān, 現在 xiàn-zài, etc.). A time phrase indicating the time of an action can go in one of the following two places:

## A. Before the subject at the very beginning of a sentence

|           |         | Predicate      |                        |
| --------- | ------- | -------------- | ---------------------- |
| Time Word | Subject | Verb/Adjective |                        |
| 今天      | 我      | 做作業。       | I do my homework today. |
| 現在      | 我      | 很忙。         | I am very busy now.     |

## B. Between the subject and the predicate verb or adjective

|  |  | Predicate |  |
| --- | --- | --- | --- |
| **Subject** | **Time Word** | **Verb/Adjective** | |
| 我 | 今天 | 不工作。 | Today I do not work. |
| 我 | 現在 | 很緊張。 | I am very tense now. |

As a noun, the time word can also be used to modify a noun. If this is the case, 的 must be placed between the time word and the modified noun. For example: 今天的作業 (today's homework). You will learn more about this in Lesson 7.

---

## 🔲 PRACTICE

Find a partner and have a short dialogue in which one person makes up two questions using the time word 今天 and the other answers the questions using the same time word. Now reverse the roles, so that the person who answered the question earlier now asks a question using 現在 and vice versa.

## II. Sentences with Multiple Verbs

In this lesson, we will learn two different verbs, either of which could be used as the first verb in a multi-verb sentence: 去 (qù, to go) and 來 (lái, to come). The phrase "去/來 + Place + Verb obj." indicates that an action is going to take place soon. The negation word is usually placed before the first verb (e.g., 不去/不來).

| Subject | Verb 1 | Verb 2 (Main Verb) | Object |
|---|---|---|---|
| 你 | 去/來 | 休息休息。 | |

You go and take a break.

| Subject | Verb 1 | Verb 2 (Main Verb) | Object |
|---|---|---|---|
| 我 不 | 去/來 | 做 | 作業。 |

I am not going to do the homework.

## *Compare:*

你現在去/來做作業嗎？    Are you going to do (the) homework?

你現在做作業嗎？    Are you doing (the) homework right now?

## PRACTICE

Find a partner and use verb phrases such as 去借書, 來做作業, 來還你的筆記, 去問一下兒, and 去休息 to create a short dialogue in which one person asks a question that uses multiple verbs and the other answers it in both positive and negative forms.

## III. Verb Repetition and the Verb 一下兒 (Yīxiàr)

There are three ways to lighten the tone of a verb to make the action sound less serious or weighty: 1) by repeating the verb; 2) by repeating the verb with a 一 in between; 3) by attaching 一下兒 to the verb.

### A. Without an Object

| Verb | Repetition | Repetition with 一 | Repetition with 一下兒 |
|---|---|---|---|
| Verb | Verb Verb | Verb 一 Verb | Verb 一下兒 |
| 看<br>to take a look | 看看 | 看一看 | 看一下兒 |
| 休息<br>to take a break | 休息休息 | N/A | 休息一下兒 |

### B. With an Object

| Verb | Repetition | Repetition with 一 | Repetition with 一下兒 |
|---|---|---|---|
| Verb-Obj. | Verb Verb-Obj. | Verb 一 Verb-Obj. | Verb 一下兒-Obj. |
| 看你的作業 | 看看你的作業 | 看一看你的作業 | 看一下兒你的作業 |

to look at your homework

*Chris Vee*

## *Notes*

1. Verb 一下兒 must always precede the object if one exists.

   CORRECT:　　　　　看一下兒你的作業。

   xxx INCORRECT:　　看你的作業一下兒。　xxx

2. When a single-character verb is repeated, you can insert 一 between the two instances of the verb. When a verb contains two characters, as in the case of 休息, the repetition takes the form of ABAB (休息休息). Do not add 一 in between the repeated verbs.

3. These forms (repetition of verbs and the "Verb 一下兒") apply only to positive statements and questions. They CANNOT be used in negative sentences.

   CORRECT:　　　　　我不看你的作業。

   xxx INCORRECT:　　我不看一下兒你的作業。　xxx

4. When there is more than one verb in a sentence, only the main verb (usually the last verb) is repeated. For example: 我去休息休息 "I am going to take a break."

## PRACTICE

Use the above structures to create your own sentences. How many more verbs can you come up with?

## IV. Tag Questions

A "tag" question is a short question attached to the end of a statement. In this lesson, we will focus on the following two groups.

### A. Using 好嗎 (Hǎoma) or 怎麼樣 (Zenmeyàng)

To make a suggestion or ask about the listener's opinion, use "..., 好嗎?" ("..., hǎo ma?")("..., is it all right with you?") or "怎麼樣?" ("Zěnmeyàng?") ("How is that with you?").

| Statement | Tag Question |
|---|---|
| 我借一下兒你的筆記， | 好嗎？ |

I'm going to borrow your notes, okay?

| | |
|---|---|
| 你現在去做作業， | 怎麼樣？ |

Now you go and do your homework, how about that?

***Responses:***

Positive: If you agree, you could respond to the above questions with 好啊, 好, or 好吧。

Negative: 不好 sounds very curt and possibly impolite. It might be more diplomatic if you provide an explanation to express disagreement. For example:

> 我們現在去做作業，好嗎？
>
> 我現在很忙。明天(míngtiān; tomorrow)，好嗎？

### B. Using 是嗎 (Shì ma?)

To confirm information, use 是嗎? (Shì ma?).

| Statement | Tag Question |
|---|---|
| 你不懂， | 是嗎？ |

You did not understand, right?

***Responses:***

Positive: 是啊。

Negative: 不是。

## *Note*

對嗎 (Duìma) can also be used as a tag question. For example:

今天的作業很難，對嗎？　　Today's homework is very difficult, right?

---

## PRACTICE

Find a partner and have a brief conversation in which one person asks a question using one of the tag words and the other provides both positive AND negative responses. The following are suggested phrases for each of the tag questions.

| | | | |
|---|---|---|---|
| 好嗎： | 借中文筆記 | 問問題 | 還你的書 |
| 怎麼樣： | 來說中文 | 去休息 | 教我 |
| 是嗎： | 學習太忙 | 工作順利 | 很糊塗 |

# 語音複習(Yǔyīn Fùxí)
# Pronunciation Review

## I. Review of Initials and Finals

The initials and finals selected for review are based on vocabulary learned in this lesson. The initials and finals in parentheses (although reviewed in previous lessons) are used with the initials and finals reviewed in this lesson.

**Initials:**     c     k     q     (z     g     j     x)

**Finals:**     -i     er/-r     ü     ui     uan     iu     iong     (u)

## II. Phonetic Spelling Rules

### A. When the Final Is *-i*

The *-i* stands for a very special vowel that is articulated by the tip of the tongue behind the upper incisors (for the *z-c-s* series). To prounce this vowel keep the tongue tip in the same position as for the preceding consonant, withdrawing it just enough to let air pass through. Because *z-c-s* are voiceless consonant initials, voicing begins just as the vowel is pronounced.

## B. When There Are No Initials

| | |
|---|---|
| *ui* → *u(e)i* | *ui* is the combination of *u* and *ei*. In syllables with no initial consonant, *u* changes to *w* and *i* changes to *ei* (e.g., *wei*). |
| *iu* → *i(o)u* | *iu* is the combination of *i* and *ou*. In syllables with no initial consonant, *i* changes to *y* and *u* changes to *ou* (e.g., *you*). |
| *iong* → *yong* | When *-iong* is not preceded by an initial consonant, *i* changes to *y*. Therefore, it should be spelled as *yong*. |
| *uan* → *wan* | When *uan* is not preceded by an initial consonant, *u* changes to *w*. Thus, *uan* will be spelled as *wan*. |
| *ü* → *yu* | When *ü* is not preceded by an initial consonant, it gains a *y* and loses the umlaut. |

## C. When There Are Initials

| | |
|---|---|
| *ui* → *u(e)i* | Although *ui* is the combination of *u* and *ei*, *e* is dropped if there is an initial and *ui* is directly attached to that initial (e.g., *kui*). |
| *iu* → *i(o)u* | Although *iu* is the combination of *i* and *ou*, *o* is dropped if there is an initial, and it is directly attached to the initial (e.g., *jiu*). |
| *ü* | If the initial is *l* or *n*, *ü* will keep the umlaut (e.g., *lü* or *nü*). However, with any other initials, *ü* loses the umlaut (e.g., *yu, ju, qu*, etc.). |

# III. Simple Final *er* and Retroflex *-r*

The *-er* is a full syllable by itself in the following words. See if you can pronounce them correctly.

| | |
|---|---|
| érzi | érnǚ |
| ěrduo | ěrchuí |
| èr shí | èryuán |

However, it also functions as a non-syllabic suffix, in which case the *e* is dropped and *r* is simply added to the syllable, or "stem," to which it is suffixed. For example:

| | | |
|---|---|---|
| yīxià + er | → | yīxiàr |
| nǎ + er | → | nǎr |

| nà + er | → | nàr |
| zhè + er | → | zhèr |
| diǎn + er | → | diǎnr |
| wan + er | → | wanr |

Please note that although the official pinyin spelling rules require that this syllable be written "dianr," it is actually pronounced "diar." The "n" sound is completely dropped when the -r suffix is added. Now it is your turn. See if you are able to pronounce the following four tones with zhèr/nàr/nǎr.

| 1st Tone: | tā zhèr | tā nàr | tā nǎr |
| 2nd Tone: | lái zhèr | shéi nàr | huí nǎr |
| 3rd Tone: | wǒ zhèr | wǒ nàr | wǒ nǎr |
| 4th Tone: | zhù zhèr | qù nàr | qù nǎr |

# 寫漢字(Xiě Hànzì)
# Character Writing

## Key Radical Presentation

The hand radical:  扌

The eye radical:  目

| Character | Practice with Chinese Characters |
|---|---|
| 借 | |
| 課 | |
| 説 | |
| 吧 | |
| 哪 | |

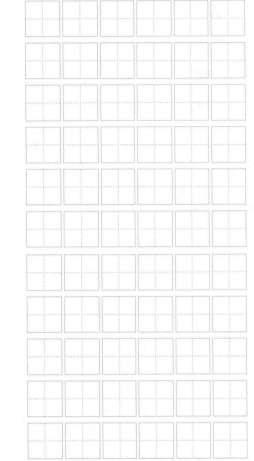

 課堂練習 (Kètáng Liànxí)

## In-Class Exercises

### 🎧📖 TASK 1. PINYIN EXERCISES

#### A. Distinguishing Tones

Listen carefully to the following syllables and mark the correct tones below. Practice saying the tones correctly, making sure that you can recognize the differences among each of the four tones.

1. ci           ci           ci           ci

2. kui          kui          kui          kui

3. qiu          qiu          qiu          qiu

4. qu           qu           qu           qu

5. huan         huan         huan         huan

6. yong         yong         yong         yong

*Browsing in a Chinese bookstore.*

## B. Distinguishing Sounds

Listen carefully to the following pairs of syllables; note the differences between them, and try to pronounce them correctly.

### Initials

| | | | | |
|---|---|---|---|---|
| 1. cuì | zuì | 2. kuǎn | guǎn |
| 3. qiū | jiū | 4. xióng | qióng |
| 5. chī | cī | | |

### Finals

| | | | | |
|---|---|---|---|---|
| 1. yǔ | wǔ | 2. qióng | qiú |
| 3. jū | zhū | 4. yǒu | ǒu |
| 5. kuī | kēi | | |

## C. Pronunciation Practice

Practice your tones and pronunciation by listening to a native speaker on your audio CD or multimedia CD-ROM.

1. huán      bǐjì      nǐ huán wǒ bǐjì, hǎo ma

2. qù      xiūxi yīxiàr      wǒ qù xiūxi yīxiàr, zěnmeyàng

3. xiànzài      lái zuò zuòyè      wǒmen xiànzài lái zuò zuòyè ba

4. jiè yīxiàr      hái yòng      wǒ jiè yīxiàr nǐde bǐjì, nǐ hái yòng ma

*A bridge overlooking the public park in Yangzhou.*

## D. Sight-reading

Read aloud the following phrases. Your sight-reading skills will be measured by your speed and accuracy. (For multimedia CD-ROM only.)

1. xuéxí tài lèi, xūyào xiūxi xiūxi
2. hǎo jiè hǎo huán, zài jiè bù nán
3. yōngrénzìrǎo, shízài bù cōngmíng

## TASK 2. GRAMMATICAL STRUCTURE PRACTICE

Check your knowledge of grammatical structures with the following exercises.

### A. Scrambled Words

Rearrange the words and phrases to form grammatically correct and meaningful sentences.

1. 我　　　　一下兒　　　去　　　　　　筆記　　　看
2. 書　　　　我　　　　去　　　　　　現在　　　看看
3. 做　　　　去　　　　他　　　　　　現在　　　作業
4. 休息　　　去　　　　還　　　　　　嗎　　　　你

## B. *Word Selection*

Select the choice that best completes each sentence.

1. 這都是你的中文書，＿＿＿＿＿＿？

    a) 是啊       b) 好嗎       c) 對嗎

2. 我借你的書看看＿＿＿＿＿＿？

    a) 是啊       b) 好嗎       c) 對嗎

3. 你來看一下兒＿＿＿＿＿＿。

    a) 吧         b) 呢         c) 嗎

4. ＿＿＿＿＿＿休息休息吧。

    a) 他們       b) 他         c) 我們

---

## TASK 3. PARAPHRASING

To find out how well you know the grammar and vocabulary covered so far, follow the steps below.

**Step 1.** Translate the following dialogue into Chinese, using your own words. To check your pronunciation, listen to the dialogue on your CD.

**Dialogue 1.**

    A:      Where are you going?
    B:      I am going to return the Chinese notes.
    A:      You are not using them now. Is it okay if I use them for a second?
    B:      Sure.

**Dialogue 2.**

    A:      Tonight's homework is very difficult, right?
    B:      That's right. How about we do the homework now?
    A:      I am very confused today. I do not understand the teacher's
            questions. I am going to take a break.
    B:      You are not confused. The homework is very difficult. You do
            not understand, and neither do I. Let's go and ask the teacher.

**Step 2.** Now that you have familiarized yourself with the dialogue, be creative! Think of other words you have learned so far that might work in this dialogue. For example, instead of asking "Where are you going?" you could ask "Where is he going?" Try to substitute as many words as possible without disrupting the structure of the dialogue.

# TASK 4. PICTURE DESCRIPTION

**Topic:** Two students are doing homework in the library. One student approaches the other, hoping to borrow something. Construct a dialogue between them, using the pictures as a guide.

1.

2.

3.

# 7

# 歡迎你們常來！
# Welcoming Guests

> **In this lesson you will:**
> - ■ Review pronunciation, tones, pinyin, and phonetic spelling rules.
> - ■ Learn to host guests and offer them a choice of drinks.
> - ■ Use Chinese to express gratitude or respond to gratitude.

Li Lili and Lin Di are having a party at their place and have invited some of their family friends. They hear a knock at the door.

李麗莉：　　　　高太太，您好。歡迎，歡迎。
Lǐ Lìlì:　　　　Gāo Tàitai, nín hǎo. Huānyíng, huānyíng.

　　　　　　　　高先生，請進，請進。
　　　　　　　　Gāo Xiānsheng, qǐng jìn, qǐng jìn.

林笛：　　　　　大家請坐！
Lín Dí:　　　　 Dàjiā qǐng zuò!

高太太：　　　　這是日本茶。
Gāo Tàitai:　　 Zhè shì Rìběn chá.

高先生：　　　　這是法國咖啡。
Gāo Xiānsheng:　Zhè shì Fǎguó kāfēi.

林笛：　　　　　哎呀！你們太客氣，帶這麼好的禮物。謝謝。
Lín Dí:　　　　 Āiya! Nǐmen tài kèqi, dài zhème hǎo de lǐwù. Xièxie.

高先生：　　　　謝什麼，這是我們的一點兒小意思。
Gāo Xiānsheng:　Xiè shénme, zhè shì wǒmen de yīdiǎnr xiǎo yìsi.

高太太：　　　　是啊，一點兒小意思。別客氣。
Gāo Tàitai:　　 Shì a, yīdiǎnr xiǎo yìsi. Bié kèqi.

After dinner, Li Lili and Lin Di begin serving drinks.

林笛：　　　　　你們誰喝咖啡？誰喝茶？誰喝酒？誰喝水？
Lín Dí:　　　　 Nǐmen shéi hē kāfēi? Shéi hē chá? Shéi hē jiǔ? Shéi hē shuǐ?

91

高太太：   我喝茶。
Gāo Tàitai:   Wǒ hē chá.

林笛：   您喝什麼茶？中國茶，英國茶，還是日本茶？
Lín Dí:   Nín hē shénme chá? Zhōngguó chá, Yīngguó chá, háishì Rìběn chá?

高太太：   我喝中國茶。多謝。
Gāo Tàitai:   Wǒ hē Zhōngguó chá. Duō xiè.

高先生：   你們有什麼酒？有白酒嗎？
Gāo Xiānsheng:   Nǐmen yǒu shénme jiǔ? Yǒu báijiǔ ma?

林笛：   沒有白酒，但是我們有紅葡萄酒，有啤酒。
Lín Dí:   Méi yǒu báijiǔ, dànshi wǒmen yǒu hóng pútáojiǔ, yǒu píjiǔ.

您喝什麼酒？
Nín hē shénme jiǔ?

高先生：   我紅葡萄酒，啤酒都不喝。我喝咖啡吧。謝謝。
Gāo Xiānsheng:   Wǒ hóng pútáojiǔ, píjiǔ dōu bù hē. Wǒ hē kāfēi ba. Xièxie.

林笛：   不用謝。你們吃水果，吃點心，還是吃糖？
Lín Dí:   Bú yòng xiè. Nǐmen chī shuǐguǒ, chī diǎnxin, háishì chī táng?

高太太：   我們都不吃糖。我吃水果。
Gāo Tàitai:   Wǒmen dōu bù chī táng. Wǒ chī shuǐguǒ.

高先生：   我吃點心。
Gāo Xiānsheng:   Wǒ chī diǎnxin.

林笛：   高太太，您的茶。高先生，這是您的咖啡。
Lín Dí:   Gāo Tàitai, nín de chá. Gāo Xiānsheng, zhè shì nín de kāfēi.

It's getting late, and everyone starts to leave.

高先生：   謝謝。
Gāo Xiānsheng:   Xièxie.

高太太：   十分感謝！
Gāo Tàitai:   Shífēn gǎnxiè!

李麗莉：   別客氣，歡迎你們常來。
Lǐ Lìlì:   Bié kèqi, huānyíng nǐmen cháng lái.

林笛：   謝謝你們的禮物。再見。
Lín Dí:   Xièxie nǐmen de lǐwù. Zàijiàn.

## *Note*

Whenever you're formally invited to someone's home for a party or a meal, it is customary to bring gifts. It is also common to return the favor and invite the hosts back to your own home for dinner. This practice of returning the favor is called "回請 (huí qǐng)."

# 生詞表 (Shēngcí Biǎo)
# Vocabulary

| | Character | Pinyin | Part of Speech | English Definition |
|---|---|---|---|---|
| 1. | 歡迎 | huānyíng | *v.* | to welcome (someone's arrival) |
| 2. | *常 | cháng | *adv.* | often, frequently |
| 3. | *請 | qǐng | *v.* | to politely request, politely ask (sb. to do sth.) |
| 4. | *進 | jìn | *v.* | to enter, come in |
| 5. | *坐 | zuò | *v.* | to sit |
| 6. | *茶 | chá | *n.* | tea |
| 7. | 咖啡 | kāfēi | *n.* | coffee |
| 8. | *客*氣 | kèqi | *adj.* | acting like a guest, courteous |
| | 客 | | *n.* | guest(s) |
| | 氣 | | *n.* | air, atmosphere |
| 9. | 帶 | dài | *v.* | to carry, bring, take |
| 10. | 這麼(那麼) | zhème (nàme) | *adv.* | such, so this/that (+adj.) |
| 11. | 禮物 | lǐwù | *n.* | gift, present |
| | 禮 | | *b.f.* | gift, present |
| | 物 | | *n.* | object(s) |
| 12. | 別 | bié | *adv.* | don't (do sth.); (ask sb.) not to (do sth.) |
| 13. | *喝 | hē | *v.* | to drink |
| 14. | *酒 | jiǔ | *n.* | wine, liquor, alcoholic drinks in general |
| | 葡萄酒 | pútáojiǔ | *n.* | grape wine |
| | 啤酒 | píjiǔ | *n.* | beer |

| 15. *水 | shuǐ | n. | water |
| 白酒 | báijiǔ | n. | a clear distilled liquor; recently also white wine |
| 16. 還是 | háishì | conj. | or (used in a question when offering two or more choices) |
| 17. *有 | yǒu | v. | to have |
| 18. *沒 | méi | adv. | no |
| 19. 紅 | hóng | adj. | red |
| 20. 白 | bái | adj. | white |
| 21. *吃 | chī | v. | to eat |
| 22. 水果 | shuǐguǒ | n. | fruit |
| 果 | | n. | fruit |
| 23. 點心 | diǎnxin | n. | snacks, light refreshment |
| 24. 糖 | táng | v. | candy, sugar |

## 專有名詞 (Zhuānyǒu Míngcí) Proper Nouns

| 1. | 日本 | Rìběn | Japan |
| 2. | 英國 | Yīngguó | England |
| 3. | 中國 | Zhōngguó | China |
| 4. | 法國 | Fǎguó | France |

*Alaric Radosh*

*Family and friends gather for dinner in a Chinese home.*

補充詞彙 (Bǔchōng Cíhuì) Supplementary Vocabulary

| | | | |
|---|---|---|---|
| 1. 冷飲 | lěngyǐn | *n.* | cool drinks |
| 2. 汽水 | qìshuǐ | *n.* | soda |
| 3. 可口可樂 | Kěkǒukělè | *n.* | Coca-Cola |
| 4. 果汁 | guǒzhī | *n.* | juice |
| 5. 客人 | kèrén | *n.* | guest |
| 6. 餅乾 | bǐnggān | *n.* | cracker, biscuit |
| 7. 吸煙 | xī yān | *v. obj.* | to smoke (cigarettes, etc.) |
| 8. 吃飯 | chī fàn | *v. obj.* | to eat |
| 9. 好喝 | hǎohē | *adj.* | good, tasty (of drink) |
| 10. 好吃 | hǎochī | *adj.* | good, tasty (of food) |
| 11. 問好 | wènhǎo | *v. phr.* | to send one's best regards |
| 12. 涼水 | liáng shuǐ | *n. phr.* | cold water |

# 口頭用語 (Kǒutóu Yòngyǔ) Spoken Expressions

## A. General Terms

| | | |
|---|---|---|
| 1. 哎呀! | Āiya! | a phrase used to express surprise |
| 2. 一點兒小意思 | yīdiǎnr xiǎo yìsi | just a small token |

## B. Expressing Gratitude

The following phrases can be used more or less interchangeably, but note the nuances as indicated by the translations.

| | | |
|---|---|---|
| 1. 謝謝 | Xièxie. | Thanks. |
| 2. 謝謝你/您 | Xièxie nǐ/nín. | Thank you. |
| 3. 多謝 | Duōxiè. | Many thanks. |
| 4. 十分感謝 | Shífēn gǎnxiè. | Thank you very much. |

## C. Responses

The phrases below can be used to respond to an expression of gratitude.

| | | |
|---|---|---|
| 1. 不謝 | Bú xiè. | You are welcome. |
| 2. 別客氣 | Bié kèqi. | You don't have to be so polite with me. |
| 3. 謝(我)什麼 | Xiè (wǒ) shénme? | What do you need to thank me for? |

4. (你/您)太客氣　　　(Nǐ/nín) tài kèqi.　　You are too polite.

5. 不用謝　　　　　　Bú yòng xiè.　　　　Don't mention it.

# 詞彙注解 (Cíhuì Zhùjiě) Featured Vocabulary

## 1. (常)常 *(Cháng) Cháng*

(常)常 is often used to describe habitual actions. Although 常常 and 常 are almost identical, the single-character "常" tends to attach itself more readily to other single- or double-character words. For example:

他常來我這兒。　　　　He often comes to my place.

他常說漢語。　　　　　He frequently speaks Chinese.

The negation of 常 and 常常 is 不常, NOT 不常常.

　　CORRECT:　　　　　　他不常說漢語。

　　xxx INCORRECT:　　　他常不說漢語。xxx

　　xxx INCORRECT:　　　他不常常說漢語。xxx

## 2. 這麼/那麼 *(Zhème/Nàme)*

這麼 and 那麼 are adverbs that can be translated as "such" or "so." They are frequently used to express the speaker's feelings. Use 這麼(那麼) in a similar way to how you would use 很. For example: 這麼好的茶！ Such good tea!

## 3. 不 *(Bù)* vs. 別 *(Bié)*

不 is placed before an adjective, adverb, or verb to form a negative sentence. It can be translated as "not." For example: 我不去 (I am not going). 別 is placed before a verb or adjective to request someone not to do something. It can be translated as "Don't." For example: 別去 (Do not go).

# 語法(Yǔfǎ)
# Grammar

## I. Noun Modifiers

Nouns can be modified not only by adjectives but also by other nouns.

### A. Nouns as Noun Modifiers

When a noun is modified by a noun, if the relationship between them is possessive, they are normally linked by the particle 的, as in 老师的书, the

馬到成功

*Chris Vee*

*Chris Vee*

*Chris Vee*

teacher's book(s) (but see Lesson 4 for exceptions to this rule). But when the relationship is simply descriptive, or further specifies a noun's nature or character, the particle 的 is not needed. For example:

| Noun | Modifier | Modified Noun |
|------|----------|---------------|
| 中國 | 茶 | Chinese tea |
| 法國 | 咖啡 | French coffee |
| 中文 | 書 | Chinese book |
| 電腦 | 課 | computer class |

## B. Adjectives as Noun Modifiers

### 1. With Monosyllabic Adjectives

When an adjective is monosyllabic and has NO adverb before it, it attaches directly to the noun.

| Adjective | Noun | |
|-----------|------|--|
| 白 | 酒 | white wine |
| 好 | 朋友 | good friends |
| 紅 | 茶 | red tea |

## Note

The adjectives 多 (duō) and 少 (shǎo) are exceptions to the rule especially in spoken language: 多 and 少 usually need an adverb when used to modify a noun and sometimes need 的 before the noun. For example: 很多朋友, many friends; 這麼少的禮物, so few gifts.

*Making a toast over a meal.*

Alaric Radosh

## 2. With Disyllabic Adjectives

When a disyllabic adjective is used to modify a noun, the modifier 的 must be placed before the noun to provide descriptive information about the noun. For example: 認真的老師, a serious teacher.

## 3. With Adjectives Preceded by Adverbs

When an adjective has an adverb before it, you should place 的 between the noun and the adjective.

| 很/這麼/那麼 | Adjective | 的 | Noun | |
|---|---|---|---|---|
| 很 | 好 | 的 | 禮物 | very good gifts |
| 很 | 好 | 的 | 朋友 | very good friends |
| 這麼 | 好 | 的 | 禮物 | such good gifts |
| 那麼 | 好 | 的 | 朋友 | such good friends |

## *Note*

When the adverb 很 + 多 is used to modify a noun, 的 usually is omitted.

For example: 很多禮物， 很多朋友， 很多老師。

## PRACTICE

Use the adjectives and nouns below to create as many phrases as possible (e.g., 好老師). Then use the combined phrases with 很/這麼/那麼 (e.g., 這麼好的老師). How many can you create?

**Adjectives:**  好 忙 緊張 認真 順利 多 少 聰明 糊塗 難

**Nouns:**  老師 學生 工作 老闆 朋友 書 問題 電腦 筆記 作業

## II. Using 還是 (Háishi) to Provide Options

When 還是 is used in questions to present multiple options to the listener, 還是 is usually placed before the last choice.

## A. Used to Link Noun Phrases

| | Noun Phrase 1 | Noun Phrase 2 | 還是 | Noun Phrase 3... |
|---|---|---|---|---|
| 你喝 | 中國茶， | 英國茶， | 還是 | 日本茶？ |

Do you want to drink Chinese tea, English tea, or Japanese tea?

| | | | | |
|---|---|---|---|---|
| 你們吃 | 水果， | 點心， | 還是 | 糖？ |

Do you want fruit, cookies, or candy?

## B. Used to Link Verb Phrases

|  | Verb Phrase 1 | Verb Phrase 2 | 還是 | Verb Phrase 3... |
|---|---|---|---|---|
| 你 | 喝中國茶， | 喝英國茶， | 還是 | 喝日本茶？ |

Do you want to drink Chinese tea, English tea, or Japanese tea?

| 你們 | 吃水果， | 吃點心， | 還是 | 吃糖？ |
|---|---|---|---|---|

Do you want fruit, cookies, or candy?

| 你 | 做作業 |  | 還是 | 去休息？ |
|---|---|---|---|---|

Are you going to do the exercises or take a break?

## PRACTICE

Come up with two kinds of sentences using 還是 — one linking noun phrases and the other linking verb phrases. (Suggested verbs are 還，借，教，學，吃，喝，看，說，搞，做，and 用.)

# III. Using 都 (Dōu) to Sum Up Objects

You have already learned that the adverb 都 can be used to modify the subject in a sentence. For example: 我們都喝中國茶。 (We all drink Chinese tea.) However, if the items being modified are objects of a sentence, then the objects should either be placed before or after the subject and 都 should still be placed before the verb.

## A. Placing Objects before the Subject

|  | Object 1 | Object 2 (...) | Subject | 都 | Verb |
|---|---|---|---|---|---|
| Positive: | 中國茶， | 日本茶 | 我 | 都 | 喝。 |

I drink both Chinese and Japanese tea.

| Negative: | 中國茶， | 日本茶 | 我 | 都 | 不喝。 |
|---|---|---|---|---|---|

I drink neither Chinese tea nor Japanese tea.

| Question: | 中國茶， | 日本茶 | 你 | 都 | 喝嗎？ |
|---|---|---|---|---|---|

Do you drink both Chinese and Japanese tea?

## B. Placing Objects after the Subject

|  | Subject | Object 1 | Object 2 (...) | 都 | Verb |
|---|---|---|---|---|---|
| Positive: | 我 | 中國茶， | 日本茶 | 都 | 喝。 |
| Negative: | 我 | 中國茶， | 日本茶 | 都 | 不喝。 |
| Question: | 你 | 中國茶， | 日本茶 | 都 | 喝嗎？ |

Can you tell what is wrong with the following two sentences?

我都不喝中國茶。 When 都 modifies the subject in this sentence, the subject must be plural, NOT singular.

都我們不喝中國茶。 都 is an adverb and can never be placed before the subject.

## PRACTICE

Find a partner and create a short dialogue in which one person asks a question using one of the 都 patterns above and the other person answers. Then switch roles and do it again. Make sure 都 is placed in the right position! For example:

> A: 你中文書，日文書都看嗎？

> B: 我看中文書，不看日文書。 or
> 我中文書，日文書都不看。

## IV. Using the Verb 有 (Yǒu)

Up to this point, you have learned two types of verbs: the verb 是 and the action verb. Now we are going to learn the verb 有, which means "to have." 有 is a special verb, because it has its own negation word, 沒. In the negative sentence, you can omit 有 entirely or you can say 沒有. Do not use 不.

*Enjoying wine and appetizers.*

|  | Subject | 有 | Object |
|---|---|---|---|
| Positive: | 我們 | 有 | 中文書。 |
|  | We have Chinese books. | | |
| Negative: | 我們 | 沒(有) | 中文書。 |
|  | We don't have Chinese books. | | |
| Question: | 你們 | 有 | 中文書 嗎？ |
|  | Do you have Chinese books? | | |

## PRACTICE

Think of a question using 有, and then answer it in both the positive and negative forms. For extra practice, find a partner and do this question-and-answer exercise in class.

# 語音複習(Yǔyīn Fùxí)
# Pronunciation Review

## I. Review of Initials and Finals

The initials and finals selected for review here are those that have not been reviewed in the previous lessons. The initials in parentheses (although reviewed in previous lessons) are used for combination practice with the finals reviewed in this lesson.

**Initials:**    f    s    (p    m    z    c    j    q    x)

**Finals:**    ing    ün    üan    ueng    iang

## II. Phonetic Spelling Rules
### A. Special "Homorganic" Final *-i*

*s(i)*    Remember that the *-i* after the initial *s* represents the homorganic final — "homorganic" because it is articulated in the same position as the preceding consonant. This is the same *-i* as after initials *z* and *c*, similar to *-i* after initials *zh*, *ch*, *sh* and *r*, and very different from *i* after any initials other than these seven.

### B. When There Are No Initials

*-ing* → *ying*    When *-ing* is not preceded by an initial consonant, add *y: ying*.

| | | |
|---|---|---|
| *-iang* → *yang* | | When *-iang* is not preceded by an initial consonant, *i* changes to *y*: *yang*. |
| *ueng* → *weng* | | The final *-ueng* does not occur with an initial consonant. Thus it is always spelled "weng." (Of the four tones, *weng* only has characters that take the first, third, and fourth tones — never the second tone.) |
| *ün* → *yun* | | When the final *-ün* is not preceded by an initial consonant, add *y*: *yun*. The umlaut is also omitted, just as it is in all other occurrences of this final. |
| *üan* → *yuan* | | When the final *üan* is not preceded by an initial consonant, add *y* and omit the umlaut: *yuan*. |

Note that the umlaut is retained ONLY in the syllables *nü, lü, nüe* and *lüe*. It is written in the BASE FORM finals to indicate the distinction between this high FRONT rounded vowel and the high BACK rounded vowel *u* (with no umlaut). But in the spellings of full syllables, the palatal initials *j, q, x* (see below), and the palatal semivowel *y* indicate this distinction and the umlaut can thus be dropped.

## C. When There Are Initials

| | |
|---|---|
| *ün* | The only initial consonants that can precede *-ün* are *j, q* and *x*: *jun, qun, xun*. |
| *üan* | The only initial consonants that can precede *-üan* are *j, q* and *x*: *juan, quan, xuan*. |

## III. Tone Combination Review

| | 1st Tone | 2nd Tone | 3rd Tone | 4th Tone |
|---|---|---|---|---|
| **1st Tone:** | yīngzī | yīngxióng | yīngwǔ | yīngjùn |
| **2nd Tone:** | yuánxiān | yuánxíng | yuánběn | yuánzhuàng |
| **3rd Tone:** | xiǎngtōng | xiǎnglái | xiǎngfǎ | xiǎngyòng |
| **4th Tone:** | sìfāng | sìhuán | sìhǎi | sìyuè |

寫漢字(Xiě Hànzì)

# Character Writing

## Key Radical Presentation

The three dot water radical (on the left):    氵

The grass radical (on top):    艹

The roof radical (on top):    宀

| Character | Practice with Chinese Characters |
|---|---|
| 歡 請 啡 喝 酒 咖 茶 客 坐 氣 進 迎 | |

 課堂練習 (Kètáng Liànxí)

## In-Class Exercises

## 🎧📖 TASK 1. PINYIN EXERCISES

### A. Distinguishing Tones

Listen carefully to the following syllables and mark the correct tones below. Practice saying the tones correctly, making sure that you can recognize the differences among each of the four tones.

*Alaric Radosh*

1. fu        fu        fu        fu

2. ci        ci        ci        ci

3. yuan       yuan      yuan      yuan

4. ying        ying       ying       ying

5. su        su        zu        cu

## B. Distinguishing Sounds

Listen carefully to the following pairs of syllables; note the differences between them, and try to pronounce them correctly.

### Initials

1. fú     wú          2. sī     zī

3. cuō    suō         4. pó     fó

5. mó     fó

### Finals

1. jīng     jīn        2. quán     qún

3. xiǎng    xǐng      4. xiàn     xiàng

5. wēng    wēn

## C. Pronunciation Practice

Practice your tones and pronunciation by listening to a native speaker on your audio CD or multimedia CD-ROM.

1. huānyíng      qǐng jìn

    Huānyíng, huānyíng, dàjiā qǐng jìn.

*Making dumplings, a household event.*

2. kèqi            lǐwù
   Nǐmen tài kèqi, dài zhème hǎo de lǐwù.

3. xiè shénme       yìdiǎn xiǎoyìsi
   Xiè shénme, zhè shì wǒmen de yìdiǎn xiǎo yìsi.

4. Yīngguó chá     Rìběn chá
   Yīngguó chá, Rìběn chá, wǒmen dōu yǒu.

## D. Sight-reading

Read aloud the following phrases. Your sight-reading skills will be measured by your speed and accuracy. (For multimedia CD-ROM only.)

1. Qiānlǐ sòng émáo, lǐ qīng qíngyì zhòng.

2. Fēngshèng de jiǔxí, bu zuì bu sàn.

3. Yīng yǒu jìn yǒu, jìn huān ér sàn.

## TASK 2. GRAMMAR STRUCTURE PRACTICE

### A. Error Identification

Can you tell incorrect sentences from correct ones? Circle all the incorrect items and provide explanations for your choices.

1. 我都不喝紅酒白酒。
2. 我常常喝茶還是咖啡。
3. 這是很好糖。
4. 您吃什麼？點心還是水果？

5. 你們有中國的茶還是日本的茶？

6. 我不常常看書。

## B. Dialogue Construction

Use the following three groups of words to construct a dialogue according to the model provided below.

Example:          英文書         法文書           中文書

A: 你借英文書還是法文書？

B: 英文書，法文書我都不借。你有中文書嗎？

A: 我沒有中文書。

1. 中國茶      日本茶       英國茶

2. 法國咖啡    英國咖啡     日本咖啡

3. 中文書      中文筆記     英文筆記

4. 水果        點心         水

5. 紅糖        白糖         水果糖

## TASK 3. PARAPHRASING

To find out how well you know the grammar and vocabulary covered so far, follow the steps below.

**Step 1.** Translate the following dialogues into Chinese, using your own words. To check your pronunciation, listen to the dialogue on your CD.

**Welcoming Guests**

A:     Grandpa Mao, welcome, welcome! Come in, come in.

B:     How are you? This is your coffee.

A:     You are too polite. You brought such a nice gift. Thank you very much.

B:     No need to thank me; it's just a small token. Don't mention it.

**Entertaining Guests**

A:     Please sit down. What do you want to drink: coffee or tea?

B:     Neither, thank you. Do you have water?

A:    Yes. Please have some water.

B:    Thank you.

A:    You are welcome.

**Step 2.** Now that you have familiarized yourself with the dialogue, be creative! Think of other words you have learned so far that might work in this dialogue. For example, instead of saying, "This is your coffee," you could say, "This is your tea." Try to substitute as many words as possible without disrupting the structure of the dialogue.

## TASK 4. PICTURE DESCRIPTION

**Topic:** A hostess is welcoming her guests, who have just arrived for the weekend. She invites them to come inside and offers them a choice of drinks. The guests give the hostess a small gift and thank her for her hospitality. The hostess has prepared a wonderful feast, and the guests are very appreciative.

1.

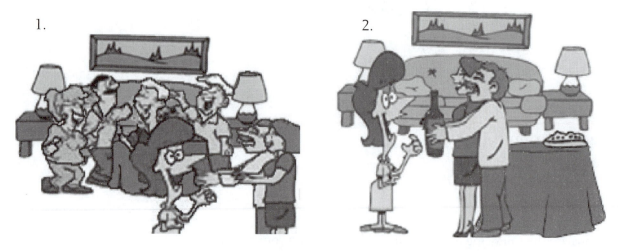

2.

3.

# 8

# 問姓名

# Asking Someone's Name

> **In this lesson you will:**
> ▓ Review pinyin combinations and try a few tongue twisters.
> ▓ Review strokes and stroke order in writing Chinese characters.
> ▓ Learn vocabulary you will need to introduce yourself to others.
> ▓ Inquire politely about someone you have just met.

(Starting in this lesson the textbook will not include pinyin for this section. If you would still like to refer to the pinyin, please see your CD-ROM, which will continue to include it.)

Wu Wende goes to a reception organized by the Chinese Department.

吳文德： 請問，您貴姓？

胡老師： 我姓胡。

吳文德： 您是胡老師？您是林笛的老師，對嗎？

胡老師： 對，我教她中文。你呢？你叫什麼名字？

吳文德： 我的中文名字叫吳文德。姓吳，叫文德。
我的中國朋友都叫我小吳。

胡老師： 你是我們學校東亞系的學生，是嗎？

吳文德： 是，我學漢語，也學日語。

胡老師： 你漢語很不錯。

吳文德： 哪裡，哪裡。我認識很多中國留學生，
我常常說漢語。 但是，我不懂中國文化，
常鬧笑話。大家常常開玩笑，
叫我小華(笑話)。

胡老師： 你們漢語老師是誰？

吳文德： 是張老師。您認識嗎？

胡老師： 老張。認識，認識。

吳文德： 他還不老啊！

胡老師： (laughs)我知道。 但是，他教書經驗豐富。
所以，我們都叫他老張。

吳文德： 張老師是哪國人？

胡老師： 是中國人。

吳文德： 他是中國哪裡人？北京人還是上海人？

胡老師： 北京人，上海人他都不是。他是四川人。
你很好奇啊。 常常問問題，對嗎？

吳文德： 對不起，我的問題太多，是嗎？

胡老師： 沒關係。

生詞表 (Shēngcí Biǎo)
# Vocabulary

| | Character | Pinyin | Part of Speech | English Definition |
|---|---|---|---|---|
| 1. | 姓名 | xìngmíng | n. | name |
| 2. | *貴*姓 | guìxìng | n. | (formal) (What is) your honorable surname? |
| | 貴 | | adj. | expensive; honorable |
| | 姓 | | n. | surname |
| | | | v. | to be surnamed |
| 3. | *對 | duì | adj. | correct, right |
| 4. | *叫 | jiào | v. | to call; to be called |
| 5. | *名*字 | míngzi | n. | given name |
| | 字 | zì | n. | Chinese character; "word" in Western languages |
| 6. | 小 | xiǎo | pref. & adj. | (placed before a personal n.); small, little |
| 7. | 學*校 | xuéxiào | n. | school |
| 8. | 系 | xì | n. | department in an academic setting |
| 9. | *漢*語 | Hànyǔ | n. | the Chinese language |
| 10. | 不錯 | búcuò | adj. | not bad, pretty good, just fine |
| | *錯 | | adj. | wrong |
| 11. | 哪裡 | nǎlǐ | phr. | where |
| 12. | 認*識 | rènshi | v. | to be acquainted with, to be familiar with |
| 13. | 留學生 | liúxuésheng | n. | foreign student (who is studying in a country other than his/her own) |
| | 學生 | | n. | student |
| | 留 | | v. | to stay, to stay behind |
| 14. | 懂 | dǒng | v. | understand, know |
| 15. | 文化 | wénhuà | n. | culture |

| 16. | 鬧笑*話 | nào xiàohua | *v. obj.* | to make a fool of oneself |
| | 鬧 | | *v.* | to make noise; to go in for; to do, make |
| | 笑 | | *v.* | to laugh (at) |
| | 話 | | *n.* | word, speech |
| | 笑話 | | *n.* | joke |
| 17. | 開玩笑 | kāi wánxiào | *v. obj.* | to joke, make fun of |
| 18. | *知*道 | zhīdào | *v.* | to know (a fact); to know that... |
| 19. | 經驗 | jīngyàn | *n.* | experience |
| 20. | 豐富 | fēngfù | *adj.* | rich, abundant |
| 21. | 所以 | suǒyǐ | *conj.* | so, therefore |
| 22. | 哪*國人 | nǎ guó rén | *phr.* | which country |
| | 哪 | | *interrog.* | which |
| | 國 | | *n.* | nation, country |
| | 人 | | *n.* | person, human being |
| 23. | 好奇 | hàoqí | *adj.* | curious/inquisitive |
| 24. | 對不起 | duìbuqǐ | *phr.* | I am sorry, I beg your pardon (lit., unable to "face" someone) |
| 25. | 沒關係 | méi guānxi | *phr.* | never mind, it doesn't matter |

## 專有名詞 (Zhuānyǒu Míngcí) Proper Nouns

| 1. | 東亞 | Dōngyà | East Asia |
| 2. | 日語 | Rìyǔ | the Japanese language |
| 3. | 小華 | Xiǎo Huá | a given name |
| 4. | 北京 | Běijīng | Beijing, the capital of China |
| 5. | 上海 | Shànghǎi | Shanghai, a large city in east China |
| 6. | 四川 | Sìchuān | Sichuan, a province in west China |

## 補充詞彙 (Bǔchōng Cíhuì) Supplementary Vocabulary

| 1. | 外語 | wàiyǔ | *n.* | foreign language |
| 2. | 美國 | Měiguó | *n.* | U.S.A. |

| | | | |
|---|---|---|---|
| 3. 明白 | míngbai | *v.* | to understand |
| 4. 告訴 | gàosu | *v.* | to tell |
| 5. 講 | jiǎng | *v.* | to speak, to say |
| 6. 有意思 | yǒu yìsi | *phr.* | very interesting |
| 7. 非常抱歉 | fēicháng bàoqiàn | *phr.* | my apologies |

## 口頭用語 (Kǒutóu Yòngyǔ) Spoken Expressions

1. 哪裡, 哪裡     nǎlǐ, nǎlǐ

   This phrase is frequently used as a modest response to a compliment.

## 詞彙注解 (Cíhuì Zhùjiě) Featured Vocabulary

### 1. 漢語 *(Hànyǔ) vs.* 中文 *(Zhōngwén)*

漢語 is frequently used to describe Chinese in a general sense (usually referring to Chinese as a second language). For example: 學漢語, 漢語書.

中文 has a similar meaning to 漢語 and can be used in any of the same places that 漢語 is used (e. g., 學中文, 中文書). It is different in

*Ringing the temple bell brings good fortune.*

that it can also be used to describe specific items that involve Chinese writing or language. For example: 中文報 (bào) Chinese newspaper

## 2. 知道 *(Zhīdào) vs.* 認識 *(Rènshi)*

Although both 知道 and 認識 can be translated as "to know," in Chinese they have distinct meanings and serve very different functions.

知道: to know a fact; to know of something. It can be followed by either a noun phrase or a clause. It cannot be used to say that you are personally acquainted with someone.

我知道史老師不是美國人。

I know that Professor Shi is not an American citizen.

CORRECT: 我知道小吳這個人。

xxx INCORRECT: 我知道小吳。xxx

認識: to be acquainted with (someone or something), to know sb./sth. through personal contact. It cannot be followed by a clause.

我認識史老師。        I know Professor Shi personally.

我不認識那個字。      I don't know that word.

xxx INCORRECT: 我認識史老師不是美國人。xxx

## 3. 意思 *(Yìsi)*

小意思 can be used as one of the responses to someone who thanks you for your gift. "Something 是甚麼意思" is used to ask for an explanation of a word or phrase or for clarification of a term. The response to the question usually employs the pattern "...就 (jiù) 是...(的意思)"。

這個字是甚麼意思？ What does this word mean?

## 4. 鬧笑話 *(Nào Xiàohua) vs.* 說笑話 *(Shuō Xiàohua) vs.* 開玩笑 *(Kāi Wánxiào)*

These three verb-object phrases may look similar, but they carry different meanings.

鬧笑話: to make a fool of someone

開玩笑: to have fun with / kid / tease someone

說笑話: to tell jokes

# 語法(Yǔfǎ)
# Grammar

## I. Verbs with Two Objects: Direct and Indirect

There are certain Chinese verbs that can take two objects: a direct and an indirect object. Generally, the direct object (referring to something) receives the action of the verb, while the indirect object (referring to someone) tells who or what was affected by the action. This lesson introduces five two-object verbs: 還 (huán), 叫 (jiào), 教 (jiāo), 借 (jiè), and 問 (wèn).

| Subject | Verb<br>叫／還／借／教／問 | Indirect Object<br>Somebody | Direct Object<br>Something |
|---|---|---|---|
| 我朋友 | 叫 | 我 | 小吳。 |

My friend calls me "Little Wu."

| | | | |
|---|---|---|---|
| (我) | 還 | 你 | 筆記。 |

I will return your notes to you.

| | | | |
|---|---|---|---|
| (我) | 借 | 你們 | 我的筆記。 |

I lend you my notes.

| | | | |
|---|---|---|---|
| 我 | 教 | 他 | 中文。 |

I teach him Chinese.

| | | | |
|---|---|---|---|
| 你 | 去問 | 老師 | 問題嗎？ |

Are you going to ask the teacher a question?

## PRACTICE

Try using 誰 to ask a question concerning an indirect object (e.g., 你借誰筆記？), using 什麼 to ask a question concerning a direct object (e.g., 你還他什麼？), and then using 嗎 to ask a question concerning the entire sentence with direct and indirect object (e.g., 你問老師問題嗎？).

## II. Inquiring about Someone's Nationality and Place of Origin

Do you remember the interrogative pronouns we have learned so far? They are 誰, 誰的, 什麼, 怎麼樣, and 哪兒. 哪 cannot be used independently. In 哪兒 ("where"), the addition of the suffix 一兒 makes it a whole word. In this lesson you see how 哪 combines with the noun 國 to form a word meaning "what country." We also see how 哪裡 combines with (i.e., modifies) the noun 人 to form an expression meaning "a person from where?" Remember that these interrogative expressions, or "question words," occupy the same position in their sentences that the key term does in the answer to the question.

### A. Questions with 哪國 (Nǎ Guó)

Note that 哪國 + Noun serves a dual purpose. If the noun refers to a person, the phrase asks for his or her nationality. If the noun is a product, the phrase asks where it was produced or manufactured.

| Question | | | Response |
|---|---|---|---|
| **Subject** | **是** | **哪國 + Noun** | |
| 他 | 是 | 哪國 人? | 他是(中國)人。 |
| What country is he from? | | | He is from China./He is Chinese. |
| 他的茶 | 是 | 哪國 茶? | 是(德國)茶。 |
| Which country does his tea come from? | | | It comes from Germany. |

### B. Questions with 哪裡 (Nǎli)

哪里 + 人 is used to ask where a person is from.

| Question | | | Response |
|---|---|---|---|
| 你 | 是 | 哪裡人? | 我是中國人。 |
| Where are you from? | | | I am from China. |
| 你 | 是 | 中國哪裡人? | 我是中國四川人。 |
| Which part of China are you from? | | | I am from Sìchuān, China. |

### *Note*

Some people also use 哪兒的人? when asking where a person is from. For example: 你是中國哪兒的人? instead of 你是中國哪裡的人?

*Chris Vee*

## PRACTICE

Talk to the student sitting next to you to find out what city and country they are from, using 哪國 and 哪裡, respectively. You may say the city name in English.

## III. Ways of Asking a Person's Name

### A. Asking for Someone's Surname

#### 1. 您貴姓 *(Nín guìxìng?)*

您貴姓 means "What is your honorable surname, please?" and is a very polite way of asking for someone's surname. It is used to address people who are older than you or just simply to show respect. 貴姓 should only be used in this question format; it is NOT appropriate in a response. Moreover, 貴姓 is usually used with the polite second-person pronoun 您. Also, 您 is often omitted, leaving just 請問，貴姓?

| Question | | Response |
|---|---|---|
| **Subject** | **Verb Object** | |
| (您) | 貴姓? | 我姓胡。 |
| What is your honorable surname, please? | | My surname is Hu. (I am surnamed Hu.) |

#### 2. 姓什麼 *(Xìng shénme?)*

For a "third person" one would ask 他姓什麼? The phrase 姓什麼 can also be used to ask someone's surname in the second person; however, that person should be approximately your age if not younger and /or should have equal or lower social status.

| Question | | | Response |
|---|---|---|---|
| **Subject** | **Verb** | **Object** | |
| 你 | 姓 | 什麼？ | 我姓李。 |
| How are you surnamed? | | | I am surnamed Li. |

## B. Asking for Someone's Given Name or Whole Name

1.  叫什麼 (Jiào shénme?)
2.  叫什麼名字 (Jiào shénme míngzì?)
3.  (Someone) 的名字是什麼 (de míngzi shì shénme?)

The above three patterns are commonly used to inquire about either someone's full name or given name.

| Question | | | Response |
|---|---|---|---|
| **Subject** | **Verb** | **Object** | |
| 她 | 叫 | 什麼？ | 她叫麗莉。 |
| What is she called? | | | Her first name is Lili. |
| 她 | 叫 | 什麼名字？ | 她的名字叫李麗莉。 |
| What is her name? | | | Her name is Li Lili. |
| 她的名字 | 是 | 什麼？ | 她的名字是李麗莉。 |
| What is her name? | | | Her name is Li Lili. |

### *Note*

你叫什麼？, 她叫什麼名字？ or 她的名字叫什麼？ are much more casual, friendly, and direct ways of inquiring about someone's name than (您)貴姓.

---

## ⧉ PRACTICE

Introduce yourself to the class and ask the students next to you for their names and surnames. If you don't know the teacher's name and you ask him or her directly, be sure to ask in a respectful manner.

## IV. Using Polite Language for Communication

The following patterns will come in handy as you start having conversations with Chinese people.

## A. 請問 (May I ask...) is a polite way to ask a question

請問 (qǐngwèn), at the beginning of a sentence, is often used as a polite way to introduce a question. Generally, it is a good idea to use this to get attention, but be careful not to overuse it.

| 請問，　Sentence |  |
|---|---|
| 請問，您是李老師嗎？ | May I ask, are you Professor Li? |
| 請問，您貴姓？ | May I ask, what is your honorable surname? |

## PRACTICE

In a group of students, use 請問 to ask each other questions.

## B. Responding to a Compliment: 哪裡，哪裡

The word 哪裡 (nǎli) is often doubled to respond to compliments. 哪裡 literally means "where?" That is, "Where can the compliment possibly apply in my case?" It is used to show one's modesty and can be translated as "It's nothing," or "You flatter me." Unlike Americans, Chinese people rarely say "Thank you" when flattered or complimented.

For example:

| Compliment | Response |
|---|---|
| 你漢語很不錯。 | 哪裡，哪裡。 |
| Your Chinese is so good! | You flatter me. |

## C. Apologies and Responses

對不起 (duìbùqǐ) literally means "being incapable of facing someone" because you realize you have done something wrong or done something that will cause inconvenience. 沒關係 (méi guānxi) is a common response, meaning "never mind" or "it does not matter." For example:

對不起，我問題太多了。　　I am sorry; I ask too many questions.

沒關係。　　　　　　　　　Never mind (no big deal).

It is NOT used to express sympathy, as one would do with "I am sorry" in English. Therefore, do not use "對不起" in response to 我身體不太好。

## V. Using Compound Verbs

So far we have learned four compound verbs — 教書(jiāoshū), 看書 (kàn-shū), 吃飯 (chīfàn), and 喝酒 (hējiǔ) — which consist of a verb and an object. The compound verb in Chinese usually keeps its object. Note that in translation the compounds' English counterparts are usually verbs.

| Verb | English | Example |
|------|---------|---------|
| 教書 | to teach | 他每天教書。 |
| 看書 | to read | 他常常看書。 |
| 吃飯 | to eat | 他去吃飯。 |
| 喝酒 | to drink | 他喝酒。 |

 語音複習 (Yǔyīn Fùxí)
# Pronunciation Review

## FINAL REVIEW OF PINYIN

This book has covered a total of twenty-one finals and thirty-eight initials as well as their combinations. The following two sections make up our final review of pinyin.

### I. Challenging Sounds

Each of the following pairs has a very similar sound. As a result, students sometimes have trouble pronouncing them correctly. What about you? Let's make sure you can pronounce them like a native speaker.

| | | | |
|------|------|------|------|
| de | te | lin | ling |
| dou | duo | chen | cheng |
| zun | cun | zhou | jiu |
| chi | che | shan | san |
| shao | xiao | xian | xiang |
| nin | lin | zhao | jiao |

### II. Tongue Twisters

Try the following tongue twisters and see how many you can say correctly on your first try. How long does it take you to perfect them? Have fun!

1. Māma mài mǎ bú mài má,          媽媽賣馬不賣麻，

   mǎ màn mā mà, mǎ kuài mā kuā.     馬慢媽罵，馬快媽誇。

*Outside a bus station in Shanghai.*

2. Zhāng Lǎoshī bù zāng,
   chéng lǎoshī bù chén,
   bù zāng lǎoshī bù rènshi bù chén
   lǎoshī.

張老師不髒，
程老師不沉，
不髒老師不認識不沉
老師。

3. Zi ci si jiùshì zi ci si,
   zhi chi shi jiùshì zhi chi shi,
   zi ci si búshì zhi chi shi,
   zhi chi shi yě búshì zi ci si.

Zi ci si 就是 zi ci si,
zhi chi shi 就是 zhi chi shi,
zi ci si 不是 zhi chi shi,
zhi chi shi 也不是 zi ci si.

4. Sì zhī shī shīzi shì sì zhī
   shī shīzi,
   shí zhī shí shīzi shì shí zhī
   shí shīzi,
   shí sì zhī sǐ shīzi shì shí
   sì zhī sǐ shīzi,
   sì shí sì zhī cí shīzi shì
   sì shí sì zhī cí shīzi.

四隻濕獅子是四隻
濕獅子，
十隻石獅子是十隻
石獅子，
十四隻死獅子是十
四隻死獅子，
四十四只瓷獅子是
四十四只瓷獅子。

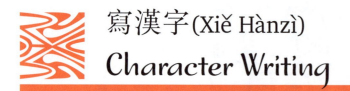

寫漢字(Xiě Hànzì)
# Character Writing

## Key Radical Presentation

The closure radical: 口

The wood radical: 木

| Character | Practice with Chinese Characters |
|---|---|
| 貴 | | | | | | | | |
| 姓 | | | | | | | | |
| 漢 | | | | | | | | |
| 語 | | | | | | | | |
| 教 | | | | | | | | |
| 叫 | | | | | | | | |
| 名 | | | | | | | | |
| 字 | | | | | | | | |
| 認 | | | | | | | | |
| 識 | | | | | | | | |
| 懂 | | | | | | | | |
| 知 | | | | | | | | |
| 道 | | | | | | | | |
| 國 | | | | | | | | |

校
就

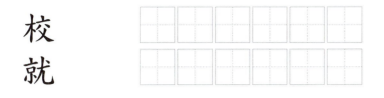

課堂練習(Kètáng Liànxí)
## In-Class Exercises

## 🎧💻 TASK 1. QUESTIONS AND ANSWERS

How well did you understand the text? Check your comprehension by answering the following questions.

1. 林笛的漢語老師姓什麼？

2. 吳文德姓什麼，叫什麼？他的中國朋友都叫他什麼？

3. 吳文德的漢語老師姓什麼？他的老師認識胡老師嗎？

## 💻 TASK 2. GRAMMATICAL STRUCTURE PRACTICE

### A. Matching
Read the following sentences carefully and then match sentences from the left column with those in the right column.

1. 請問，您是胡先生，對嗎？    (a) 不對，她是我們老師！

2. 你們叫我小吳，好嗎？    (b) 他不姓林，他姓史。

3. 她也是這兒的學生，對嗎？    (c) 不，我是李老師。

4. 你叫什麼名字？    (d) 好啊。

5. 你們老師姓林嗎？    (e) 姓吳，叫文德。你呢？

## B. Word Selection

Select the choice that best completes each sentence.

1. 我不_____他。

   a) 知道          b) 認識          c) 懂

2. 我們老師_____。

   a) 叫史          b) 姓史          c) 姓史小英

3. 我不_____你朋友是哪兒人。

   a) 知道          b) 認識          c) 懂

4. 請問，他老師的_____是什麼？

   a) 貴姓          b) 叫          c) 名字

## C. Scrambled Words

Rearrange the words and phrases to form grammatically correct and meaningful sentences.

**1.** 茶      是      哪國      他的茶

2. 是      人      你      中國      哪裡

3. 的      叫      名字      甚麼      你朋友

4. 人      是      他      我不      哪裡      知道

*Chinese brush painting with flowers and birds.*

Chris Vee

## 📔 TASK 3. PARAPHRASING

How well do you remember the grammar and vocabulary we've covered so far? Test yourself by translating the following sentences into Chinese.

1. A: What is your name?

   B: My Chinese name is Li Wen, (my) surname is Li. My friends call me Xiao Li.

2. A: Excuse me — may I ask what your honorable surname is, please?

   B: My last name is Hu. You may call me Hu Laoshi.

3. A: Where is he from?

   B: I know he is from China, but I don't know which part.

4. A: Your Chinese is very good now.

   B: You flatter me. I know lots of Chinese students, and we frequently speak Chinese.

5. A: Do you often ask your teachers questions?

   B: No, I don't ask questions very often.

6. A: Thank you for teaching me Chinese. But I have too many questions — my apologies.

   B: It is okay.

## 📔 TASK 4. SITUATIONAL DIALOGUE

| | |
|---|---|
| **Setting:** | Outside an office building |
| **Cast:** | Two business associates |
| **Situation:** | Mr. 李 has just started working as an engineer in a computer company and meets one of his business associates, Ms. 張. The two introduce themselves, exchange surnames, and then talk a bit about themselves, their positions, and the company. |

# 9
# 找人
# Looking for Someone

> **In this lesson you will:**
> * Learn to use Chinese numbers.
> * Inquire about a person's whereabouts.
> * Ask for and write Chinese addresses.

Li Lili sits in her dorm room. She hears someone knock at the door.

| | |
|---|---|
| 李麗莉： | 請問，你找誰？ |
| 高朋： | 我找林笛，她住這兒，對嗎？ |
| 李麗莉： | 對，她住這兒。你好，我叫李麗莉，<br>是林笛的室友。 |
| 高朋： | 你好，我是林笛的同學。我姓高，叫朋。 |
| 李麗莉： | 高朋？久聞大名[1]。林笛說你中文很好！ |
| 高朋： | 哪裡，你太客氣了。林笛在嗎？ |
| 李麗莉： | 她現在不在。她在吳文德那兒做作業。 |
| 高朋： | 吳文德住哪兒？ |
| 李麗莉： | 他住學生宿舍九二五樓。 |
| 高朋： | 他住幾層，多少號？ |
| 李麗莉： | 二層二〇九號。 |
| 高朋： | 吳文德的電話號碼是多少？ |
| 李麗莉： | 他的電話是二八六一九五七三。<br>我們的電話在那兒，你用吧。 |
| 高朋： | 謝謝。 |

After the phone call:

高朋：　　　林笛還在吳文德那兒，我現在去找她。
　　　　　　麻煩你了。歡迎你以後去我那兒玩兒。

李麗莉：　　好啊，多一個朋友，多一條路[2]。你
　　　　　　住哪兒？

高朋：　　　我住學生宿舍七五六樓，三層三一二號。
　　　　　　以後你一定來玩兒啊！

李麗莉：　　一定。

Forty-five minutes later, Gao Peng returns.

高朋：　　　真不好意思。我去學生宿舍九二五樓
　　　　　　三層找吳文德，但是他不住在那兒。

李麗莉：　　吳文德不住那層樓。 他的地址是九二
　　　　　　五樓，二層，二〇九號。我們一起去找他吧。

高朋：　　　好啊。我的車在樓下。

Li Lili and Gao Peng are standing in the parking lot.

李麗莉：　　這是你的車嗎？這麼漂亮的德國車。

高朋：　　　不是。我的車是美國車，你看，在那兒。

Chris Vee

## Notes

1. 久聞大名。(Jiǔ wén dà míng.) Literally, "I heard your name long ago." In other words, "Although we have not met, I know who you are."

2. 多一個朋友，多一條路。(Duō yī gè péngyou, duō yī tiáo lù.) Literally, "one more friend, one more road," which means "The more friends you have, the better."

# 生詞表 (Shēngcí Biǎo)
# Vocabulary

| Character | Pinyin | Part of Speech | English Definition |
|---|---|---|---|
| 1.*找 | zhǎo | *v.* | to look for; to call on, visit (someone) |
| 2.*住 | zhù | *v.* | to stay at/in; to dwell in/at |
| 3. 這兒 | zhèr | *n.* | here, this place |
| 4.*室友 | shìyǒu | *n.* | roommate |
| 室 | | *n.* | room |
| 5.*同學 | tóngxué | *n.* | classmate |
| 同 | | *adj.* | same, similar; together with |
| 6. 在 | zài | *prep.* | to be located (in, on, at) |
| 7. 那兒 | nàr | *pron.* | that place |
| 8.*宿*舍 | sùshè | *n.* | dormitory |
| 9.*樓 | lóu | *n.* | multi-storied building |
| 10.*幾 | jǐ | *num.* | several, a few; how many (used mostly when the estimated response is less than 10) |
| 11. 層 | céng | *m.w.* | floor, story (in a building), (lit.) layer |
| 12. 多少 | duōshǎo | *adj.* | how many, how much (esp. when the estimated response is greater than 10) |
| 13.*號 | hào | *m.w.* | number in a series |
| 14. 電話 | diànhuà | *n.* | telephone |
| 15. 號碼 | hàomǎ | *n.* | number |
| 16. 麻煩 | máfan | *v.* | to bother |
| | | *adj.* | trouble |

| | | | |
|---|---|---|---|
| 17. *以*後 | yǐhòu | *n.* | later on, in the future |
| 18. *玩兒 | wánr | *v.* | to have fun; to play; to relax and enjoy oneself |
| 19. 一*定 | yídìng | *adv.* | surely, certainly |
| 20. *地址 | dìzhǐ | *n.* | address |
|      地 | | *n.* | ground, floor |
| 21. 一*起 | yìqǐ | *adv.* | together |
| 22. *車 | chē | *n.* | car, vehicles in general |
| 23. 樓下 | lóu xià | *n.* | downstairs |
| 24. 漂亮 | piàoliang | *adj.* | good-looking, beautiful |
| 25. *個 | gè | *m.w.* | general classifier |

## 專有名詞 (Zhuānyǒu Míngcí) Proper Nouns

| | | |
|---|---|---|
| 1. 高朋 | Gāo Péng | a person's name |
| 2. 德國 | Déguó | Germany |
| 3. 美國 | Měiguó | U. S. A. |

## 補充詞彙 (Bǔchōng Cíhuì) Supplementary Vocabulary

| | | | |
|---|---|---|---|
| 1. 同屋 | tóngwū | *n.* | roommate |
| 2  同事 | tóngshì | *n.* | colleague |
| 3. 賓館 | bīnguǎn | *n.* | hotel |
| 4. 飯店 | fàndiàn | *n.* | hotel |
| 5. 房間 | fángjiān | *n.* | room |
| 6. 樓上 | lóu shàng | *n.* | upstairs |
| 7. 打電話 | dǎ diànhuà | *v.* | to make a phone call |

## 口頭用語 (Kǒutóu Yòngyǔ) Spoken Expressions

1. 麻煩你了(Máfan nǐ le.) This is used to apologize for bothering some-one or to express thanks when someone has done you a favor.

2. 不好意思 (Bù hǎo yìsi.) (I am) embarrassed (to put you to all the trouble).

## 詞彙注解 (Cíhuì Zhùjiě) Featured Vocabulary

### 1. The Verb 住 (Zhù)

The verb 住 means "to live, reside, stay at." It has many different usages.
For example:

住 + **Specific Location:** (more colloquial)

| | | | |
|---|---|---|---|
| 住哪兒 | live where? | 住那兒 | live there |
| 住哪個樓 | live in which building? | 住那個樓 | live in that building |
| 住多少號 | live in which room? | | |

住 + 在 + **Place (country, city, institution or dorm):** (more formal)

| | | | |
|---|---|---|---|
| 住在中國 | live in China | 住在北京 | live in Beijing |
| 住在學校 | live at school | 住在宿舍 | live in a dorm |

The short form of 住在學校 is 住校.

住在 + 一起 **live together**

林笛和李麗莉住在一起。 Lin Di and Li Lili live together.

### 2. 幾層 (Jǐcéng) vs. 哪層 (Nǎcéng)

幾層 and 哪層 ask questions with different meanings; thus, their responses are different.

| Questions | | Responses | |
|---|---|---|---|
| 幾層 How many floors? | | 兩 (liǎng) 層 | There are two floors. |
| 哪層 Which floor? | | 二層 | Second floor. |

## Numerals 0–10

Chinese uses a decimal counting system. For the first eleven digits (0-10), each number has its own character. For example:

| 零 | 一 | 二(兩) | 三 | 四 | 五 | 六 | 七 | 八 | 九 | 十 |
|---|---|---|---|---|---|---|---|---|---|---|
| líng | yī | èr (liǎng) | sān | sì | wǔ | liù | qī | bā | jiǔ | shí |
| zero | one | two | three | four | five | six | seven | eight | nine | ten |

## *Notes*

1. The Chinese number 一 has two different pronounciations: yī and yāo. Yī is more commonly used, while yāo is used by people from Northern China.

2. When two is used before a measure word, use 两, NOT 二.

# Numerals 11–99

For numbers between 11 and 19, there are two characters each. The first character is simply 十, and the second fills the ones position (see Row 1 in the table on page 130 for more examples).

The 10s (20, 30, 40, etc.) also consist of two characters: The first character stands in the tens position, and the second is 十 itself (see Column 1 in the table on page 130 for more examples).

For all other numbers greater than 20 but less than 100, there are three characters: The first character expresses the number of tens, the second character is 十 itself, and the third character expresses the number of ones.

## *Numbers*

|        | X+1 | X+2 | X+3 | X+4 | X+5 | X+6 | X+7 | X+8 | X+9 |
|--------|-----|-----|-----|-----|-----|-----|-----|-----|-----|
|        | 十一 | 十二 | 十三 | 十四 | 十五 | 十六 | 十七 | 十八 | 十九 |
| 20 二十 | 二十一 | 二十二 | 二十三 | 二十四 | 二十五 | 二十六 | 二十七 | 二十八 | 二十九 |
| 30 三十 | 三十一 | 三十二 | 三十三 | 三十四 | 三十五 | 三十六 | 三十七 | 三十八 | 三十九 |
| 40 四十 | 四十一 | 四十二 | 四十三 | 四十四 | 四十五 | 四十六 | 四十七 | 四十八 | 四十九 |
| 50 五十 | 五十一 | 五十二 | 五十三 | 五十四 | 五十五 | 五十六 | 五十七 | 五十八 | 五十九 |
| 60 六十 | 六十一 | 六十二 | 六十三 | 六十四 | 六十五 | 六十六 | 六十七 | 六十八 | 六十九 |
| 70 七十 | 七十一 | 七十二 | 七十三 | 七十四 | 七十五 | 七十六 | 七十七 | 七十八 | 七十九 |
| 80 八十 | 八十一 | 八十二 | 八十三 | 八十四 | 八十五 | 八十六 | 八十七 | 八十八 | 八十九 |
| 90 九十 | 九十一 | 九十二 | 九十三 | 九十四 | 九十五 | 九十六 | 九十七 | 九十八 | 九十九 |

 語法(Yǔfǎ)
# Grammar

## I. Location Words

In this lesson, we will learn how to use the location words 這兒 "here" and 那兒 "there."

### A. Using the Noun/Pronoun + 這兒/那兒 (Zhèr/Nàr)

這兒 and 那兒 frequently follow nouns or pronouns to indicate a location.

| Noun/Pronoun | 這兒/那兒 | |
|---|---|---|
| 她 | 這兒 | (Here at) her place... |
| 我 | 這兒 | My place over here... |
| 史老師 | 這兒 | (Here at) Professor Shi's place... |
| 我 | 那兒 | My place over there... |
| 你哥哥 | 那兒 | Your brother's place over there... |
| 誰 | 那兒 | Whose place |

### B. Using the Interrogative Pronoun 哪兒 (Nǎr)

In Lesson 6, you learned that 哪兒 means "which place/what place" or "where." Like all the other question words covered so far (誰, 甚麼, etc.), it replaces the missing information in a sentence WITHOUT changing the word order. This lesson will focus on "Verb + 哪兒 + Verb Phrase" and its responses.

| | Subject | Verb | Place | Verb Phrase |
|---|---|---|---|---|
| Question: | 她 | 去 | 哪兒? | |

Where is she going?

| | | | | |
|---|---|---|---|---|
| Response: | 她 | 去 | 史老師那兒。 | |

She is going to Professor Shi's place.

| | | | | |
|---|---|---|---|---|
| Question: | 你 | 去 | 哪兒 | 喝咖啡? |

Where do you go for coffee?

| | | | | |
|---|---|---|---|---|
| Response: | 我 | 去 | 我哥哥那兒 | 喝咖啡。 |

I am going to my brother's place to drink coffee.

*Margaret Vee*

*Morning mist dissipating over Huang Shan.*

---

## ❖ PRACTICE

Can you think of any more phrases using "Noun/Pronoun + 這兒/那兒?"
Take a few minutes in class to work with the student sitting next to you. Ask
and respond to each other's questions using the 哪兒 and 這兒 or 那兒
patterns above. For example:

Q: 你去哪兒做作業？           A: 我去同學那兒做作業。

Q: 你來我這兒做作業嗎？       A: 我去你那兒做作業。

For your convenience, we have provided below two groups of words for this
practice.

Location:    朋友　奶奶　室友　醫生　他的老闆

Action:      借筆記　找工作　吃點心　休息　玩兒

## II. Ways to Use the Location Verb 在 (Zài)

在 can function as a verb or a preposition, and it has various meanings.

### A. As a Verb

When used with an object, it means "to be located at/in a certain place." The
subject is a person or a thing.

|  | Subject | 在 | Place |  |
|---|---|---|---|---|
| Question: | 你的車 | 在 | 哪兒? | Where is your car? |
| Response: | 我的車 | 在 | 樓下。 | My car is downstairs. |

| | | | |
|---|---|---|---|
| Question: | 林笛 | 在 | 哪兒? | Where is Lin Di? |
| Question: | 她 | 在 | 吳文德那兒嗎? | Is she at Wu Wende's place (over there)? |
| Response: | 她 | 在 | 吳文德那兒。 | She is at Wu Wende's place (over there). |
| Negative: | 她朋友 | 不在 | 吳文德那兒。 | Her friend is not at Wu Wende's place (over there). |

| | **Subject** | 在 | 嗎? | |
|---|---|---|---|---|
| Question: | 林笛 | 在 | 嗎? | Is Lin Di in? |
| Response: | 她 | 在。 | | She is at home. |
| Negative: | 她朋友 | 不在。 | | Her friend is not at home. |

When used without an object, it means "to be in, to be at home." The subject is usually a person.

## B. As a Preposition

In the structure below, 在 is a preposition. You will learn more about prepositional phrases in the next lesson; for now, all you need to know is that "在 + Location" must be placed before the verb.

| | **Subject** | 在 + Place | **Verb Phrase** |
|---|---|---|---|
| Question: | 林笛 | 在哪兒 | 做作業? |
| | Where is Lin Di doing her homework? | | |
| Response: | 她 | 在吳文德那兒 | 做作業。 |
| | She is at Wu Wende's place, doing her homework. | | |

---

## ⧉ PRACTICE

Use the words given below with 在 (both as a verb or a preposition) to ask a question, and then provide a positive and a negative response.

Location:    宿舍　樓下　中國　朋友家　老師那兒

Action:    用電話　問問題　搞電腦　做生意　喝酒

## III. Brief Introduction to Measure Words

In Chinese, numbers or demonstrative pronouns such as 這 and 那, and interrogative pronouns such as 哪, 幾, and 多少, cannot be used directly to quantify people or things; you always need to use a measure word. Measure words function as a unit to qualify nouns. Measure words are placed after

*Chinese brush painting on eggshells.*

the number or the demonstrative pronoun. Please keep in mind that different nouns take different measure words. In this lesson, you have learned 個 (gè), 號 (hào), and 層 (céng).

個: 個 is the most commonly used measure word. For example: 一個工作, 兩個朋友, 三個老闆, 四個護士, 五個電腦, 六個問題, 七個水果, and so on. Or 這／那／哪／幾個工作, 這／那／哪／幾個朋友, 這／那／哪／幾個老闆, 這／那個電腦, and so on.

號: 號 is frequently used with rooms. For example: 一號教室 Classroom No. 1.

層: 層 is frequently used with 樓. For example: 一層樓 the first floor, or 這／那／哪／幾層樓 (this / that / which / how many floors).

You will learn more about measure words in Lesson 12.

## IV. The Interrogative Words 多少 (Duōshǎo) and 幾 (Jǐ)

When used interrogatively, 多少 and 幾 mean "how many/much." 多少 is used when the number is expected to exceed ten; 幾 is used when the number is expected to be under ten. Remember that when using interrogative words to form questions, the word order remains the same as in a statement.

### A. Estimated Number >10

| Subject | Verb | 多少 | Measure Word | |
|---------|------|------|--------------|---|
| 你 | 住 | 多少 | 號？ | What is your room number? |
| 我 | 住 | 209 | 號。 | I live in room 209. |

## B. Estimated Number <10

| Subject | Verb | 幾 | Measure Word | |
|---------|------|---|--------------|---|
| 你 | 住 | 幾 | 層？ | On which floor do you live? |
| 我 | 住 | 五 | 層。 | I live on the fifth floor. |

### *Note*

The interrogative pronoun 幾 must be followed by a measure word. As for the interrogative pronoun 多少, sometimes the measure word can be omitted.

---

## 🔲 PRACTICE

With a partner, create a short dialogue in which one person asks a question with 幾 or 多少 and the other answers. When you're done, switch roles and do it again! Here are some words you can use to create your own questions:
幾層 幾號 幾個醫生 幾個電腦 多少號
多少朋友 多少學生 多少問題

## V. Chinese Addresses

In Chinese addresses, the largest unit comes first and the other units follow in descending order, with the smallest unit at the end. For example:

Largest ——————————————————————> Smallest

| Largest Unit | 2nd Largest | 3rd ... | 4th... | Smallest Unit |
|--------------|-------------|---------|--------|---------------|
| 北京大學 | 學生宿舍 | 七五六樓 | 三層 | 三〇一五號。 |

---

## 🔲 PRACTICE

Practice saying your own address aloud — first on your own, and then for the whole class. If your address is too difficult to say, make up one in Chinese.

# 寫漢字(Xiě Hànzì)
# Character Writing

## Key Radical Presentation

The hand radical: 扌

The field radical: 士

| Character | Practice with Chinese Characters |
|---|---|
| 找 | |
| 住 | |
| 室 | |
| 同 | |
| 宿 | |
| 舍 | |
| 樓 | |
| 幾 | |
| 號 | |
| 話 | |
| 以 | |
| 後 | |
| 玩 | |
| 定 | |

地
車

課堂練習 (Kètáng Liànxí)

# In-Class Exercises

## TASK 1. QUESTIONS AND ANSWERS

How well did you understand the text? Test your comprehension by answering the following questions.

1. 李麗莉認識不認識高朋？你怎麼知道？

2. 林笛在那兒？她的宿舍有人嗎？有電話嗎？

3. 吳文德是不是高朋室友？你怎麼知道？

## TASK 2. GRAMMATICAL STRUCTURE PRACTICE

### A. Matching

Read the following sentences carefully and then match sentences from the left column with those in the right column.

**Part 1.**

1. 我的筆記在哪兒？    a) 我住三二五號。
2. 李太太，請問，林林在嗎？    b) 我不住學生宿舍。
3. 你住多少號？    c) 在我那兒。
4. 你住學生宿舍嗎？    d) 她不在。

**Part 2.**

1. 她住哪層？    a) 不住，他住學生宿舍。
2. 你哥哥住你爸爸媽媽那兒嗎？    b) 不，他住四層。
3. 你弟弟也住三層嗎？    c) 不在，我們這兒的
    四二九號在三層。
4. 四二九號不在四層嗎？    d) 六層，六零九號。

*A stone statue of a well-known Chinese hero.*

## B. Word Selection

Select the choice that best completes each sentence.

1. 我奶奶不_____。

    a) 住          b) 在            c) 那兒            d) 這兒

2. 你的電話號碼是_____?

    a) 幾          b) 幾號          c) 多少          d) 多少號

3. 我朋友的筆記在_____?

    a) 誰哪兒     b) 誰那兒        c) 你哪兒        d) 你那兒

4. 你住我_____, 好嗎?

    a) 的這兒     b) 這兒          c) 這兒宿舍      d) 的這兒宿舍

5. 他住學生_____。

    a) 的宿舍四層十四號四十四樓

    b) 的宿舍四十四樓十四號四層

    c) 宿舍四十四樓十四號四層

    d) 宿舍四十四樓四層十四號

## TASK 3. PARAPHRASING

How well do you remember the grammar and vocabulary we've covered so far? Test yourself by translating the following sentences into Chinese.

*Nanjing Normal University.*

1. A: Is Wu Wende in?
   B: Sorry, Wu Wende is not in right now. He is still at his friend's place.

2. A: Where is his friend? Do you know the floor and the room number of where his friend lives?
   B: Sorry, I don't know. But I have his friend's phone number. It is 536-3295.

3. A: Where do you live now?
   B: I live in the student dorm, building 845, second floor, number 201.

4. A: Can I use your phone for a second?
   B: It's over there. Go ahead.

## TASK 4. SITUATIONAL DIALOGUE

**Setting:** Outside a residential building

**Cast:** A student and a resident

**Situation:** The student goes to return a book to a friend but knocks on someone else's door by mistake. The student must provide an explanation to the resident and ask for directions to the correct apartment.

# 10
# 介紹朋友
# Introducing Friends

**In this lesson you will:**
- Learn to make introductions.
- Set up a date and time to meet someone.
- Politely accept and decline invitations.

Li Lili and Wu Wende walk across campus. They see a female student standing next to a car.

吳文德： 李麗莉，你看，那是誰？

李麗莉： 怎麼？你不認識她？她是我的老朋友，
姓張，叫子倩。

吳文德： 她名字好聽，車也那麼漂亮。她是不
是我們學校的學生？

李麗莉： 不是。她的男朋友陳大勇是我們學校
的學生。她常常來這兒看陳大勇。

吳文德： 噢,她是陳大勇的女朋友。陳大勇說
她很聰明。

李麗莉： 張子倩，好久不見，你最近怎麼樣？

張子倩： 我還好。李麗莉，你呢？

李麗莉： 馬馬虎虎。(to 吳文德 and 張子倩)
你們不認識吧。來，我給你們介紹
一下兒。
這是吳文德。這是張子倩。

吳文德：　你好，張子倩。

張子倩：　你好。你們現在去哪兒？

李麗莉：　我和吳文德現在去咖啡館，你去不去？

張子倩：　以後吧[1]。我現在去商店買東西。對了，
　　　　　今天晚上你們忙不忙？陳大勇的同學
　　　　　跟我們一起去中國飯館兒吃晚飯，
　　　　　你們有沒有時間來？

李麗莉：　對不起，我今天晚上很忙，沒有時間。

張子倩：　明天呢？我們一起去看電影，放鬆一
　　　　　下兒，好不好？

李麗莉：　我明天上午、下午都有課，非常忙。
　　　　　後天行不行？

張子倩：　行，沒問題。吳文德你來不來？

吳文德：　來，我一定來。

張子倩：　好，後天見。

After 張子倩 leaves:

李麗莉：　吳文德，你不是後天下午很忙嗎？
　　　　　你是不是不好意思跟張子倩說"不"？

吳文德：　不是。跟大家一起去看電影，
　　　　　放鬆放鬆，我當然去啦[2]。

## Notes

1. 以後吧。　Yǐhòu ba. 以後 means in the future. 吧 indicates suggestion.

2. 我當然去啦。　　Wǒ dāngrán qù la. 啦 is placed at the end of the
sentence for emphasis.

# 生詞表 (Shēngcí Biǎo)
# Vocabulary

| | Character | Pinyin | Part of Speech | English Definition |
|---|---|---|---|---|
| 1. | *介*紹 | jièshào | v. | to introduce |
| 2. | 好聽 | hǎotīng | adj. | (lit.) pretty to listen to |
| | 聽 | | v. | to listen |
| 3. | *男 | nán | adj. & n. | male |
| 4. | *女 | nǚ | adj. & n. | female |
| 5. | *最*近 | zuìjìn | adv. | recently, lately |
| 6. | 給 | gěi | v. | to give |
| | | | prep. | to, for, towards |
| 7. | *和 | hé | conj. | and, with |
| 8. | 咖啡*館 | kāfēiguǎn | n. | coffee shop |
| | 館 | | n. | (originally) guesthouse, hotel; (now) a place for eating, gathering, etc. |
| 9. | *商*店 | shāngdiàn | n. | store, department store |
| | 商 | | n. | commerce |
| | 店 | | n. | shop, store |
| 10. | *買*東*西 | mǎi dōngxi | v. obj. | to buy things, to go shopping |
| | 買 | | v. | to buy, purchase |
| | 東西 | | n. | object, thing |
| 11. | *晚上 | wǎnshang | n. | evening |
| | 晚 | | adj. | late (in time) |
| | 上 | | suff. | suffix commonly found in nouns |

| | | | |
|---|---|---|---|
| 12. *跟 | gēn | *prep.* | with, together with |
| 13. *飯館 | fànguǎn(r) | *n.* | restaurant |
| 飯 | | *n.* | cooked rice; meal |
| 14. 晚飯 | wǎnfàn | *n.* | the evening meal, supper, dinner |
| 15. 時間 | shíjiān | *n.* | time |
| 16. *明天 | míngtiān | *n.* | tomorrow |
| 17. 電影 | diànyǐng | *n.* | movie |
| 18. 放鬆 | fàngsōng | *v. comp.* | to relax, loosen |
| 19. 上午 | shàngwǔ | *n.* | morning |
| 20. 下午 | xiàwǔ | *n.* | afternoon |
| 21. 非常 | fēicháng | *adv.* | very, extremely |
| 22. 後天 | hòutiān | *n.* | the day after tomorrow |
| 23. 行 | xíng | *adj.* | to be okay, permissible, feasible |
| 24. 當然 | dāngrán | *adv.* | of course, certainly |

## 專有名詞 (Zhuānyǒu Míngcí) **Proper Nouns**

| | | |
|---|---|---|
| 1. 張子倩 | Zhāng Zǐqiàn | a woman's name |
| 2. 陳大勇 | Chén Dàyǒng | a man's name |

## 補充詞彙 (Bǔchōng Cíhuì) **Supplementary Vocabulary**

| | | | |
|---|---|---|---|
| 1. 圖書館 | túshūguǎn | *n.* | library |
| 2. 書店 | shūdiàn | *n.* | bookstore |
| 3. 早飯 | zǎofàn | *n.* | breakfast |
| 4. 午飯 | wǔfàn | *n.* | lunch |
| 5. 昨天 | zuótiān | *n.* | yesterday |
| 6. 前天 | qiántiān | *n.* | the day before yesterday |
| 7. 以前 | yǐqián | *n* | before, ago |
| 8. 中午 | zhōngwǔ | *n.* | noon |

## 口頭用語 (Kǒutóu Yòngyǔ) Spoken Expressions

1. 噢    ō    Oh! (used when someone realizes something)

2. 怎麼    zěnme    What! What?

3. 老朋友    lǎo péngyou    (lit.) old friend (i.e., someone who has been a friend for a long time)

4. 對了    Duì le!    Oh, right! By the way...

5. 沒問題    Méi wèntí.    No problem.

## 詞彙注解 (Cíhuì Zhùjiě) Featured Vocabulary

### 看(Kàn) Someone vs. 去看(Qù Kàn) / 來看 (Lái Kàn) Someone

看 someone and 去/來看 someone look very similar in Chinese, but they have very different meanings:

1. 看 **Someone** = to watch somebody; to look at somebody
   她的男朋友常常看她。
   Her boyfriend often stares at her.

2. 去/來 **(Place) Someone** = to go/come to visit someone
   她的男朋友常常來(這兒)看她。
   Her boyfriend often comes (here) to see her.

## 語法(Yǔfǎ)
# Grammar

## Review

In Lesson 6, you learned that time phrases in Chinese are nouns and that they can be placed either before or right after the subject. This lesson introduces five more time words: 後天,下午,上午, 明天, and 晚上.

## I. Affirmative-Negative Questions

In this lesson, you are going to learn the affirmative-negative question pattern, which is formed by an affirmative predicate plus a negative predicate without 嗎 at the end. This structure requires a positive/negative response (literally "yes/no"), much like the 嗎 questions in Lessons 3 and 4. But Chinese has no literal "yes/no" response. You simply repeat the main verb or the main adjective in a sentence if you agree and negate the main verb/adjective if you disagree. See the examples below.

## A. With Predicate Verbs

### 1. Verb 是

| Subject | Verb | 不 | Verb | Object |
|---------|------|-----|------|--------|
| 她 | 是 | 不 | 是 | 學生? |

Literally: "Is she a student or not?"

Positive response: 是 or 她是學生。

Negative response: 不是 or 她不是學生。

### 2. Verb 有

| Subject | Verb | 没 | Verb | Object |
|---------|------|-----|------|--------|
| 她 | 有 | 没 | 有 | 課? |

Literally: "Does she have class or not?"

Positive response: 有 or 她有課。

Negative response: 没有 or 她没有課。

### 3. Verb 在

| Subject | Verb | 不 | Verb | Object |
|---------|------|-----|------|--------|
| 她 | 在 | 不 | 在 | 宿舍? |

Literally: "Is she in the dorm or not?"

Positive response: 在 or 她在宿舍。

Negative response: 不在 or 她不在宿舍。

*Classical Chinese architecture in a public park.*

### 4. Action Verb

| Subject | Verb | 不 | Verb | Object |
|---|---|---|---|---|
| 她 | 去 | 不 | 去 | 商店？ |

Literally: "Is she going to the store or not?"

Positive response: 去 or 她去商店。

Negative response: 不去 or 她不去商店。

In addition, the object in each of the preceding four affirmative-negative questions could also be placed between the positive and negative predicate, which is a little more colloquial.

| Subject | Verb | Object | Negative Word | Verb |
|---|---|---|---|---|
| 她 | 是 | 學生 | 不 | 是？ |
| 她 | 有 | 課 | 沒 | 有？ |
| 她 | 在 | 酒吧 | 不 | 在？ |
| 他 | 去 | 商店 | 不 | 去？ |

## Notes

1. When several verbs are used in the same sentence, the affirmative-negative change usually applies to the first verb, unless you want to emphasize the second verb. For example:

   她去不去商店買東西？
   Emphasizing whether or not she is going to the store.

   她去商店買不買東西？
   Emphasizing whether or not she is going to buy anything.

2. 是不是 can also be used before an action verb to confirm whether or not the subject is going to carry out the action. For example:

   她是不是去商店？ "Is it true that she is going to the shop?"

3. Adverbs like "常," "很," and "也," which are used in the 嗎-type question, CANNOT be used in the affirmative-negative question. These adverbs can be used in questions with 是不是.

   CORRECT: 她去不去? or 他也去嗎? or 她是不是也去?

   xxx INCORRECT: 她也去不去? xxx

## B. With Predicate Adjectives

| Subject | Adjective | 不 | Adjective |
|---------|-----------|-----|-----------|
| 你們 | 忙 | 不 | 忙? |

Literally: "Are you busy this evening or not?"

Positive response: 忙 or 我們很忙。

Negative response: 不忙 or 我們不忙。

> CORRECT: 你忙不忙? or 你很忙嗎? or 你是不是很忙?
>
> xxx INCORRECT: 你很忙不忙? xxx

## C. With Tag Questions

| Main Sentence | | | Tag Question |
| Subject | Verb | Object | Adjective 不 Adjective |
|---------|------|--------|------------------------|
| 我們現在一起 | 去 | 咖啡館, | 好 不 好? |

Literally: "Let's go to a coffee shop right now. Is that all right with you?"

Positive response: 好 or 好啊。

Negative Response: 不好 is too abrupt and is rarely used.

Alternative Response: 以後吧。

---

## ❖ PRACTICE

Have a short dialogue in which one person asks an affirmative-negative question and the other provides both positive and negative responses. In your conversation, include the following:

1. Verbs: 做 搞 用 看 吃 喝 學 教 說 來 有

2. Adjectives: 忙 累 難 多 少 認真 漂亮 緊張 麻煩 豐富

3. Tag questions: 好不好 對不對 行不行

4. Adverbs: 常 都 很 也 還

## II. Using the Prepositions 給(Gěi) and 跟(Gēn)

The prepositional phrase consists of the preposition and the noun or noun phrase object of the preposition. In Chinese sentences containing prepositions, a verb phrase usually follows the prepositional phrase. For example, Lesson 9 introduced our first preposition, and its pattern is "+ Location + Verb + Object (at a place do something)."

In addition, when a sentence contains a prepositional phrase, it is usually the preposition — not the verb — that is negated or otherwise modified by an adverb. For example, 不 is placed before the preposition, not the verb, to form a negative sentence. Likewise, affirmative-negative questions are formed by "Prep + 不 + Prep." This lesson introduces two more prepositions:

A. 跟 means "with (somebody)."

B. 給 introduces the recipient of an action. It means "for (somebody)" or "for the benefit of (somebody)."

## A. Using the Preposition 跟

| | Subject | Prepositional Phrase | | Verb Phrase |
|---|---|---|---|---|
| | | 跟 | Somebody | Verb (Object) |
| Affirm.-neg.: | 他 今天 | 跟不跟 | 我們 | 去吃晚飯？ |

Is he going to have dinner with us or not?

| | | | | |
|---|---|---|---|---|
| 嗎-question: | 他 今天 | 跟 | 我們 | 去吃晚飯嗎？ |

Is he going to have dinner with us or not?

| | | | | |
|---|---|---|---|---|
| Positive: | 他 今天 | 跟 | 我們 | 去吃晚飯。 |

He is going to have dinner with us.

| | | | | |
|---|---|---|---|---|
| Negative: | 他 今天 | 不跟 | 我們 | 去吃晚飯。 |

He is not going to have dinner with us.

## B. Using the Preposition 給

| | Subject | Prepositional Phrase | | Verb Phrase |
|---|---|---|---|---|
| | | 嗎 | Somebody | Verb (Object) |
| Affirm.-neg.: | 你 今天 | 給不給 | 我們 | 介紹你的女朋友？ |

Are you going to introduce your girlfriend today or not?

| | | | | |
|---|---|---|---|---|
| 嗎-question: | 你 今天 | 給 | 我們 | 介紹你的女朋友嗎？ |

Are you going to introduce your girlfriend to us today?

| | | | | |
|---|---|---|---|---|
| Positive: | 我 來 | 給 | 你們 | 介紹一下兒我的女朋友。 |

Let me introduce my girlfriend to you.

Negative:    我 今天　不給　　你們　　　介紹我的女朋友。 明天吧。

I will not introduce my girlfriend to you today. Maybe tomorrow.

---

## PRACTICE

Use each of the following prepositions and the given verb phrase to ask a question and provide a positive and negative response to it.

1. 在：工作 上課 做作業
2. 給：介紹 買禮物 做晚飯 打電話
3. 跟：去飯館 一起玩兒 看電影

## III. Topic-Comment Sentences (Cont'd.)

Lesson 4 briefly discussed a few topic-comment sentences, such as 您太太身體好嗎 and 他們工作順利嗎？ Each of these sentences consists of a subject (as a topic) and a sentence that provides more information on the subject (as a comment). The comment can be a simple sentence or a series of sentences. Sentences of this type are called Topic-Comment Sentences. For example:

### A. With One Comment

|  | Subject | Sentence |
|---|---|---|
| Positive: | 他 | 工作很忙。 |

Literally, "He is very busy, in terms of his work."

|  | Subject | Sentence |
|---|---|---|
| Negative: | 他 | 身體不太好。 |

Literally, "He is not very good, in terms of his health."

|  | Subject | Sentence |
|---|---|---|
| Question: | 她 | 人聰明嗎？ |

Literally, "Is she, as a person, smart?"

### B. With More Than One Comment

| Subject | Sentence 1 | Sentence 2 | Sentence 3 |
|---|---|---|---|
| 她 | 人聰明， | （她）車也漂亮， | （她）名字也這麼好聽。 |

Literally, "She is smart, her car is pretty, and her name is also very nice."

*Chris Vee*

## PRACTICE

Here are some words you could use as topics when forming a topic-comment sentence: 中文課, 我們的老師, 我們學校, 我的老闆, 那個飯館. Can you add some comments when creating sentences of your own?

A new student has just arrived at your school. Talk to your friends about this person, using the topic-comment construction.

## IV. 和 (Hé) as a Conjunction

The Chinese conjunction 和 is very different from the English conjunction "and." 和 can ONLY be used to link nouns or certain other constructions, while the English "and" can link words belonging to any part of speech and even whole clauses or sentences.

| Nominal 1 | | Nominal 2 |
| --- | --- | --- |
| **Noun/Pronoun 1  和** | | **Noun/Pronoun 2** |

我　　　　　和　　吳文德　　　去喝咖啡。

Wu Wende and I are going to get a cup of coffee.

| Nominal 1 | | Nominal 2 |
| --- | --- | --- |
| **Verb-Object 1** | **和** | **Verb-Object 2** |

喝咖啡　　　和　　吸烟　　　　都不好。

Drinking coffee and smoking are bad for your health.

## *Note*

1. The verb-object construction can sometimes act as a noun phrase, much like the gerund (-ing) form in English. Take the sentence 喝咖啡和吸烟都不好 for example, where the verb-object constructions 喝咖啡 and 吸烟 function as nominal constructions in the syntax of the larger sentence.

2. Never place 和 between two clauses nor use it to join verbs. It can only join nouns or phrases that function as nominal constructions in a larger sentence.

   > xxx INCORRECT: 他來美國，和我去中國。 xxx
   >
   > CORRECT: 他來美國，我去中國。
   >
   > xxx INCORRECT: 他喝咖啡和吸烟。　xxx
   >
   > CORRECT: 他喝咖啡也吸烟。

   In this sentence, 喝咖啡 and 吸烟 are verb phrases functioning as entire predicates.

---

## ◪◩ PRACTICE

Make a sentence with 和 that connects two verb-object phrases.

## V. Rhetorical Questions

A rhetorical question is a statement formulated as a question. It is usually used to make a point or produce a certain effect. 不/不是 and the interrogative particle 嗎 together make a rhetorical question. For example:

## A. Subject + 不 + Predicate Verb (+ Object) + 嗎

你不跟我們一起去酒吧嗎？

Aren't you going to the bar with us?

(I thought you were going but now you are not. What is going on?)

## B. Subject + 不是 + Predicate Adjective + 嗎

你不是下午很忙嗎？

Aren't you supposed to be busy this afternoon?

(I thought you were very busy this afternoon, but you don't seem to be that busy.)

*Chris Vee*

*A wooden statuette of a Happy Buddha.*

 **PRACTICE**

Try using predicate verbs and adjectives to form at least two of your own rhetorical questions.

# 部首小結 (Bùshǒu Xiǎojié)
# Summary of Radicals

Chinese characters have over two hundred radicals. These are useful when you need to look up the words in the dictionary. So far we have covered twenty-five of them. Due to limited space, we will cover only the most commonly used radicals in the following table.

## Table of Key Radicals

| | Radical | Number of Strokes | Definition | Character |
|---|---|---|---|---|
| 1. | 亻 | 2 | man (erect) | 你 |
| 2. | 力 | 2 | strength | 努 |
| 3. | 阝 | 2 | ear | 都 |
| 4. | 言 | 7 | speech | 認 |
| 5. | 口 | 3 | mouth | 吃 |
| 6. | 土 | 3 | earth | 地 |
| 7. | 大 | 3 | great | 大 |
| 8. | 女 | 3 | female | 好 |
| 9. | 宀 | 3 | roof | 字 |
| 10. | 彳 | 3 | double-man radical | 很 |
| 11. | 忄 | 3 | heart | 忙 |
| 12. | 扌 | 3 | hand | 搞 |
| 13. | 糹 | 6 | silk | 經 |
| 14. | 氵 | 3 | water | 酒 |
| 15. | 艹 | 3 | grass | 茶 |
| 16. | 辶 | 3 | running | 進 |
| 17. | 食 | 8 | food | 飯 |
| 18. | 馬 | 10 | horse | 驗 |
| 19. | 門 | 8 | door | 問 |
| 20. | 弓 | 3 | bow | 張 |
| 21. | 日 | 4 | sun | 是 |
| 22. | 木 | 4 | wood, tree | 校 |
| 23. | 月 | 4 | moon, month | 朋 |

| | Radical | Number of Strokes | Definition | Character |
|---|---|---|---|---|
| 24. | 貝 | 7 | cowry shell | 貴 |
| 25. | 衤 | 5 | clothing | 衫 |
| 26. | 牛 | 4 | ox | 物 |
| 27. | 車 | 4 | vehicle | 車 |
| 28. | 田 | 5 | field | 男 |
| 29. | 目 | 5 | eye | 看 |
| 30. | 禾 | 5 | grain | 程 |
| 31. | 金 | 8 | gold, metal | 錯 |
| 32. | 竹 | 6 | bamboo | 筆 |
| 33. | 米 | 6 | rice | 糖 |
| 34. | 頁 | 9 | page | 順 |

## 課堂練習 (Kètáng Liànxí)

## In-Class Exercises

## 🎧 TASK 1. QUESTIONS AND ANSWERS

How well did you understand the text? Check your comprehension by answering the following questions.

1. 張子倩是誰？張子倩來學校做什麼？

2. 吳文德認識不認識張子倩和她的男朋友？李麗莉呢？

3. 現在他們三個人做什麼呢？今天晚上呢？

4. 明天張子倩和李麗莉要做什麼？還有誰跟他們一起去？

# 📖 TASK 2. GRAMMATICAL STRUCTURE PRACTICE

## A. Fill in the Blanks

Fill in the blanks by taking a word from below and placing it into the appropriate place in the sentence. When you're done, translate the sentence into English.

認識不認識　行不行　跟

去不去　　　給　　　是不是

1. 你明天下午（ ＿＿＿＿＿ ）有中文課？
2. 那是誰？你（ ＿＿＿＿＿ ）他？
3. A:你來（ ＿＿＿＿＿ ）我介紹一下兒，好嗎？
   B:好啊。來，你（ ＿＿＿＿＿ ）我來。
4. A:今天下午我們去咖啡館放鬆一下兒，你
   （ ＿＿＿＿＿ ）？
   B:今天下午我很忙。明天下午（ ＿＿＿＿＿ ）？

## B. Error Identification

Can you tell incorrect sentences from correct ones? Circle all the incorrect items and provide explanations for your choices.

1. 你去不去那兒買東西嗎？
2. 她常常工作順利不順利？
3. 她人聰明，和學習也很好。
4. 他跟我們去不去喝咖啡。
5. 我去飯館吃飯跟他們。
6. 我介紹你我們老師。他姓張。

# 📖 TASK 3. PARAPHRASING

How well do you remember the grammar and vocabulary we've covered so far? Test yourself by translating the following sentences into Chinese. To find out how well you know the grammar and vocabulary covered so far, follow the steps below.

1. A: Do you know each other?
   B: No, we don't. Would you please introduce us?

*Huang Shan in early afternoon.*

2.  A: We are going to the store to do some shopping. Are you going?

    B: Maybe later. Right now I'm going to do my homework. I don't have any time.

3.  A: This evening I am going to a Chinese restaurant for dinner with some friends. Do you want to come?

    B: With a pretty girl like you? Of course! I'll see you tonight.

4.  A: Do you have classes in the morning?

    B: I don't have classes in the morning, but I have classes in the afternoon.

5.  A: Are you going to the movie?

    B: Yes, do you want to go with us and relax for a little while?

## TASK 4. SITUATIONAL DIALOGUE

**Setting:** A restaurant

**Cast:** Mr. Li and Ms. Lin

**Situation:** Mr. Li and Ms. Lin are business acquaintances. They are eating dinner at a fancy restaurant when someone stops by to talk to Mr. Li. Mr. Li introduces him as an old friend from China, and they take a moment to talk about his family, his old home, his former profession, etc.

# Appendix:

# List of Grammar Points

# Chinese-English Vocabulary Glossary, Arranged Alphabetically by Pinyin

This vocabulary glossary includes all regular vocabulary, spoken expressions, and supplementary vocabulary. An "s" after a lesson number means that the word comes from a supplementary vocabulary list. For proper nouns, see the Glossary of Proper Nouns.

| Simplified | Traditional | Pinyin | Part of Speech | Definition | Lesson |
|---|---|---|---|---|---|
| 啊 | 啊 | a | s.e. | This is used at the end of a sentence for emphasis. | 5 |
| 唉 | 唉 | ài | s.e. | the sound of a sigh | 6 |
| 哎呀 | 哎呀 | Āiyā! | s.e. | a phrase used to express surprise | 7 |
| 阿姨 | 阿姨 | āyí | n. | auntie (mother's sister); used to address a woman of one's parents' generation | 3 |
| 吧 | 吧 | ba | part. | used at the end of a sentence to indicate uncertainty, to make a suggestion, etc. | 6 |
| 八 | 八 | bā | num. | eight | 9s |
| 爸爸 | 爸爸 | bàba | n. | dad, daddy | 3 |
| 白 | 白 | bái | adj. | white | 7 |
| 白酒 | 白酒 | báijiǔ | n. | a clear distilled liquor; recently also white wine | 7 |
| 笔 | 筆 | bǐ | n. | pen | 6 |
| 别 | 別 | bié | adv. | don't (do sth.); (ask sb.) not to (do sth.) | 7 |
| 别客气 | 別客氣 | Bié kèqi. | s.e. | You don't have to be so polite with me. | 7 |
| 笔记 | 筆記 | bǐjì | n. | notes | 6 |

163

| Simplified | Traditional | Pinyin | Part of Speech | Definition | Lesson |
|---|---|---|---|---|---|
| 饼干 | 餅乾 | bǐnggān | n. | cracker, biscuit | 7s |
| 宾馆 | 賓館 | bīnguǎn | n. | hotel | 9s |
| 不 | 不 | bù | adv. | not, no | 4 |
| 不错 | 不錯 | búcuò | adj. | not bad, pretty good, just fine | 8 |
| 不好意思 | 不好意思 | Bù hǎo yìsi | s.e. | (I am) embarrassed (to put you to all the trouble). | 9 |
| 不谢 | 不謝 | Búxiè. | s.e. | You are welcome. | 7s |
| 不用谢 | 不用謝 | Bú yòng xiè | s.e. | Don't mention it. | 7s |
| 层 | 層 | céng | m.w. | floor, story (in a building), (lit.) layer | 9 |
| 茶 | 茶 | chá | n. | tea | 7 |
| 常 | 常 | cháng | adv. | often, frequently | 7 |
| 车 | 車 | chē | n. | car, vehicles in general | 9 |
| 吃 | 吃 | chī | v. | to eat | 7 |
| 吃饭 | 吃飯 | chīfàn | v. obj. | to eat | 7s |
| 词典 | 詞典 | cídiǎn | n. | dictionary | 6s |
| 聪明 | 聰明 | cōngmíng | adj. | smart, intelligent | 6 |
| 错 | 錯 | cuò | adj. & n. | error; wrong | 6s, 8 |
| 打电话 | 打電話 | dǎ diànhuà | v. obj. | to make a phone call | 9s |
| 带 | 帶 | dài | v. | to carry, bring, take | 7 |
| 大夫 | 大夫 | dàifu | n. | medical doctor | 5s |
| 大家 | 大家 | dàjiā | n. | everybody | 4s |
| 当然 | 當然 | dāngrán | adv. | of course, certainly | 10 |
| 但是 | 但是 | dànshì | conj. | but, however | 4 |
| 的 | 的 | de | part. | a particle used to indicate possession, similar to the English "apostrophe + s" | 5 |
| 地 | 地 | dì | n. | ground, floor | 9 |
| 电 | 電 | diàn | n. & adj. | electricity; electronic | 5 |
| 店 | 店 | diàn | n. | shop, store | 10 |

| Simplified | Traditional | Pinyin | Part of Speech | Definition | Lesson |
|---|---|---|---|---|---|
| 电话 | 電話 | diànhuà | n. | telephone | 9 |
| 点心 | 點心 | diǎnxin | n. | snacks, light refreshments | 7 |
| 电影 | 電影 | diànyǐng | n. | movie | 10 |
| 弟弟 | 弟弟 | dìdi | n. | younger brother | 3s |
| 地址 | 地址 | dìzhǐ | n. | address | 9 |
| 懂 | 懂 | dǒng | v. | to understand | 6 |
| 都 | 都 | dōu | adv. | all, both | 4 |
| 对 | 對 | duì | adj. | correct, right | 8 |
| 对不起 | 對不起 | duìbuqǐ | phr. | I am sorry, I beg your pardon (lit., unable to "face" someone) | 8 |
| 对了 | 對了 | Duì le! | s.e. | Oh, right! By the way... | 10 |
| 多 | 多 | duō | adj. | many, much (opposite of 少) | 5 |
| 多少 | 多少 | duōshǎo | adj. | how many, how much (esp. when the estimated response is greater than 10) | 9 |
| 多谢 | 多謝 | Duōxiè. | s.e. | Many thanks. | 7s |
| 二 | 二 | èr | num. | two | 9s |
| 饭 | 飯 | fàn | n. | cooked rice; meal | 10 |
| 饭店 | 飯店 | fàndiàn | n. | hotel | 9s |
| 房间 | 房間 | fángjiān | n. | room | 9s |
| 放松 | 放鬆 | fàngsōng | v. comp. | to relax, loosen | 10 |
| 饭馆 | 飯館 | fànguǎn(r) | n. | restaurant | 10 |
| 非常 | 非常 | fēicháng | adv. | very, extremely | 10 |
| 非常抱歉 | 非常抱歉 | fēicháng bàoqiàn | phr. | my apologies | 8s |
| 丰富 | 豐富 | fēngfù | adj. | rich, abundant | 8 |
| 父母 | 父母 | fùmǔ | n. | parents | 3s |
| 父亲 | 父親 | fùqin | n. | father | 3s |
| 搞 | 搞 | gǎo | v. | to work on, to specialize in, to be engaged in (a certain field) [colloq.] | 5 |

| Simplified | Traditional | Pinyin | Part of Speech | Definition | Lesson |
|---|---|---|---|---|---|
| 搞电脑 | 搞電腦 | gǎo diànnǎo | v. obj. | to specialize in computers (colloq.) | 5 |
| 告诉 | 告訴 | gàosu | v. | to tell | 8s |
| 个 | 個 | gè | m.w. | general classifier | 9 |
| 哥哥 | 哥哥 | gēge | n. | elder brother | 3s, 5 |
| 给 | 給 | gěi | v. & prep. | to give; to, towards for | 10 |
| 跟 | 跟 | gēn | prep. | with, together with | 10 |
| 工程 | 工程 | gōngchéng | n. | engineering | 5 |
| 工程师 | 工程師 | gōngchéngshī | n. | engineer | 5 |
| 功课 | 功課 | gōngkè | n. | assignment | 6s |
| 工作 | 工作 | gōngzuò | n. & v. | occupation, profession, job; to work | 4 |
| 馆 | 館 | guǎn | n. | (originally) guesthouse, hotel; (now) a place for eating, gathering, etc. | 10 |
| 贵 | 貴 | guì | adj. | expensive; honourable | 8 |
| 贵姓 | 貴姓 | guìxìng | n. | (formal) (What is) your honourable surname? | 8 |
| 国 | 國 | guó | n. | nation, country | 8 |
| 果 | 果 | guǒ | n. | fruit | 7 |
| 果汁 | 果汁 | guǒzhī | n. | juice | 7s |
| 还 | 還 | hái | adv. | still | 4, 6 |
| 还好 | 還好 | háihǎo | adj. phr. | "OK"—not very good, but not very bad either | 4 |
| 还是 | 還是 | háishì | conj. | or (used in a question when offering two or more choices) | 7 |
| 汉语 | 漢語 | Hànyǔ | n. | the Chinese language | 8 |
| 好 | 好 | hǎo | adj. | good, well | 2 |
| 号 | 號 | hào | m.w. | number in a series | 9 |
| 好吃 | 好吃 | hǎochī | adj. | good, tasty (of food) | 7s |
| 好喝 | 好喝 | hǎohē | adj. | good, tasty (of drink) | 7s |
| 好久不见 | 好久不見 | Hǎojiǔ bújiàn! | s.e. | Long time no see! | 4 |

| Simplified | Traditional | Pinyin | Part of Speech | Definition | Lesson |
|---|---|---|---|---|---|
| 号码 | 號碼 | hàomǎ | n. | number | 9 |
| 好奇 | 好奇 | hàoqí | adj. | curious/inquisitive | 8 |
| 好听 | 好聽 | hǎotīng | adj. | (lit.) pretty to listen to, pleasant to | 10 |
| 喝 | 喝 | hē | v. | to drink | 7 |
| 和 | 和 | hé | conj. | and, with | 10 |
| 很 | 很 | hěn | adv. | very | 3 |
| 红 | 紅 | hóng | adj. | red | 7 |
| 后天 | 後天 | hòutiān | n. | the day after tomorrow | 10 |
| 话 | 話 | huà | n. | word, speech | 8 |
| 还 | 還 | huán | v. | to return (sth. to sb.) | 6 |
| 欢迎 | 歡迎 | huānyíng | v. | to welcome (someone's arrival) | 7 |
| 护士 | 護士 | hùshi | n. | nurse | 5 |
| 糊涂 | 糊塗 | hútu | adj. | muddle-headed, confused | 6 |
| 几 | 幾 | jǐ | num. | several, a few; how many (used mostly when the estimated response is less than 10) | 9 |
| 记 | 記 | jì | v. | to record | 6 |
| 家 | 家 | jiā | n. | family, home | 4 |
| 见 | 見 | jiàn | v. | to see, to meet | 3 |
| 讲 | 講 | jiǎng | v. | to speak, to say | 8s |
| 健康 | 健康 | jiànkāng | adj. | healthy | 4s |
| 教 | 教 | jiāo | v. | to teach | 6 |
| 叫 | 叫 | jiào | v. | to call; to be called | 8 |
| 教授 | 教授 | jiàoshòu | n. | professor | 5 |
| 教书 | 教書 | jiāo shū | v. obj. | to teach | 8 |
| 借 | 借 | jiè | v. | to borrow, to lend | 6 |
| 姐姐 | 姐姐 | jiějie | n. | elder sister | 3s |
| 介绍 | 介紹 | jièshào | v. | to introduce | 10 |
| 进 | 進 | jìn | v. | to enter, come in | 7 |

| Simplified | Traditional | Pinyin | Part of Speech | Definition | Lesson |
|---|---|---|---|---|---|
| 经理 | 經理 | jīnglǐ | n. | manager | 5s |
| 经验 | 經驗 | jīngyàn | n. | experience | 8 |
| 今天 | 今天 | jīntiān | n. | today | 6 |
| 紧张 | 緊張 | jǐnzhāng | adj. | tense, stressed, stressful | 4 |
| 酒 | 酒 | jiǔ | n. | wine, liquor, alcoholic drinks in general | 7 |
| 九 | 九 | jiǔ | num. | nine | 9s |
| 咖啡 | 咖啡 | kāfēi | n. | coffee | 7 |
| 咖啡馆 | 咖啡館 | kāfēiguǎn | n. | coffee shop | 10 |
| 开玩笑 | 開玩笑 | kāi wánxiào | v. obj. | to joke, make fun of | 8 |
| 看 | 看 | kàn | v. | to look, watch, read | 6 |
| 看电视 | 看電視 | kàn diànshì | v. obj. | to watch TV | 5s |
| 看电影 | 看電影 | kàn diànyǐng | v. obj. | to see a movie | 5s |
| 看书 | 看書 | kàn shū | v. obj. | to read, read a book | 5s |
| 考试 | 考試 | kǎoshì | n. & v. | test, exam; to take a test or exam | 6s |
| 课 | 課 | kè | n. | class | 6 |
| 客 | 客 | kè | n. | guest(s) | 7 |
| 可口可乐 | 可口可樂 | Kěkǒukělè | n. | Coca-Cola | 7s |
| 客气 | 客氣 | kèqi | adj. | acting like a guest, courteous | 7 |
| 客人 | 客人 | kèrén | n. | guest | 7s |
| 可是 | 可是 | kěshì | adv | but | 4s |
| 来 | 來 | lái | v. | to come | 6 |
| 老 | 老 | lǎo | adj. | old, respected | 2 |
| 老板 | 老闆 | lǎobǎn | n. | boss (colloq.) | 5 |
| 老朋友 | 老朋友 | lǎo péngyou | s.e. | (lit.) old friend (i.e., someone who has been a friend for a long time) | 10 |
| 老师 | 老師 | lǎoshī | n. | teacher, professor | 2 |
| 累 | 累 | lèi | adj. | tired | 4 |
| 冷饮 | 冷飲 | lěngyǐn | n. | cool drinks | 7s |

| Simplified | Traditional | Pinyin | Part of Speech | Definition | Lesson |
|---|---|---|---|---|---|
| 礼 | 禮 | lǐ | b.f. | gift, present | 7 |
| 两 | 兩 | liǎng | num. | two | 9s |
| 凉水 | 涼水 | liángshuǐ | n. | cold water | 7s |
| 零 | 零 | líng | num. | zero | 9s |
| 留 | 留 | liú | v. | to stay, to stay behind | 8 |
| 六 | 六 | liù | num. | six | 9s |
| 留学生 | 留學生 | liúxuéshēng | n. | foreign student (who is studying in a country other than his/her own) | 8 |
| 礼物 | 禮物 | lǐwù | n. | gift, present | 7 |
| 楼 | 樓 | lóu | n. | multi-storied building | 9 |
| 楼上 | 樓上 | lóushàng | n. | upstairs | 9s |
| 楼下 | 樓下 | lóuxià | n. | downstairs | 9 |
| 吗 | 嗎 | ma | part. | an interrogative particle used to form questions | 3 |
| 嘛 | 嘛 | ma | s.e. | This is used at the end of the sentence to indicate that something is obvious. | 5 |
| 麻烦 | 麻煩 | máfan | v. & adj. | trouble, to bother | 9 |
| 麻烦你了。 | 麻煩你了。 | máfan nǐ le | s.e. | This is used to apologize for bothering someone or to express thanks when someone has done you a favor | 9 |
| 买 | 買 | mǎi | v. | to buy, purchase | 10 |
| 买东西 | 買東西 | mǎi dōngxi | v. obj. | to buy things, to go shopping | 10 |
| 妈妈 | 媽媽 | māma | n. | mom, mommy | 3 |
| 马马虎虎 | 馬馬虎虎 | mǎmahūhū | s.e. | neither good nor bad, so-so | 4 |
| 忙 | 忙 | máng | adj. | busy | 4 |
| 没 | 沒 | méi | adv. | no | 7 |
| 没关系 | 沒關係 | méi guānxi | phr. | never mind, it doesn't matter | 8 |
| 美国 | 美國 | Měiguó | n. | U.S.A. | 8s |
| 妹妹 | 妹妹 | mèimei | n. | younger sister | 3s |

| Simplified | Traditional | Pinyin | Part of Speech | Definition | Lesson |
|---|---|---|---|---|---|
| 没问题 | 沒問題 | Méi wèntí. | s.e. | No problem. | 10 |
| 们 | 們 | men | suff. | used to pluralize the singular personal pronouns | 3 |
| 明白 | 明白 | míngbai | v. | to understand | 8s |
| 明天 | 明天 | míngtiān | n. | tomorrow | 10 |
| 名字 | 名字 | míngzi | n. | given name | 8 |
| 母亲 | 母親 | mǔqin | n. | mother | 3s |
| 哪 | 哪 | nǎ | interrog. | which | 8 |
| 那 | 那 | nà | pron. | that | 5 |
| 哪国人 | 哪國人 | nǎ guó rén | phr. | which country | 8 |
| 奶奶 | 奶奶 | nǎinai | n. | grandma (father's mother) | 3 |
| 哪里, 哪里 | 哪裡, 哪裡 | nǎli, nǎli | s.e. | This phrase is frequently used as a modest response to a compliment. | 8 |
| 那么（这么） | 那麼 (這麼) | nàme (zhème) | s.e. | such/so this/that (+adj.) | 7 |
| 难 | 難 | nán | adj. | difficult, hard | 6 |
| 男 | 男 | nán | adj. & n. | male | 10 |
| 脑 | 腦 | nǎo | n. | brain | 5 |
| 闹 | 鬧 | nào | v. | to make noise; to go in for; to do, make | 8 |
| 哪儿 | 哪兒 | nǎr | pron. | which place, where | 6 |
| 那儿 | 那兒 | nàr | pron. | that place | 9 |
| 闹笑话 | 鬧笑話 | nào xiàohua | v. obj. | to make a fool of oneself | 8 |
| 呢 | 呢 | ne | part. | an interrogative particle used to make up questions | 3 |
| 你 | 你 | nǐ | pron. | you (singular) | 2 |
| (你/您) 太客气 | (你/您) 太客氣 | (Nǐ/nín) tài kèqi. | s.e. | You are too polite. | 7s |
| 你们 | 你們 | nǐmen | pron. | you (pl.) | 3 |

| Simplified | Traditional | Pinyin | Part of Speech | Definition | Lesson |
|---|---|---|---|---|---|
| 您 | 您 | nín | pron. | you (singular in formal or polite form) | 2 |
| 女 | 女 | nǚ | adj. & n. | female | 10 |
| 噢 | 噢 | ō | s.e. | "Oh!" (used when someone realizes something) | 10 |
| 朋友 | 朋友 | péngyou | n. | friend | 5 |
| 漂亮 | 漂亮 | piàoliang | adj. | good-looking, beautiful | 9 |
| 啤酒 | 啤酒 | píjiǔ | n. | beer | 7 |
| 葡萄酒 | 葡萄酒 | pútáojiǔ | n. | grape wine | 7 |
| 七 | 七 | qī | num. | seven | 9s |
| 气 | 氣 | qì | n. | air, atmosphere | 7 |
| 前天 | 前天 | qiántiān | n. | the day before yesterday | 10s |
| 请 | 請 | qǐng | v. | to politely request, politely ask (sb. do sth.) | 7 |
| 轻松 | 輕鬆 | qīngsōng | adj. | easy | 4s |
| 汽水 | 汽水 | qìshuǐ | n. | soda | 7s |
| 去 | 去 | qù | v. | to go; to be going to (do sth.) | 6 |
| 人 | 人 | rén | n. | person, human being | 8 |
| 认识 | 認識 | rènshi | v. | to be acquainted with, to be familiar with | 8 |
| 认真 | 認真 | rènzhēn | adj. | serious, earnest, conscientious | 4 |
| 容易 | 容易 | róngyì | adj. | easy | 6s |
| 三 | 三 | sān | num. | three | 9s |
| 商 | 商 | shāng | n. | commerce | 10 |
| 上 | 上 | shàng | suff. | suffix commonly found in nouns | 10 |
| 商店 | 商店 | shāngdiàn | n. | store, department store | 10 |
| 上课 | 上課 | shàng kè | v. obj. | to go to class | 6s |
| 上司 | 上司 | shàngsī | n. | boss | 5s |
| 上午 | 上午 | shàngwǔ | n. | morning | 10 |

| Simplified | Traditional | Pinyin | Part of Speech | Definition | Lesson |
|---|---|---|---|---|---|
| 少 | 少 | shǎo | adj. | few, little (opposite of 多) | 5 |
| 谁 | 誰 | shéi | pron. | who, whom | 5 |
| 生意 | 生意 | shēngyì | n. | business | 5 |
| 什么 | 什麼 | shénme | pron. | what? | 5 |
| 身体 | 身體 | shēntǐ | n. | the human body; health condition | 4 |
| 师 | 師 | shī | b.f. | teacher, master | 2 |
| 十 | 十 | shí | num. | ten | 9s |
| 是 | 是 | shì | v. | to be | 5 |
| 室 | 室 | shì | n. | room | 9 |
| 是啊 | 是啊 | Shì a. | s.e. | You are right. (indicating agreement) | 4 |
| 十分感谢 | 十分感謝 | Shífēn gǎnxiè. | s.e. | Thank you very much. | 7s |
| 时间 | 時間 | shíjiān | n. | time | 10 |
| 是吗 | 是嗎 | Shì ma? | s.e. | "Is that true?" or "Really?" This is often used to express surprise or disbelief. | 5 |
| 室友 | 室友 | shìyǒu | n. | roommate | 9 |
| 书 | 書 | shū | n. | book | 5 |
| 书店 | 書店 | shūdiàn | n. | bookstore | 10s |
| 水 | 水 | shuǐ | n. | water | 7 |
| 水果 | 水果 | shuǐguǒ | n. | fruit | 7 |
| 顺利 | 順利 | shùnlì | adj. | smooth (going smoothly) | 4 |
| 说 | 說 | shuō | v. | to speak; to say (sth.) | 6 |
| 叔叔 | 叔叔 | shūshu | n. | uncle (father's younger brother); used to address a man of one's parents' generation | 3 |
| 四 | 四 | sì | num. | four | 9s |
| 所以 | 所以 | suǒyǐ | conj. | so, therefore | 8 |

| Simplified | Traditional | Pinyin | Part of Speech | Definition | Lesson |
|---|---|---|---|---|---|
| 宿舍 | 宿舍 | sùshè | n. | dormitory | 9 |
| 他 | 他 | tā | pron. | he, him | 3 |
| 她 | 她 | tā | pron. | she, her | 3 |
| 太 | 太 | tài | adv. | too, extremely | 4 |
| 太太 | 太太 | tàitai | n. | Mrs., Madam; wife | 2s, 4 |
| 他们 | 他們 | tāmen | pron. | they, them | 3 |
| 糖 | 糖 | táng | n. | candy, sugar | 7 |
| 听 | 聽 | tīng | v. | to listen | 10 |
| 同 | 同 | tóng | adj. | same, similar; together with | 9 |
| 同事 | 同事 | tóngshì | n. | colleague | 9s |
| 同屋 | 同屋 | tóngwū | n. | roommate | 9s |
| 同学 | 同學 | tóngxué | n. | classmate | 6s, 9 |
| 图书馆 | 圖書館 | túshūguǎn | n. | library | 10s |
| 外语 | 外語 | wàiyǔ | n. | foreign language | 8s |
| 晚 | 晚 | wǎn | adj. | late (in time) | 10 |
| 晚安。 | 晚安。 | Wǎn'ān. | sent. | Good night. | 2s |
| 晚饭 | 晚飯 | wǎnfàn | n. | the evening meal, supper, dinner | 10 |
| 玩儿 | 玩兒 | wánr | v. | to have fun; to play; to relax and enjoy oneself | 9 |
| 晚上 | 晚上 | wǎnshang | n. | evening | 10 |
| 问 | 問 | wèn | v. | to ask, to inquire | 5 |
| 问好 | 問好 | wènhǎo | v. phr. | to send one's best regards | 7s |
| 文化 | 文化 | wénhuà | n. | culture | 8 |
| 问题 | 問題 | wèntí | n. | question, problem, issue | 5 |
| 问问题 | 問問題 | wèn wèntí | v. obj. | to ask a question | 5s |
| 我 | 我 | wǒ | pron. | I, me | 3 |
| 我们 | 我們 | wǒmen | pron. | we, us | 3s, 8 |
| 五 | 五 | wǔ | num. | five | 9s |
| 物 | 物 | wù | n. | object(s) | 7 |

| Simplified | Traditional | Pinyin | Part of Speech | Definition | Lesson |
|---|---|---|---|---|---|
| 午饭 | 午飯 | wǔfàn | n. | lunch | 10s |
| 系 | 系 | xì | n. | department in an academic setting | 8 |
| 下课 | 下課 | xià kè | v. obj. | to get out of class | 6s |
| 先生 | 先生 | xiānsheng | n. | gentleman, Mr., Sir, husband | 2s, 4 |
| 现在 | 現在 | xiànzài | n. | now, the present time | 6 |
| 小 | 小 | xiǎo | pref. & adj. | (placed before a personal noun); small, little | 8 |
| 笑 | 笑 | xiào | v. | to laugh (at) | 8 |
| 笑话 | 笑話 | xiàohua | n. | joke | 8 |
| 小姐 | 小姐 | xiǎojiě | n. | young lady, Miss | 2s |
| 下午 | 下午 | xiàwǔ | n. | afternoon | 10 |
| 谢(我)什么? | 謝(我)什麼? | Xiè (wǒ) shénme? | s.e. | What do you need to thank me for? | 7s |
| 谢谢 | 謝謝 | xièxie | v. & s.e. | to thank; Thanks. | 6, 7s |
| 谢谢你/您 | 謝謝你/您 | Xièxie nǐ/nín | s.e. | Thank you. | 7 |
| 行 | 行 | xíng | adj. | to be okay, permissible, feasible | 10 |
| 姓 | 姓 | xìng | n. & v. | surname; to be surnamed | 8 |
| 姓名 | 姓名 | xìngmíng | n. | name | 8 |
| 兄弟姐妹 | 兄弟姐妹 | xiōngdì jiěmèi | n. | siblings | 3s |
| 休息 | 休息 | xiūxi | v. | to rest, to relax | 6 |
| 吸烟 | 吸煙 | xīyān | v. obj. | to smoke (cigarettes, etc.) | 7s |
| 学生 | 學生 | xuésheng | n. | student | 8 |
| 学习 | 學習 | xuéxí | n. & v. | study; to study | 4 |
| 学校 | 學校 | xuéxiào | n. | school | 8, 10 |
| 也 | 也 | yě | adv. | also, too | 3 |
| 爷爷 | 爺爺 | yéye | n. | grandpa (father's father) | 3 |
| 医 | 醫 | yī | n. | medicine; medical science | 5 |
| 一 | 一 | yī | num. | one | 6, 9s |

| Simplified | Traditional | Pinyin | Part of Speech | Definition | Lesson |
|---|---|---|---|---|---|
| 一点儿<br>小意思 | 一點兒<br>小意思 | yīdiǎnr<br>xiǎoyìsi | s.e. | just a small token | 7 |
| 一定 | 一定 | yídìng | adv. | surely, certainly | 9 |
| 以后 | 以後 | yǐhòu | adv. | later on, in the future | 9 |
| 一起 | 一起 | yìqǐ | adv. | together | 9 |
| 以前 | 以前 | yǐqián | adv. | before, ago | 10s |
| 医生 | 醫生 | yīshēng | n. | medical doctor | 5 |
| 意思 | 意思 | yìsi | n. | meaning | 6 |
| 一下儿 | 一下兒 | yīxiàr | phr. | (lit.) "one stroke," often used immediately after the verb to indicate a short period of time | 6 |
| 用 | 用 | yòng | v. | to use, need | 6 |
| 有 | 有 | yǒu | v. | to have | 7 |
| 有意思 | 有意思 | yǒu yìsi | phr. | very interesting | 8s |
| 再 | 再 | zài | adv. | again | 3 |
| 在 | 在 | zài | prep. | to be located (in, on, at) | 9 |
| 再见 | 再見 | zàijiàn | v. phr. | "Good-bye," "Farewell," "See you again!" | 3 |
| 早 | 早 | zǎo | adj. | early | 2 |
| 早安。 | 早安。 | Zǎoān. | sent. | Good morning (more formal). | 2s |
| 早饭 | 早飯 | zǎofàn | n. | breakfast | 10s |
| 早上好。 | 早上好。 | Zǎoshang hǎo. | sent. | Good morning. | 2s |
| 怎么 | 怎麼 | zěnme | s.e. | What! What? | 10 |
| 怎么样 | 怎麼樣 | zěnmeyàng | interrog. | how | 4 |
| 找 | 找 | zhǎo | v. | to look for; to call on, visit (someone) | 9 |
| 这 | 這 | zhè | pron. | this | 5 |
| 这么(那么) | 這麼 (那麼) | zhème (nàme) | adv. | such/so this/that (+adj.) | 7 |
| 真的 | 真的 | zhēn de | s.e. | really | 6 |

| Simplified | Traditional | Pinyin | Part of Speech | Definition | Lesson |
|---|---|---|---|---|---|
| 这儿 | 這兒 | zhèr | n. | here, this place | 9 |
| 知道 | 知道 | zhīdào | v. | to know (a fact); to know that... | 8 |
| 中文 | 中文 | Zhōngwén | n. | the Chinese language | 6 |
| 中文班 | 中文班 | Zhōngwén bān | n. | Chinese class | 6s |
| 中文课 | 中文課 | Zhōngwén kè | phr. | Chinese class | 6 |
| 中午 | 中午 | zhōngwǔ | n. | noon | 10s |
| 住 | 住 | zhù | v. | to stay at/in; to dwell in/at | 9 |
| 字 | 字 | zì | n. | Chinese character; "word" in Western languages) | 8 |
| 最近 | 最近 | zuìjìn | adv. | recently, lately | 10 |
| 做 | 做 | zuò | v. | to do | 5 |
| 坐 | 坐 | zuò | v. | to sit | 7 |
| 做买卖 | 做買賣 | zuò mǎimai | v. obj. | to do business, buy and sell | 5s |
| 昨天 | 昨天 | zuótiān | n. | yesterday | 10s |
| 作业 | 作業 | zuòyè | n. | homework, assignment | 6 |